Anthropological Papers
Museum of Anthropology, University of Michigan
No. 84

Debating Oaxaca
Archaeology

edited by
Joyce Marcus

Ann Arbor, Michigan
1990

©1990 by the Regents of The University of Michigan
The Museum of Anthropology
All rights reserved

Printed in the United States of America

ISBN 0-915703-22-X

Library of Congress Cataloging-in-Publication Data

Debating Oaxaca archaeology / edited by Joyce Marcus.
    p. cm. – (Anthropological papers / Museum of Anthropology, University of Michigan ; no. 84)
    "This volume grew out of the 1987 meeting of the Northeast Mesoamericanists Society, held at the University of Pennsylvania Museum in Philadelphia"–Pref.
    Includes bibliographical references.
    ISBN 0-915703-22-X
    1. Indians of Mexico–Mexico–Oaxaca–Antiquities–Congresses. 2. Excavations (Archaeology)–Mexico–Oaxaca–Congresses. 3. Oaxaca (Mexico)–Antiquities–Congresses. 4. Mexico–Antiquities–Congresses. I. Marcus, Joyce. II. Northeast Mesoamericanists Society. III. Series: Anthropological papers (University of Michigan. Museum of Anthropology) ; no. 84.
GN2.M5 no. 84
[F1219.1.O11]
306 –dc20
[972'.74]   90-42333
                                                                                                                        CIP

Contents

List of figures, *iv*
List of tables, *vii*
Preface, *ix*
    by Joyce Marcus

CHAPTER 1
    Theory and Practice in Mesoamerican Archaeology: A Comparison of Two Modes of Scientific Inquiry, *1*
        by Richard E. Blanton

CHAPTER 2
    Borrón, y Cuenta Nueva: Setting Oaxaca's Archaeological Record Straight, *17*
        by Kent V. Flannery and Joyce Marcus

CHAPTER 3
    Settlement and Land Use in Ancient Oaxaca, *71*
        by Gary M. Feinman and Linda M. Nicholas

CHAPTER 4
    Irrigated Agriculture at Hierve el Agua, Oaxaca, Mexico, *115*
        by J. A. Neely, S. C. Caran, and B. M. Winsborough

CHAPTER 5
    Science and Science Fiction in Postclassic Oaxaca: Or, "Yes, Virginia, There is a Monte Albán IV," *191*
        by Joyce Marcus and Kent V. Flannery

CHAPTER 6
    Scale and Complexity: Issues in the Archaeology of the Valley of Oaxaca, *207*
        by Stephen A. Kowalewski

List of Figures

2.1 Two views of Tierras Largas phase public buildings from San José Mogote, 24
2.2 Views of plastered corners in Early Formative public buildings from San José Mogote, 25
2.3 Lime-plastered pits from two Tierras Largas phase public buildings at San José Mogote, 26
2.4 Plan of Structure 6, San José Mogote, a Tierras Largas phase public building, 27
2.5 Two views of Structure 8, San José Mogote, a Guadalupe phase public building, 28
2.6 Seven miniature Socorro Fine Gray vessels from Burial 68, San José Mogote, 33
2.7 Effigy *brasero* from Monte Albán II temple at San José Mogote, 36
2.8 Typical Monte Albán II bowl with mammiform supports and *xicalcoliuhqui* motif, 36
2.9 Plan showing relationship of Structures 19, 19A, 19B, 28, and 14, 37
2.10 Structure 28, a Rosario phase adobe platform, 38
2.11 Stairway of Structure 19A, San José Mogote, 39
2.12 View of Structure 19 from the northeast, showing how building stages were dated, 40
2.13 View of Structure 19 from the northwest, 41
2.14 Monument 3, San José Mogote, showing the layer of *lajas* (flagstones) laid below it to level it, 43
2.15 Drawing of top and side of Monument 3, San José Mogote, 44
2.16 Decorated Socorro Fine Gray bowl sherds found below Monument 3, San José Mogote, 45
2.17 Additional examples of decorated Socorro Fine Gray bowl sherds found below Monument 3, San José Mogote, 49
2.18 Typical effigy bridgespout vessel of Monte Albán Ic date, 51
2.19 Roussanou, near Meteora, Greece, 55
2.20 Concentric defensive walls at "La Corona Grande," a fortified hilltop site in the northern (Etla) part of the Valley of Oaxaca, 56
2.21 Examples of prostrate, sprawling captives from Maya stone monuments from Naranjo, Guatemala, 57
2.22 Examples of *danzantes* or sprawled captives from steps in Building L, Monte Albán, 58
3.1 Map showing Valley of Oaxaca and Ejutla Valley survey areas, 83
3.2 Population trends in Oaxaca and Ejutla, 84
3.3 Rates of population change in Oaxaca, 84
3.4 Population trends in each subregion of the Valley of Oaxaca, 85
3.5 Population density during Monte Albán V in the valleys of Oaxaca and Ejutla, 89
3.6 Distribution of Rosario phase population and good land, 90

3.7   Scatterplot of Late I (Monte Albán Ic) populations (actual and potential) in Ejutla, *91*
3.8   Colonization map for the San José phase in the Valley of Oaxaca, *93*
3.9   Colonization map for the Rosario phase in the Valley of Oaxaca, *94*
3.10 Colonization map for the Late I (Ic) phase in the Valley of Oaxaca, *95*
3.11 Potential population levels in the Valley of Oaxaca, *96*
3.12 Distribution of surplus during the San José phase, *97*
3.13 Distribution of surplus during Late I (Period Ic), *98*
3.14 Monte Albán support zones during Early and Late I (Ia and Ic), *99*
3.15 Distribution of population for maximum production during the San José phase, *100*
3.16 Ideal maximum surplus versus potential surplus, *101*
4.1   Topographic map of the southeast portion of the Valley of Oaxaca, showing the location of Hierve el Agua, *117*
4.2   A view of Hierve el Agua from the air, *121*
4.3   Map of Hierve el Agua, showing the terrace and canal system as well as architectural features, *122*
4.4   Map of Hierve el Agua, showing the locations of 41 test pits excavated in 1966, *124*
4.5   Terrace walls located near Test Pit 24, *131*
4.6   View of the central portion of Hierve el Agua, looking southwest, *132*
4.7   View of the central portion of Hierve el Agua, looking northeast, *133*
4.8   Modern solar evaporation saltworks at Zapotitlán Salinas west of the Tehuacán Valley, *137*
4.9   Another view of the modern solar evaporation saltworks at Zapotitlán Salinas west of the Tehuacán Valley, *138*
4.10 A canal and *pocito* that have been cross-sectioned to show the layering of the travertine filling it, *144*
4.11 A terrace wall near Test Pit 24, showing small canal and *pocitos*, *147*
4.12 Map of the upper central portion of Hierve el Agua, *167*
4.13 Graph showing changes in hydrochemistry along a direct flow path at Hierve el Agua, *172*
5.1   Example of a G-23 gray bowl with "pseudo-glyphs" in a cartouche, a diagnostic of Monte Albán IIIa, *198*
5.2   Examples of tripod polychrome bowls, diagnostic of Monte Albán V, *200*
6.1   Aerial view of Cerro de Atzompa, *217*
6.2   View of Monte Albán from the east, *219*
6.3   Aerial view of the piedmont north of Oaxaca City, *221*
6.4   View of the middle piedmont north of Oaxaca City, *223*
6.5   View to the northwest of Monte Albán, *225*
6.6   Aerial view of the hills west of San Andrés Ixtlahuaca, *227*
6.7   The El Mirador site, looking north, *229*
6.8   A terraced site above San Felipe Tejalapan, *231*
6.9   Plaza 1 at terraced site above San Felipe Tejalapan, *233*
6.10 View of ancient terraces above San Mateo Macuilxochitl, *235*
6.11 Teotitlán del Valle, *237*
6.12 Group of mounds at Cerro Guirún, *239*
6.13 Ballcourt at Cerro Guirún, *241*
6.14 Xoxocotlán, *243*
6.15 Sites at Santa Ana Tlapacoyan, about 34 km south of Monte Albán, *245*

6.16   Two terraced sites on the Río Mixtepec, *247*
6.17   El Choco, west of Santa María Ayoquezco, *249*
6.18   Aerial view of southern Ocotlán, *251*
6.19   Aerial view of Jalieza, *253*
6.20   View from atop eastern ridge at Jalieza, *255*
6.21   Center of Jalieza during Early Classic times, *257*
6.22   Jalieza during Monte Albán IV, *259*
6.23   Terrace retaining wall at Jalieza, *261*
6.24   Inspecting artifacts on a terrace at Jalieza, *263*
6.25   A scatter of chert tools and debitage near San Marcos Tlapazola, southern Tlacolula, *265*
6.26   Structure 3 at Unión Zapata (Loma Larga), *267*

List of Tables

2.1 Sherds found below Monument 3, San José Mogote, 46
2.2 Total inventory of Socorro Fine Gray bowls associated with Monument 3, San José Mogote, 48
3.1 Distribution of good land in Oaxaca, 86
3.2 Wilcoxon sum scores for catchment circles and large sites, 86
3.3 Surplus production by distance from major centers, 103
3.4 Maximum potential production in dry years (valley population distributed on best land), 103
4.1 Percentages of the relative abundance of the most common diatoms at Hierve el Agua, 156
4.2 Previously published analyses of water from Hierve el Agua, 159
4.3 Major-ion hydrochemistry of the spring water at Hierve el Agua, 164
4.4 Major-ion hydrochemistry of the water in pools located along the flow paths at Hierve el Agua, 166
4.5 Seasonal variation of the spring-water hydrochemistry at Hierve el Agua, 174

Preface

This volume grew out of the 1987 meeting of the Northeast Mesoamericanists Society, held at the University of Pennsylvania Museum in Philadelphia. The meeting organizers, Robert Sharer and Elin Danien, asked Kent Flannery and me to chair a morning symposium on Oaxaca archaeology. Following our opening lecture, Richard Blanton, Gary Feinman, Laura Finsten, Stephen Kowalewski, and Linda Nicholas all presented papers.

Our talks in Philadelphia addressed two main topics. The first of these was the intensely negative reaction of William T. Sanders and his students to the discoveries and theoretical conclusions of the Oaxaca Project. We had not anticipated that our Oaxaca results would touch such a nerve at University Park, Pennsylvania. To begin with, our conclusion that Zapotec civilization could not be explained simply as the result of population pressure and the manipulation of soil and water drew loud protestations. Further, our conclusion that the layout and location of Oaxaca's first urban center could not be explained by land use variables alone proved utterly unacceptable to Sanders. We had anticipated that our explanations for cultural evolution in Oaxaca might not be the same as Sanders's explanations for the Basin of Mexico; we were, after all, working in two different regions. What we had not realized was that, for Sanders, all cultural evolution everywhere must fit his theory.

In this volume, Blanton (Chapter 1) proposes an epistemological reason why Sanders's approach and ours are incompatible: two very different views of science are involved. Feinman and Nicholas (Chapter 3) present land use data which explain why we find Sanders's interpretation of our evolutionary sequence unconvincing. On a more general plane, Kowalewski (Chapter 6) argues that prehistoric civilizations have so many levels of scale and complexity that a simple analytical approach, however rigorous, cannot be applied throughout.

A second topic addressed by our symposium was the proliferation of factual misinformation about Oaxaca archaeology which one finds in the recent literature. Hardly a month goes by that we do not find ourselves misquoted, or our discoveries misdated or inaccurately described. Since our conclusions depend on correct interpretations of our raw data, from time to time we need to correct the most significant of these errors. This seems to be as good a time as any.

In Chapter 2, Flannery and I review a number of recent errors, presenting fuller archaeological data in the hope of clarifying the problem. In Chapter 5 we deal with the chronology of Classic and Postclassic Oaxaca and, we hope, lay to rest the amusing but ill-considered notion that the valley was once abandoned for half a millennium.

One Oaxaca site which has recently been the subject of a great deal of speculation and misinformation is Hierve el Agua. When Laura Finsten declined to publish her Philadelphia presentation in this volume, we invited James A. Neely, the excavator of Hierve el Agua, to contribute a paper clarifying the nature of the site. In Chapter 4, Neely, Caran, and Winsborough leave no doubt that Hierve el Agua was used for irrigation—not saltmaking, as has been recently suggested.

My old high school instructor, Mr. Faubion, defined debate as "a dialogue with empirical support given by both parties." Obviously, this volume contains only our side of the debate. However, it should be clear from the bibliographic citations that our adversaries have already had their say. In other words, we are following the precedent set by Lewis Binford in *Debating Archaeology*,* a volume in which we hear from Binford, but not from his opponents Gould, Bunn, Isaac, Schiffer et al. Binford will be hearing from many of those adversaries again, and undoubtedly, we will be hearing from ours. Thus, we have taken the precaution of saving our best lines for the future.

Joyce Marcus
Ann Arbor, 1990

---

*Academic Press, 1989.

1

THEORY AND PRACTICE IN MESOAMERICAN ARCHAEOLOGY
A Comparison of Two Modes of Scientific Inquiry

Richard E. Blanton, Purdue University

In "Ecological Theory and Cultural Evolution in the Valley of Oaxaca," Sanders and Nichols (1988) express substantial disagreements with conclusions that I (and others) have made, based on the Valley of Oaxaca settlement pattern survey. Their stance is enigmatic because my colleagues and I have a problem orientation, theoretical framework, and field methodology very similar to those of Sanders and his students. In fact, the Oaxaca survey is the direct outcome of an archaeological method developed largely by Sanders in the Valley of Mexico; cultural evolutionary ideas from Leslie White and Julian Steward provide a theoretical stimulus shared by both survey projects. But now, according to Sanders and Nichols (ibid.), there is virtually complete dissonance between the two groups. This schism is a fascinating one, which I attempt to explain in this chapter. It has implications not only for an expanded understanding of the history of research in Mesoamerican archaeology, but also for the nature of scientific inquiry in general. By comparing two modes of scientific inquiry described by philosophers of science Thomas Kuhn and Karl Popper, I propose several hypotheses to explain this schism.

TWO MODES OF SCIENCE

In the works of Kuhn (1970) and Popper (1959), there are two highly divergent opinions regarding the nature of scientific inquiry (cf. Suppe [ed.] 1977; Suppe 1977a, 1977b; Lakatos and Musgrave [eds.] 1970). Kuhn's famous presentation dissects scientific *Weltan-*

schauungen. In his conceptualization, science is conducted within the confines of cognitive models (paradigms) consisting of exemplars (strategies for solving scientific problems recognized by the particular community of scientists) and disciplinary matrices (shared culture, values, and norms that promote communication among members of the scientific community) (Kuhn 1970, 1977). Normally, according to Kuhn, scientific investigation consists of the resolution of "puzzles" presented by the paradigm ("normal science"). Research is not conducted in order to challenge theory or evaluate it. Instead, puzzle-solving is carried out because "the results gained . . . add to the scope and precision with which the paradigm can be applied" (Kuhn 1970:36). Scientists whose understanding of the world is filtered through a particular collection of exemplars, and whose professional success is linked to continued participation in a particular disciplinary matrix, are understandably not likely to challenge the status quo. Nor are these scientists likely to view anomalous results as challenges to the paradigm or its theory, at least not in the context of normal science. If anomalies accumulate, however, a loss of faith could follow, and in such extraordinary times a scientific revolution may occur in which a new paradigm is developed to replace the failed paradigm (a "gestalt switch").

In Popper's more rationalist interpretation, the scientist starts with a problem and develops a theory or theories capable of solving the problem. These theories must be falsifiable, and scientific research is aimed at falsification of theories, in whole or part. Successful parts of theories—that is, parts that have survived sincere attempts at falsification—may be incorporated into new, broader theory. In this way human knowledge is expanded. Ideally, Popper's scientists are not committed to exemplars and a disciplinary matrix. Instead, they are rational falsificationists, always looking for ways to subject their theories to maximum strain. As he puts it, the scientist must maintain a "wonderfully self-critical attitude" (1983:190), and, he argues: "The proper counsel to the scientist is that he will always hold, consciously or unconsciously, a host of theories and that he is well advised to adopt a critical attitude towards them" (1983:233).

It has been suggested that Kuhn's model presents an excessively irrationalistic and pessimistic opinion of science (e.g. Suppe 1977a:150), and that Popper, in contrast, ignores *Weltanschauungen* and is a "naive falsificationist" (e.g. Lakatos 1970). Perhaps the real nature of scientific inquiry resides somewhere between the extremes of the two idealized structures, but I suggest that certain elements of each throw light on the conflict between Sanders and ourselves. I hypothesize that neither Kuhn's nor Popper's model describes the way science is done, in a whole sense, but instead are models of contrasting styles of scientific inquiry, styles that may coexist within a community of scientists concerned with the same kinds of problems. When two world views as different as these collide, conflict between their practitioners is inevitable. I propose that Sanders' style of scientific inquiry is very much like that described by Kuhn's idea of paradigm and normal science, while the style my colleagues and I have pursued is more like what Popper describes, in general if not in detail. I do not mean to imply that Sanders has modeled himself after the paradigmatic scientists described by Kuhn. So far as I know (judging from references in Sanders' published works), he may not even have read Kuhn. Similarly, I do not imply that I have consciously followed Popper's advice down to the last detail, although I am sure I have been influenced by several post-positivists, including Popper, however indirectly. The point I am trying to make is that these two models of science perceptively describe two kinds of science being done by two groups of people whose problems, methods, and data overlap. There is conflict between Sanders and the Oaxaca researchers because he thinks our activities gratuitously undermine a theory he has devoted a lifetime to developing and promoting, while we, in turn, view him as a theoretical dinosaur who refuses to accept the reality of the falsification of critical parts of his theory.

CULTURAL ECOLOGY AS NORMAL SCIENCE

According to Sanders and his followers:

> [because] densely settled populations are socially and politically more complex than are small, less dense groups . . . we can conclude that when a society increases in size over time and this expansion is ongoing, locally contained, and adequately supported, then that society must develop more complex features of subsistence, economic exchange, and political integration. [Logan and Sanders 1976:32]

This is, of course, a *non sequitur*, since we can never make an inference about causality from an association or correlation. But logic seemingly has no place here. To be a follower, one must accept such statements as true; this is the source of the "epistemological strength" described by Sanders and Nichols (1988:34). Falsification has no role to play either, since ultimately the accepted causal variables will maintain an "analytical priority," no matter what the results of research might indicate about causal sequence (1988:35). It seems to me legitimate to ask (as I did in Blanton 1981): Why engage in research at all?

I was perplexed about this until I recalled Kuhn's discussion of the puzzle-solving that takes place in the context of paradigmatic normal science. Even though the cultural ecologists have long ago arrived at their main conclusions, the theory still poses questions regarding the exact connections between population pressure and social change, such as: At what level of population pressure do changes take place? As Logan and Sanders put it: "A major theoretical point is the specific quantitative aspect of responses to rising population. How nearly does a population, in terms of a given system, approach carrying capacity before responses are triggered?" (1976:52). Or, exactly how does population pressure interact with a variable like circumscription, for example, to produce varying rates of social evolution (cf. Logan and Sanders 1976:53–56; Sanders and Webster 1978)?

Even though it may at first seem counterintuitive, normal science requires method because it has puzzles to solve. And Sanders has labored over much of his career to develop a method to measure population size and population density in relation to carrying capacity. To accomplish this, he has become probably the foremost authority on the early Colonial population history of the Valley of Mexico and adjacent regions (Sanders 1970). He and his colleagues have done most of the basic research in the area of environmental variation in the Central Highlands and the way this is related to variation in traditional agricultural practices (e.g. Sanders 1965; Sanders et al. 1970; Sanders, Parsons, and Santley 1979). And he is largely responsible for the development of the systematic settlement pattern survey method that has been so widely applied in the Central Highlands and Southern Highlands of Mexico, a research effort that has provided the best information, from archaeological data, on past population trends for any world region (Blanton et al. 1982; Kowalewski et al. 1989; Millon 1973; Parsons 1971; Parsons et al. 1982; Sanders, Parsons, and Santley 1979). Thus Sanders has had a key role to play in one of the most important research efforts in the history of Mesoamerican archaeology, namely the settlement pattern surveys of the Valleys of Oaxaca and Mexico. I return to this point below.

I consider myself extremely fortunate to have been able to participate in the development of this method and in the carrying out of the archaeological surveys. But since my days as a graduate student working on the Valley of Mexico survey, I have come to regard the settlement pattern survey method in a new light. I now consider the settlement pattern survey a highly appropriate tool for evaluating the efficacy of cultural ecological theories such as those proposed by Sanders and his followers. I admit (having just reexamined my dissertation and an early article based on it [Blanton 1972a, 1972b]) that at the time I was engaged in Valley of Mexico research and studying with Jeffrey Parsons, my research consisted of an application of the method in order to solve puzzles contained within the specified scope of interest of the dominant paradigm. These two works are replete with assumptions held by cultural ecologists, which I had evidently embraced with little critical thought. Evidently, I was not yet aware of the dynamics of paradigmatic science.

But by the early 1970s, I was beginning to have doubts about the causal priority of population growth and population pressure, based mostly on theoretical grounds (Blanton 1975, 1976). At the same time, George Cowgill (1975a, 1975b) was raising some of the same issues — at the 1974 meeting of the American Association of Physical Anthropologists, Cowgill and I independently gave very similar papers. In addition, as I proceeded with the Valley of Oaxaca archaeological survey, I began to find many things that were anomalous in light of population determinist theory, especially in connection with the founding of Monte Albán. As the survey expanded to encompass the entire Valley of Oaxaca, my colleagues and I encountered more and more evidence that population pressure and environmental determinist theory were inadequate and misleading. We have written extensively about these matters, and I will not repeat the arguments (Blanton 1980, 1983a, 1983b; Feinman et al. 1985; Blanton, Kowalewski, Feinman, and Appel 1981).

Throughout this time I had assumed, naively, that my efforts to find weak spots in our theory, and to expand theory and method, would be favorably received; however, the opposite occurred. What I had failed to realize is that in paradigmatic science there develops a strong personal attachment to ideas, especially for a person like Sanders, who has devoted his professional career to a single idea. But there is more to it than just emotional ties; to refer back to Kuhn again, another reason for the energetically negative response to my work is found in the fact that I represent a particularly worrisome threat to the integrity of Sanders' paradigm, because I was trained within it. According to Kuhn, a crisis that can threaten a paradigm is more likely to be precipitated by a person who " . . . knowing with precision what he should expect, is able to recognize that something has gone wrong. Anomaly appears only against the background provided by the paradigm" (Kuhn 1970:65).

AGAINST METHOD

Intellectual honesty does not consist in trying to entrench, or establish one's position by proving . . . it—intellectual honesty consists rather in specifying precisely the conditions under which one is willing to give up one's position. Committed Marxists and Freudians refuse to specify such conditions: this is the hallmark of their intellectual dishonesty.

[Lakatos 1970:92]

Up to this point, I have largely discussed the two types of science, paradigmatic and Popperian, as simply two alternative modes of doing science. But these are not simply two types of science that can be viewed as equals, or two different strategies that can achieve the same end result. They are radically different in terms of their potential for contributing to the growth of knowledge. What Lakatos says of the committed Freudians and Marxists in the quotation above can be said of Sanders and his students and followers. Sanders' paradigm is intellectually dishonest. Paradigmatic science is misguided science. In Popper's words: "In my view the 'normal' scientist, as Kuhn describes him, is a person one ought to be sorry for. . . . The 'normal' scientist . . . has been taught badly. . . . He has been taught in a dogmatic spirit: he is the victim of indoctrination" (1970:52–53). In the hands of an overly ambitious, domineering individual who is excessively committed to an idea, science can easily become the kind of degraded science Kuhn describes.

In paradigmatic science, criticism is anathema, and anything goes when it comes to protecting the integrity of the paradigm and its ideas. In several recent publications (especially Sanders and Nichols 1988), Sanders and his followers have shown they are willing to go to extreme lengths to defend their theory. It is astonishing to me that in order to protect themselves from falsification, they display in this and other recent publications a willingness to trivialize, and, in essence, dismantle, a method they have devoted years to working out and applying. As I mentioned above, puzzle-solving in the paradigm is dependent on a method for measuring population and resource variables, and with great effort techniques were developed that are highly suitable for doing this. The sophistication of these methods is the result of years of work, and they have been successfully applied over large areas of the Mexican highlands, involving hundreds of thousands of dollars of research funding and many years of fieldwork. These methods have provided an abundance of data, data that are better and more encompassing than any available from elsewhere. But when research using the method brings the theory into question, do we abandon the theory or try to improve it? No: not in paradigmatic science. Instead, Sanders and his followers have begun a campaign to retroactively modify and discredit the method and its results in order to shelter the theory.

Methodological deconstructionism has taken primarily three forms: (1) creating population pressure where the established method failed to find it (this is discussed also by Feinman and Nicholas in this volume); (2) discrediting the value of surface evidence of craft specialization, since we found less evidence of craft specialization at Monte Albán than Sanders thinks there should be;* (3) minimizing the importance of early Monte Albán, and arguing that political unification did not occur in the Valley of Oaxaca until the Late Classic (their "Stage 3"). Oddly, this last assertion conflicts with an earlier argument of Sanders and Webster (1978:286) that, given the environmental characteristics and size of the Valley of Oaxaca, Monte Albán would have been a "... major urban and political center by the time of Christ." Evidently Sanders has now decided that the interaction of population growth and circumscription did not act in the manner suggested by the earlier "systemic" social evolutionary model, but there is no explanation as to why this abrupt about-face occurred.

Sanders and Nichols (1988:45) say they do not challenge the assumptions of the method of population reconstruction, but they do. Most of their methodological revisionism is based on manipulations of estimated rates of early post-Conquest population decline, which, they argue, indicate that the archaeological survey estimates (both for the Valleys of Mexico and Oaxaca) are too low (1988:43,44). But any attempt to estimate the 1519 population on the basis of rates of decline between the Conquest and the time of the earliest censuses will fail for one simple reason: There is no dependable information on population size pertaining to the earliest period of European contact from areas coterminous with the archaeological survey areas, in either the Valley of Mexico or the Valley of Oaxaca (cf. Feinman and Nicholas 1988a). Thus estimates of rates of decline will lack any solid empirical foundation, and any attempt to use them to reconstruct prehispanic population size or to modify our methods of archaeological reconstruction of population trends will fail.

The only empirically based method of estimating post-Conquest rates of decline is to compare the archaeological estimates for the Late Postclassic with the early census data. The archaeological estimates have been based on a method first laid out by Sanders in his disserta-

---

*According to their argument (Sanders and Nichols 1988:47–49) agriculture and "marketing potential" would have been more important factors determining the location of the city than the political factors I emphasized.

tion (Sanders 1957), in which he identified several major contemporary community types in highland Mexico, and established for each type a range of population density. This basic method has survived many field seasons of archaeological application with only minor modifications, because the range of community types Sanders described can be reasonably well distinguished in the archaeological record. While I am sure this method can be improved with knowledge that will be gained from excavation, it has a better-established empirical basis than any method of measuring population decline rates using early Colonial sources.

To cast additional doubt on the method of population estimation, Sanders and Nichols (1988:45) approvingly review Santley's (1983) revision of my Monte Albán population estimates, although they don't agree with him in terms of specific numbers. But it is difficult to follow their discussion of modifications of population estimates, since in the one article they alternate between five different versions of Monte Albán's population history (as I discuss in Blanton 1988). Santley (1983) also has trouble establishing a firm method of estimation that will substitute for the one I used. For example, while he initially makes the argument that the Period IIIa population of Monte Albán must have been much less than I estimated, because there are so few IIIa diagnostic sherds, later in the same article (p. 76) he reverses himself and concludes that the small size he estimated is due to the nature of the period's ceramics, " . . . so the Early Classic site may have been larger than the periodized materials would suggest." Was the site smaller than I estimated or not? This kind of obfuscation and methodological meddling, whether intentional or unintentional, only serves to create confusion and promote pessimism in the community of Mesoamerican researchers. I do not mean to imply that any method is above criticism, or that the method of estimating population size archaeologically cannot be improved. It can. But we should be wary of those who question and modify methods *post hoc* simply because they fail to give desired results. I will be much more impressed by critics or innovators who have no axes to grind.

Sanders' and Nichols' critique of the survey method extends to the issue of identifying craft production from surface survey. They argue (p. 70) that "[s]mall opportunistic or grab samples and 'density observations of lithic artifacts' . . . do not allow a researcher to determine the presence of workshops or what was being manufactured, much less the type and organization of craft specialization." This very strong statement flies in the face of many previous statements along these lines made by Sanders and his students, and is clearly false. Of course, more intensively collected data using systematic collection methods and excavation will produce more refined information regarding the nature of craft production, but it is wrong to say that nothing at all can be learned through surface inspection and grab-bag surface collections. While it might be the case that a more intensive survey of Otumba, mentioned by Sanders and Nichols (p. 70), produced additional evidence of craft production not noted in the original survey, it still is the case that the initial surveys correctly identified Otumba as an important locus of craft production (Sanders 1965:83). Sanders seems unsure of exactly what kind of method we should apply in locating craft production. In Sanders and Nichols the argument is made that we must restrict ourselves to systematic collection methods, but in criticizing Elizabeth Brumfiel's systematic surface collection methodology at Huexotla, Sanders (1980) argues that visual survey would have been more productive than her systematic surface collection!

CRITICISM AND THE GROWTH OF KNOWLEDGE

The controversy discussed in this book would be interpreted by Kuhn as evidence for the beginning of a paradigm shift—a scientific revolution. Anomalies have been discovered. A conflict has ensued, authorities questioned, and there is a search for a new world view. But I would strongly disagree with such an interpretation. According to Kuhn, the kind of critical, exploratory science that takes place during a scientific revolution is "extraordinary science," whose outcome will be a "gestalt switch." In such a period of extraordinary science, Kuhn says, researchers look for a way to replace a paradigm. And when they do, he argues, the change is likely to be so complete that "we may want to say that after a revolution scientists are responding to a different world" (Kuhn 1970:111). In the more Popperian world I favor, "extraordinary science" is in reality "normal science." Anomalies were found because that is what research is for. Theories have been questioned, because we should always question theories. Disagreements are encouraged because they can lead to fruitful dialogue. But there is no sense among the Oaxaca researchers that we are about to foment a revolution that will lead to a gestalt switch and the establishment of a radical alternative paradigm. If this were to happen, we would be guilty of making the same mistake that the cultural ecologists made in establishing a rigid, unresponsive, dogmatic world view that invited revolution. Our new motto in Mesoamerican archaeology should be: Down with Paradigms.

The systematic archaeological surveys and related work done under the rubric of cultural ecology have provided data on several of the most important variables relevant to understanding the evolution and dynamics of complex society, including environmental variation, risk, carrying capacity, agricultural strategies, and population dynamics, among others. While these might not be the only variables of concern to the student of cultural evolution, they are important. It would be a mistake to overreact to the faults of population determinism in particular, or of cultural materialism in general, and turn to a polar opposite position that favors only the cognitivistic, structuralist, critical, or cultural historical arguments, as Sahlins (1976) and Hodder (1986) suggest we should do (or, closer to home, Conrad and Demarest [1984]). Harris (1979) perpetuates the paradigmatic fallacy in the way he promotes his cultural materialism, but his critique of the alternative paradigms (Part II) contains many valid points. We need to avoid the mistake of gestalt switching from one paradigm to another, and instead concentrate on ways to transcend paradigmatic thinking by establishing critically based theory building. In this transcendent mode of science, hypotheses may come from any quarter, including (but not exclusively) those usually associated with cognitive or structuralist theory such as ritual, religion, and myth—or any other area. The source of an idea is irrelevant. What is important is that theories must be falsifiable and viewed critically. If this means that we will be accused of suffering from "multicausalitis" (Carneiro 1987), then so be it. I would rather be multicausal than dogmatic.

IMPLICATIONS FOR METHOD AND THEORY

While doing the Valley of Oaxaca survey, my colleagues and I began to ask new kinds of questions, and to develop new problem orientations, expressed as our concern with the interrelationships of our main variables—scale, integration, complexity, and boundedness. Related to these questions, we wanted to understand more about such things as the origin and dynamics of the region's market system, and the relationship of local sociopolitical structures to regional-scale institutions, as well as other matters of concern to regional analysis. We wanted to know more about changing household strategies of production, consumption, and migration. And we wanted to learn more about change in locations and permeabilities of regional boundaries. Although the method of systematic regional settlement pattern survey pioneered by Sanders was designed primarily to collect data on population and resource variables, it encouraged the archaeologist to collect other categories of information during the normal course of survey—for example, drawings of floor plans, sketch maps of civic-ceremonial architecture, evidence for specialized activities (production, ritual, etc.), and recording of carved stone monuments. The serendipitous result is that the method, with only minor modifications, proved highly adaptable in the light of the new questions we were asking.

A goal of the surveys has always been to cover large expanses of territory as completely and systematically as possible, in order to maximize the accuracy of regional population estimates; thus we avoided using regional sampling strategies (at times over the objections of grant review panels). This tactic proved beneficial, as it facilitated the use of the resulting data for regional analyses—for example, rank-size measures of urban primacy that would be impossible using sampled data (Kowalewski et al. 1989; cf. Fish and Kowalewski 1990). And as a normal part of our survey method, we made numerous ceramic collections (roughly 3000 from the Valley of Oaxaca survey). The original intent of these collections was to facilitate chronological placement of sites, especially complex ones, so the samples are not probability samples of populations of sherds. Thus they have limited utility for statistical analysis. But we found the data very useful for conducting preliminary studies of the spatial distribution of ceramic types, a source of data useful in our measures of regional integration (e.g. Feinman 1982; Kowalewski et al. 1989).

I was able to use the data collected on the morphology and positioning of public buildings to examine the nature of change in the way the elite manipulated the architectural rhetoric of public spaces (Blanton 1989). This type of analysis would have been impossible without the large sample of building plans collected from all over the Valley of Oaxaca. Today the same (or similar) survey methods are being used to address questions related to the nature of the intersocietal interactions (Feinman and Nicholas 1988b; Stark 1985, Redmond 1983), drawing from theoretical frameworks unlike the region-centered orientation of cultural ecology. All of these are kinds of questions well outside the domain of those originally asked by the cultural ecologists, but their method has proven highly adaptable. This is another important reason for avoiding a Kuhnian-style gestalt switch as we build new theory and reformulate our research strategies.

The survey data already collected will be useful for many kinds of analyses related to new questions we may find ourselves asking in the coming years. We would be foolish to disregard these hard-won data. At the same time, we should do more surveys in more Mesoamerican regions using the same methods, to assure comparability between studies, and the cultural ecologists should be encouraged to publish more fully the information they have collected. Sanders and his followers may not be happy about our questioning of his paradigm, but he should be proud of the fact that he was instrumental in the development of one of the most productive methods ever utilized in Mesoamerican archaeology. That is his main legacy to the field.

References Cited

Blanton, Richard E.
1972a Prehispanic Settlement Patterns of the Ixtapalapa Peninsula Region, Mexico. The Pennsylvania State University, Occasional Contributions in Anthropology, 6. University Park: Pennsylvania State University.
1972b Prehispanic adaptation in the Ixtapalapa region, Mexico. Science, 175:1317–26.
1975 The cybernetic analysis of human population growth. In: Population Studies in Archaeology and Biological Anthropology: A Symposium, edited by Alan Swedlund, pp. 116–26. American Antiquity Memoirs, 30.
1976 Appendix: Comment on Sanders, Parsons, and Logan. In: The Valley of Mexico: Studies in Pre-Hispanic Ecology and Society, edited by Eric R. Wolf, pp. 179–80. Albuquerque: University of New Mexico Press.
1980 Cultural ecology reconsidered. American Antiquity, 45:1:145–50.
1981 Review of The Basin of Mexico (William T. Sanders, Jeffrey Parsons, and Robert Santley). American Anthropologist, 83(1):223–24.
1983a The ecological approach in highland Mesoamerican archaeology. In: Archaeological Hammers and Theories, edited by James A. Moore and Arthur S. Keene, pp. 221–33. New York: Academic Press.
1983b Advances in the study of cultural evolution in prehispanic highland Mesoamerica. In: Advances in World Archaeology, edited by Fred Wendorf and Angela E. Close, pp. 245–88. New York: Academic Press.
1988 Comment on Ecological Theory and Cultural Evolution in the Valley of Oaxaca (William T. Sanders and Deborah Nichols). Current Anthropology, 29(1):52–54.
1989 Continuity and change in public architecture: Periods I through V in the Valley of Oaxaca, Mexico. In: Monte Albán's Hinterland, Part II: Prehispanic Settlement Patterns in Tlacolula, Etla, and Ocotlán, the Valley of Oaxaca, Mexico, by Stephen A. Kowalewski, Gary M. Feinman, Laura Finsten, Richard E. Blanton, and Linda M. Nicholas, pp 409–47. Memoirs, 23. Museum of Anthropology, University of Michigan. Ann Arbor.

Blanton, Richard E., Stephen A. Kowalewski, Gary M. Feinman, and Jill Appel
1981 Ancient Mesoamerica: A Comparison of Change in Three Regions. Cambridge: Cambridge University Press.
1982 Monte Alban's Hinterland, Part I: Prehispanic Settlement Patterns of the Central and Southern Parts of the Valley of Oaxaca, Mexico. Prehistory and Human Ecology of the Valley of Oaxaca, Vol. 7, edited by Kent V. Flannery and Richard E. Blanton. Memoirs, 15. Museum of Anthropology, University of Michigan. Ann Arbor.

Carneiro, Robert
1987 Review of Development and Decline: The Evolution of Sociopolitical Organization (edited by Henri J. M. Claessen, Pieter van de Velde, and M. Estellie Smith). American Ethnologist, 14(4):756–70.

Conrad, Geoffrey W., and Arthur A. Demarest
1984 Religion and Empire: The Dynamics of Aztec and Inca Expansionism. Cambridge: Cambridge University Press.

Cowgill, George
1975a Population pressure as a non-explanation. In: Population Studies in Archaeology and Biological Anthropology: A Symposium, edited by Alan Swedlund, pp. 127–31. American Antiquity Memoir, 30.
1975b On causes and consequences of ancient and modern population change. American Anthropologist, 77(3):505–25.

Feinman, Gary M.
1982 Patterns in ceramic production and distribution, Periods I through V. In: Monte Albán's Hinterland, Part I: Prehispanic Settlement Patterns of the Central and Southern Parts of the Valley of Oaxaca. Prehistory and Human Ecology of the Valley of Oaxaca, Vol. 7, edited by Kent V. Flannery and Richard E. Blanton, pp. 181–206. Memoirs, 15. Museum of Anthropology, University of Michigan. Ann Arbor.

Feinman, Gary M., Stephen A. Kowalewski, Laura Finsten, Richard E. Blanton, and Linda Nicholas
1985 Long-term demographic change: A perspective from the Valley of Oaxaca. Journal of Field Archaeology, 12:333–62.

Feinman, Gary M., and Linda M. Nicholas
1988a Comment on Ecological Theory and Cultural Evolution in the Valley of Oaxaca (William T. Sanders and Deborah L. Nichols). Current Anthropology, 29(1):52–54.
1988b The prehispanic settlement history of the Ejutla Valley, Mexico: A preliminary perspective. Mexicon, 10(1):5–13.

Fish, Suzanne K., and Stephen A. Kowalewski (eds.)
1990 The Archaeology of Regions: A Case for Full-Coverage Survey. Washington, D.C.: Smithsonian Institution Press.

Harris, Marvin
1979 Cultural Materialism: The Struggle for a Science of Culture. New York: Random House.

Hodder, Ian
1986 Reading the Past: Current Approaches to Interpretation in Archaeology. New York: Cambridge University Press.

Kowalewski, Stephen A.
1980 Population-resource balances in Period I of Oaxaca, Mexico. American Antiquity 45(1):151-65.
1982 Population and agricultural potential: Early I through V. In: Monte Alban's Hinterland, Part I: Prehispanic Settlement Patterns of the Central and Southern Parts of the Valley of Oaxaca, Mexico. Prehistory and Human Ecology of the Valley of Oaxaca, Vol. 7, edited by Kent V. Flannery and Richard E. Blanton. Memoirs, 15. Museum of Anthropology, University of Michigan. Ann Arbor.

Kowalewski, Stephen A., Gary M. Feinman, Laura Finsten, Richard E. Blanton, and Linda M. Nicholas
1989 Monte Albán's Hinterland, Part II: Prehispanic Settlement Patterns in Tlacolula, Etla, and Ocotlán, the Valley of Oaxaca, Mexico. Memoirs, 23. Museum of Anthropology, University of Michigan. Ann Arbor.

Kuhn, Thomas S.
1970 The Structure of Scientific Revolutions, 2nd ed. Chicago: University of Chicago Press.
1977 Second thoughts on paradigms. In: The Structure of Scientific Theories, 2nd ed., edited by Frederick Suppe, pp. 459-82. Urbana and Chicago: University of Illinois Press.

Lakatos, Imre
1970 Falsification and the methodology of scientific research programmes. In: Criticism and the Growth of Knowledge, edited by Imre Lakatos and Alan Musgrave, pp. 91-196. Cambridge: Cambridge University Press.

Lakatos, Imre, and Alan Musgrave (eds.)
1970 Criticism and the Growth of Knowledge. Cambridge: Cambridge University Press.

Logan, Michael H., and William T. Sanders
1976 The model. In: The Valley of Mexico: Studies in Pre-Hispanic Ecology and Society, edited by Eric R. Wolf, pp. 31-58. Albuquerque: University of New Mexico Press.

Millon, René
1973 Urbanization at Teotihuacán, Mexico, Vol. 1. The Teotihuacán Map. Austin: University of Texas Press.

Nicholas, Linda M., Gary M. Feinman, Stephen A. Kowalewski, Richard E. Blanton, and Laura Finsten
1986 Prehispanic colonization of the Valley of Oaxaca, Mexico. Human Ecology, 14(2):131–62.

Parsons, Jeffrey R.
1971 Prehispanic Settlement Patterns in the Texcoco Region, Mexico. Memoirs, 3. Museum of Anthropology, University of Michigan. Ann Arbor.

Parsons, Jeffrey R., Elizabeth Brumfiel, Mary H. Parsons, and David J. Wilson
1982 Prehispanic Settlement Patterns in the Southern Valley of Mexico: The Chalco-Xochimilco Region. Memoirs, 14. Museum of Anthropology, University of Michigan. Ann Arbor.

Popper, Karl R.
1959 The Logic of Scientific Discovery. New York: Basic Books.
1970 Normal science and its dangers. In: Criticism and the Growth of Knowledge, edited by Imre Lakatos and Alan Musgrave, pp. 51–58. Cambridge: Cambridge University Press.
1983 Realism and the Aim of Science. Totowa, New Jersey: Rowman and Littlefield.

Redmond, Elsa M.
1983 A Fuego y Sangre: Early Zapotec Imperialism in the Cuicatlán Cañada, Oaxaca. Studies in Latin American Ethnohistory & Archaeology, Vol. 1, edited by Joyce Marcus. Memoirs, 16. Museum of Anthropology, University of Michigan. Ann Arbor.

Sahlins, Marshall D.
1976 Culture and Practical Reason. Chicago: University of Chicago Press.

Sanders, William T.
1957 Tierra y Agua. Ph.D. dissertation, Harvard University.
1965 The Cultural Ecology of the Teotihuacán Valley. University Park: Department of Sociology and Anthropology, The Pennsylvania State University.
1970 The population of the Teotihuacan Valley, the Basin of Mexico, and the central Mexican symbiotic region in the 16th century. In: The Natural Environment, Contemporary Occupation, and 16th Century Population of the Valley, by William T. Sanders, Anton Kovar, Thomas Charlton, and Richard Diehl, pp. 385–457. Teotihuacan Valley Final Report, Vol. 1. Occasional Papers, 3. Department of Anthropology, Pennsylvania State University.
1980 Comment on Specialization, Market Exchange, and the Aztec State: A View from Huexotla, by Elizabeth Brumfiel. Current Anthropology, 21(4):474.

Sanders, William T., Anton Kovar, Thomas Charlton, and Richard Diehl
1970   The Natural Environment, Contemporary Occupation, and 16th Century Population of the Valley. Teotihuacan Valley Final Report, Vol. 1. Occasional Papers, 3. Department of Anthropology, Pennsylvania State University.

Sanders, William T., and David Webster
1978   Unilinealism, multilinealism, and the evolution of complex societies. In: Social Archaeology, edited by Charles Redman et al., pp. 249–302. New York: Academic Press.

Sanders, William T., Jeffrey R. Parsons, and Robert Santley
1979   The Basin of Mexico: Ecological Processes in the Evolution of a Civilization. New York: Academic Press.

Sanders, William T., and Deborah L. Nichols
1988   Ecological theory and cultural evolution in the Valley of Oaxaca. Current Anthropology, 29(1):33–80.

Santley, Robert
1983   Ancient population at Monte Albán: A reconsideration of methodology and culture history. Haliksa'i, University of New Mexico Contributions to Anthropology, 2:64–84.

Stark, Barbara
1985   Prehistoric Political and Economic Change in La Mixtequilla, Veracruz, Mexico. Proposal to the National Endowment for the Humanities.

Suppe, Frederick
1977a The search for philosophical understanding of scientific theories. In: The Structure of Scientific Theories, 2nd ed., edited by Frederick Suppe, pp. 3–241. Urbana and Chicago: University of Illinois Press.
1977b Afterward-1977. In: The Structure of Scientific Theories, 2nd ed., edited by Frederick Suppe, pp. 617–730. Urbana and Chicago: University of Illinois Press.

Suppe, Frederick (ed.)
1977   The Structure of Scientific Theories, 2nd ed. Urbana and Chicago: University of Illinois Press.

2

BORRÓN, Y CUENTA NUEVA
Setting Oaxaca's Archaeological Record Straight

Kent V. Flannery and Joyce Marcus,
University of Michigan

I

As graduate students years ago, learning archaeology from our professors, we took our first glimpse of the field through idealistic eyes. Most of an archaeologist's time, we assumed, would be spent recovering data, analyzing that data, and presenting the results to a cohort of enthusiastic and supportive colleagues.

Boy, were we wrong.

To be sure, we knew that some colleagues would disagree with a particularly controversial opinion, or debate our interpretation of those phenomena which could be explained in alternative ways. That's fair enough; it just challenges you to explain why you think the preponderance of the data supports your position. But we assumed there would be no problem communicating the rawest, most rudimentary, most basic factual data, such as the depth of a pit, the size of a building, or the age of an easily dated level.

Boy, were we wrong.

We thought that if we recovered a building 5.2 meters on a side, facing north, and dated by the associated ceramics to Period B, those innocuous data would not be difficult to get across. The function of the building might be debatable, but not its size, orientation, and well-documented date.

Wrong again. To be sure, nine out of ten of our fellow archaeologists will get it right, but there will always be one turkey whose "synthesis" reports that Flannery and Marcus found a building "6.2 meters on a side, facing south, and dated to Period C." He'll be the one guy who never checks with us for accuracy, and with our luck, his error will be published in a textbook used by ten thousand archaeology students.

So all you idealistic young prehistorians, write this down: Archaeologists spend only about half their time recovering data, analyzing that material, and presenting the results to their colleagues. The other half of their time is spent correcting the errors of colleagues who misquoted them, or made factual misstatements about what they found. That is one reason archaeology proceeds so slowly.

This book is devoted largely to debates about the interpretation of Valley of Oaxaca prehistory. Such debates can be intellectually entertaining. Unfortunately, there are also a lot of factual errors in the recent literature on Oaxaca. Correcting those errors is important, but rarely intellectually entertaining.

We will devote this chapter largely to the correction of errors, while allowing our colleagues Blanton, Neely, Kowalewski, Feinman, and Nicholas the more enjoyable task of interpretive debate. And because historical perspective often has clarifying power, we will present our critique in the form of a retrospective look at Oaxaca archaeology.

In our discussions, we take the most charitable position on the mistakes made by others while citing our work. We do not assume that they have done it deliberately, in an effort to be difficult or contrary (although there are one or two cases where that motive could be suspected). Rather, we assume that we simply didn't do a good enough job of explaining things the first time around. As we go over each point in this chapter, we will therefore give fuller documentation than we did in our original publications. For the vast majority of our colleagues, we are sure that that will be more than enough. Or are we still being too idealistic?

II

Our project, The Prehistory and Human Ecology of the Valley of Oaxaca, began with the discovery of Cueva Blanca, near Mitla, in December of 1964 (Flannery [ed.] 1986:37). A quarter of a century has passed since that discovery, and a great deal of information on Oaxaca has accumulated—so much that it is often taken for granted. Let us therefore look back to November of 1964, and remind ourselves exactly what we knew about the Valley of Oaxaca at that moment.

We knew, among other things, about Monte Albán. We knew it was one of the largest and earliest cities in Mesoamerica, and occupied one of the most spectacular mountaintop locations. It also had an eight-period sequence (Monte Albán Ia, Ib, Ic, II, IIIa, IIIb, IV, and V) worked out stratigraphically by Caso, Bernal, and Acosta (1967; see also Bernal 1946, 1949a, and 1949b). But Monte Albán had no apparent antecedents in the area; its Period Ia, then thought to date back perhaps as far as 600 B.C., was the earliest period known in the valley. Even a survey of some 275 important sites in the valleys of Etla, Tlacolula, Zaachila-Zimatlán, and Ejutla by Bernal (1965) had not recovered earlier materials. This meant that the Valley of Oaxaca so far had no Preceramic and no Early Formative. This lacuna was explained by reference to a giant lake which some ethnohistoric documents claimed to have filled the ancient Valley of Oaxaca. It was widely believed that this lake had drained around 600 B.C., allowing settlement to take place on the valley floor.

As for the earliest occupants of Monte Albán, they were thought perhaps to have come from Monte Negro, a site in the Tilantongo Valley of the Mixteca Alta, which was important at a time roughly contemporaneous with Monte Albán I. At the same time, the art of Monte Albán I was also thought to show "Olmec influence." In particular, the series of Period I carved stones popularly called *danzantes* ("dancers") and *nadadores* ("swimmers") were thought to have Olmec stylistic traits. Originally described by Dupaix in 1806 (Dupaix 1969), these stones had been dated to Monte Albán Ia by Caso on the basis of the associated ceramics, and were thought by many to represent nude dancers or people swimming, perhaps in the giant lake.

While many scholars remained confused as to whether Monte Albán I was Mixtec-derived or Olmec-derived, Monte Albán II was thought to be "Maya influenced." Many of the ceramic attributes appearing for the first time in Period II, such as waxy red and orange slips, rim flanges, and swollen mammiform supports, brought to mind the Protoclassic pottery of Chiapas and Guatemala. Then came Monte Albán IIIa, with its "Teotihuacán-influenced" Thin Orange vessels with ring bases, adding another region to the list of outside influences on the Valley of Oaxaca. In the former Regional Museum in Oaxaca, which used to stand on the north side of the Alameda during the 1950s and 1960s, one label read: "During Monte Albán IIIa, the Olmec tradition fused with Maya and Teotihuacán influence to produce the Zapotec culture." Thus, while it was generally acknowledged that Monte Albán was the product of the Zapotec Indians, Zapotec culture was seen as a rather late development brought about by the hybridization of powerful influences from at least three different regions of Mesoamerica.

Archaeological research over the last twenty years, recently summarized in a volume called *The Cloud People* (Flannery and Marcus [eds.] 1983), has gradually changed our understanding of Valley of Oaxaca prehistory. Unfortunately, old myths and legends die hard, and new data take decades to reach the secondary literature. Perhaps the slowest to change are the tourist guide books, which often lag years behind the cutting edge of research.

Today there are two tourist booklets on Oaxaca. The one we recommend is the Official Guide of the Instituto Nacional de Antropología e Historia, written by Ignacio Bernal (1985), one of the original excavators of Monte Albán, Cuilapan, Dainzú, Mitla, Yagul, and other important sites in Oaxaca. In it, Bernal not only draws on his forty years of experience in the area, but also incorporates many of the discoveries made by the Universities of Michigan, Purdue, Georgia, and Wisconsin in recent years. The other tourist booklet (Winter 1989) appears to have been written by someone with a copy of *The Cloud People* open on the desk beside him, but with some inadvertent and occasionally humorous errors made in summarizing our results. Perhaps these errors are understandable, because the electric lighting in Oaxaca fluctuates a lot and, as Barbara Voorhies (1984:762) pointed out in her review, *The Cloud People* "is printed on glaring paper with small type, which makes reading unnecessarily tiring." We hope that some clarification of our findings, printed on non-glaring paper in this chapter, will eliminate future errors.

Winter's tourist guide does have one curious omission which probably can't be blamed on glaring paper: There is no mention of the fact that the Valley of Oaxaca has now been intensively surveyed, with approximately 2700 archaeological sites and 6153 components recorded (Blanton et al. 1982; Kowalewski et al. 1989). This omission suggests that the staff of the second largest settlement pattern survey in the history of Mesoamerican archaeology slipped into the valley, did their research, and left without Winter's noticing them. Now, we realize that Winter has a "killer" schedule of gluing together restorable vessels, but he really owes it to himself to get out of his office more often.

III

One of the first things our project did in Oaxaca was to bring down a team of British geomorphologist-geographers to study the soil, water, and geological history of the Valley of Oaxaca. It took Michael and Anne Kirkby only a few weeks to determine that there had never been a giant lake in the Valley of Oaxaca. It was, and had been for all of the Pleistocene, a river valley, the product of the Atoyac River and its tributary, the Río Salado. There was therefore no reason why the valley should not have been occupied prior to Monte Albán I.

As we began our survey for earlier sites, we soon found evidence that the valley had in fact been inhabited far back into Preceramic times. First, a series of caves and rockshelters near Mitla yielded the remains of Archaic hunter-gatherers and early agriculturalists, back to at least 8000 B.C. More recently, a Clovis-type fluted point was found by the Oaxaca Settlement Pattern Project near San Juan Guelavía (Finsten, Flannery, and Macnider 1989); this point may have been contemporaneous with the broken and burned Late Pleistocene fauna we found in Zone F of Cueva Blanca (Flannery 1983).

The circumstances under which Early Formative remains were first found in the Valley of Oaxaca are not familiar to the average reader, so let us briefly review them. In the collections of the Museo Frissell de Arte Zapoteca in Mitla in 1966 were dozens of figurines which, by any stylistic criterion, should have been Early and Middle Formative. Those figurines had been purchased over the years from Oaxaca villagers who regularly came to Mitla. Many were without provenience, but one large sample was said to have come from San Sebastián Etla.

One day in 1966, when Richard S. MacNeish had come to visit our project, we decided to visit San Sebastián Etla as a kind of busman's holiday. The immediate environs of the town, which lies in the eastern piedmont of the Etla valley, revealed no Formative, so we moved west toward the border between the lands of San Sebastián Etla and the neighboring village of San José Mogote. Here a series of dry arroyos on the slope overlooking San José Mogote had Formative material eroding from their lower levels, and our conversations with local farmers indicated that this must be the place from which the figurines in the Frissell Museum had come.

Following MacNeish's visit, we decided to survey San José Mogote itself. This was a large site with many impressive mounds, a ballcourt, and a main plaza, features which a *priori* had led us to suspect a Classic date (much as Kidder, Jennings, and Shook [1946] had expected Kaminaljuyú to be a Classic site because of its many impressive mounds). To our surprise, it turned out that most of the deposits at San José Mogote were Monte Albán II or earlier. In a dry arroyo coming down from the east edge of the main plaza, we found a rocker-stamped *tecomate* eroding out of a deeply-buried level. Now we knew where the Early Formative was and what it looked like.

Over the course of the next three field seasons, as we became more and more familiar with the Early and Middle Formative of the Valley of Oaxaca, we began finding more and more sites of that period. In the first stages of our survey for Formative sites, Dr. Ignacio Bernal generously supplied us with a list of the 275 sites he had already located. We systematically visited all those at which he had found Monte Albán I pottery. As it turned out, many of the Formative sites we later excavated—including San José Mogote, Barrio del Rosario Huitzo, Tierras Largas, Fábrica San José, Abasolo, Tomaltepec, and Mitla—had already been visited by Dr. Bernal and given numbers in his system.

It should be remembered that Bernal did much of his survey in the early 1950s, before the Early Formative ceramics of Chiapa de Corzo, the Tehuacán Valley, or the Ocós region of Guatemala had been published. Therefore, the Early and Middle Formative ceramics of southern Mexico were not yet well known, and when Bernal found occasional sherds of this material, he could not be sure that they were anything more than trade wares of the Monte Albán I period (Bernal, personal communication) . Only in the 1960s, with the explosion of work on the Formative from Puebla to Soconusco, did it become easier to recognize Early Formative horizon markers on the surface of Oaxaca sites.

As survey continued in the 1970s under Blanton, Kowalewski, Feinman, and the other members of the Oaxaca Settlement Pattern Project, it became apparent that the Valley of Oaxaca had not only been occupied prior to Monte Albán I, but in fact had one of the highest densities of early villages anywhere in Mesoamerica. At this writing, there are 18 to 20 sites known from the Tierras Largas phase (1450–1150 B.C.), 40 sites known from the San José phase (1150–850 B.C.), and 85 sites known from the Rosario phase (700–500 B.C.). (It is more difficult to estimate the number of sites of the period 850–700 B.C. because the ceramic complexes in the various arms of the valley are not uniform.)

Our study of the Oaxaca Formative has changed our pre-1966 view of the region in other ways. First of all, one no longer has to look outside the Valley of Oaxaca to find the origins of Monte Albán I. At Barrio del Rosario Huitzo, for example, one can see a long ceramic sequence gradually evolving *in situ* into that of Monte Albán I, and at San José Mogote one can see a long architectural sequence evolving into the Monte Albán I architectural style. A second point is that Monte Albán I is not Olmec at all, but post-Olmec. The period that shows the greatest interaction with the Gulf Coast Olmec is the San José phase, when motifs like the fire-serpent and were-jaguar occurred on Oaxaca pottery (Marcus 1989). And even in this case, it is not clear that Oaxaca potters were imitating Gulf Coast themes; there are more than 600 examples of fire-serpent or were-jaguar motifs from San José Mogote alone, more than are known from any site on the Gulf Coast.

Perhaps the biggest difference between the Valley of Oaxaca and the Gulf Coast Olmec, however, lies in ceremonial architecture (Flannery and Marcus 1976a, 1976b; Marcus 1989). Most Gulf Coast public architecture of 1200–850 B.C. consists of clay mounds and clay platforms, with no use of stone or of lime plaster. As early as the Tierras Largas phase, Oaxaca villagers were building small public buildings on crushed bedrock foundations and coating them inside and out with lime plaster. At least as early as 900 B.C., they were placing them on dry-laid stone masonry platforms with small stairways, and by 700 B.C. they were building those platforms out of multi-ton limestone blocks. This type of architecture leads directly into the masonry buildings of Monte Albán I, but finds no parallels in the Olmec region. Oaxaca masonry buildings of the period 700–400 B.C. are also accompanied by calendric inscriptions carved in stone, which are earlier than any calendric monument known so far from the Gulf Coast. Thus, we would now reject the old, pre-1966 view that early complex society in Oaxaca was derived either from the Olmec or from Monte Negro in the Mixteca. We see it developing *in situ* in the Valley of Oaxaca over thousands of years and contributing its own special features, such as lime plaster, stone masonry, and early calendrics.

Let us say a few words about our Tierras Largas phase public buildings, for they have been erroneously portrayed in Winter's tourist guide. The Tierras Largas phase, so far as we can tell archaeologically, was a time of egalitarian society. All known residences of the period are small, wattle-and-daub houses, perhaps whitewashed on the outside, but never lime-plastered on the inside. They do not have a consistent orientation, their sand floors are littered with artifacts and sherds, and we can detect no differences in artifact content that might indicate social ranking. The burials of the period are generally simple and, while they may include pottery vessels or occasional figurines, the differences among them do not suggest the existence of inherited status. We do have two Tierras Largas phase burials from San José Mogote that appear to have been of the seated type, like some later high-status burials, but their offerings were modest.

The small public buildings of the Tierras Largas phase, which so far have been found only at San José Mogote, are so different from the residences of the period as to leave no doubt that they are different in function (Figs. 2.1–2.4). First of all, they are all oriented 8 degrees west of true north, an orientation which is widespread among public buildings at early Mesoamerican sites, but not among residences.

Figure 2.1. Tierras Largas phase public buildings from San José Mogote. *Top*: Structure 6, showing a step or altar at left, and a pit, Feature 56, near the center. *Bottom*: Bedrock below the southeast corner of Structure 3, showing a posthole density which is twice that of the typical Early Formative residence.

Figure 2.2. Early Formative public buildings from San José Mogote. *Top*: Northeast corner of Structure 7, Area C. Note hollows for posts within the wall stubs. (This yellow-plastered, one-room public building dated to the San José phase.) *Bottom*: Northeast corner of Structure 6, Area C. The fallen fragment displays a patch of white, lime-plastered upper surface from a "sitting bench" that ran along one wall of the room. (Tierras Largas phase.)

Figure 2.3. Lime-plastered pits from Tierras Largas phase public buildings at San José Mogote. *Top*: Feature 55 in Structure 15. *Bottom*: Feature 56 in Structure 6. (When found, both pits were filled to the brim with powdered lime; such features are not found in ordinary residences of the phase.)

SETTING THE RECORD STRAIGHT 27

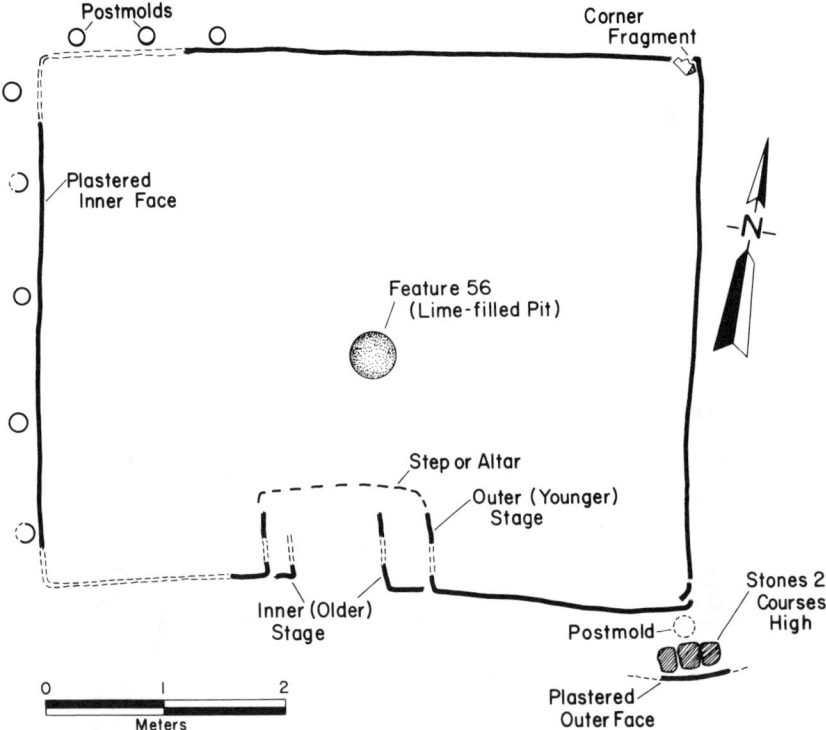

Figure 2.4. Plan view of Structure 6 at San José Mogote, showing that the structure was definitely a one-room building with a plastered outer face (see lower right).

Figure 2.5. Structure 8 at San José Mogote, a Guadalupe phase public building. *Top*: South end, showing dry-laid stone masonry exterior walls (foreground) and fill-retaining interior walls constructed with plano-convex adobes (background). *Bottom*: North end, showing plano-convex adobe retaining wall and a remnant of the puddled adobe upper surface.

Second, they have many times the number of posts used in ordinary residences (Fig. 2.1). Third, they are plastered and replastered with pure white lime stucco inside as well as outside, and are swept clean of artifacts (Fig. 2.2). Fourth, each contains a centrally placed circular pit, filled to the brim with powdered lime, which we suspect may have been used in association with some ritual plant, such as tobacco (Fig. 2.3). Fifth, these structures may contain a large step or altar just inside the doorway, or a well-made sitting bench, which residences of the period do not have. The buildings were roofed with pine poles, over which went reed matting and a thatch of reed canary grass (*Phalaris* sp.); in one case, the roof had burned and collapsed into the building, providing us with numerous details.

Unfortunately, Winter's tourist booklet is quite confused about these buildings, calling them "relatively elaborate and well-preserved Tierras Largas phase residences," and adding that "some had adobe walls about 1 meter high, and apparently consisted of patios surrounded by rooms" (Winter 1989:117). This is erroneous on several counts. First of all, each structure consists of a single room (see Fig. 2.4), of which both the inside and outside have been found; no patios were involved, and in fact, patios are not known until much later in the Formative sequence. Second, as we have already seen, the buildings are roofed and thatched; after all, one would hardly store powdered lime in an open patio in a region receiving 550 mm of rain a year! Third, there were absolutely no adobes associated with these buildings. In fact, adobes were unknown in the Tierras Largas phase; they first appeared around 850 B.C. Evidently Winter has confused our Structure 6, a Tierras Largas phase public building (Fig. 2.1), with our Structure 8, an adobe platform of the Guadalupe phase (850–700 B.C.), which was found stratigraphically well above Structure 6 (see Fig. 2.5 and Flannery and Marcus 1976b: Fig. 10.5).

Winter's confusion is all the more puzzling because, on page 23 of the same tourist booklet, he has already described Tierras Largas phase village organization as "egalitarian." If it was egalitarian, why would one family out of the entire community have an elaborate, astronomically oriented, lime-plastered residence with no utilitarian artifacts in it, while everyone else in the valley lived in a modest wattle-and-daub hut? You can't have it both ways. Our position, which will be spelled out in detail in future publications, is that these small buildings were analogous to the "men's houses" in some ethnographically documented egalitarian farming societies.

For the record, the actual sequence of architectural features in Oaxaca is as follows. Lime plaster appears by 1350 B.C.; bun-shaped adobes appear by 850 B.C.; rectangular adobes appear by 700 B.C.;

pyramidal mounds with relatively crude stone masonry facades and simple stairways appear by 900 B.C.; and more sophisticated stone masonry buildings with vertical walls, wide stairways, and stones weighing a half-ton or more appear by 650 B.C. While households of the late San José phase could consist of wattle-and-daub structures on two sides of a dooryard or open-air work space, actual patios (surrounded on all four sides by rooms) are so far not known prior to the adobe residences of high-status Rosario phase families. Future work might one day extend any of these features backward in time, but this is where we stand at the moment.

Before leaving the Early Formative, let us also correct a bit of confusion about the burials of the period. As we have suggested, our relatively small sample of burials of the Tierras Largas phase does not provide us with evidence for hereditary social inequality. Such evidence first emerges, in a modest way, in our much larger sample of San José phase burials. As discussed more fully in *The Cloud People*, the San José phase also gives us our first evidence for differential treatment of men and women. Only men seem to have received cylindrical vessels with carvings of the were-jaguar or fire-serpent, while women tended to receive bowls and jars of other kinds. Since some infants (too young for the sex to be determined) had fire-serpent vessels like those found with men, and other infants (also too young to be sexed) had vessels like those found with adult women, we conclude that the association of males with "Olmec" motifs was present from birth.

However, just as reported by Tolstoy (1989) for the Valley of Mexico, "Olmec" motifs were not necessarily predictors of rank. Other features—such as jade artifacts, mother-of-pearl artifacts, magnetite mirrors, and the presence of stone slabs around the grave—may be better indicators of rank. So also, apparently, was burial position. At the San José phase cemetery at Tomaltepec, which yielded 80 individuals, the most common burial position was fully extended, face down, with arms folded across the chest. (Although Whalen [1981] claims that Tomaltepec was "unusual" in its high frequency of this burial position, this is in fact the most common burial position everywhere in the San José phase.) However, the group of male burials described by Whalen as "flexed"—although it comprised only 12.7% of the individuals in the cemetery—was accompanied by 88% of the jade beads, 66% of the slab coverings, and 50% of the vessels with fire-serpent motifs. We conclude, as did Whalen, that these "flexed" males were some of the higher-status members of the community. However, based not only on burial data, but also on differences in house construction, access to deer meat, and exotic raw material, we see status differentiation in the San José phase as forming a continuum from relatively high to relatively low status, without a sharp division into actual strata or classes.

Recently, we have had an opportunity to re-examine photographs and drawings of all the burials of this period which have been described as "flexed," and to compare them with other examples from Mexico and Central America. We now feel that most, if not all, of those burials could be described as "seated crosslegged." In some cases, it appears that burials which had originally been seated, tailor-fashion, had slumped under the weight of the overburden to a face-down position, while others had slumped backwards to a face-up position. In addition to the flexed males at Tomaltepec, such male interments as Burial 3 at Abasolo, Burials 28 and 29 at San José Mogote, and perhaps even Burial 42 at Tierras Largas, could be interpreted as burials that were originally seated upright in conical or bell-shaped pits, but eventually collapsed under the weight of the earth as the flesh disintegrated.

There are precedents for such burials elsewhere; Vaillant (1931:422) found a seated male burial at Ticomán, as did Lothrop (1937) at Coclé. In cases where the details are known, such a burial position often indicates high status; for example, Panamanian chiefs were typically buried in this position, while commoners were buried fully extended so that their heads would be lower than the chief's. Such "seated" burials may even have been wrapped tightly in a bundle of some kind, like the seated high-status bundle burials shown in the later codices of the Mixtec and Aztec. Our oldest example of this burial type comes from the very end of the Tierras Largas phase at San José Mogote, and such burials become more common in the San José phase.

IV

In Topic 19 of *The Cloud People*, "The Rosario Phase and the Origins of Monte Albán I," we have summarized the evolution in ceramics and architecture which indicates conclusively that Monte Albán I developed *in situ* out of the Rosario phase (Flannery and Marcus 1983b:74–77). We suggest that anyone interested in that transition take a look at those pages.

Winter clearly has read Topic 19, but an electrical power surge evidently reflected off the glaring paper of *The Cloud People* that day, causing him to misdate some of our Rosario buildings and features in his tourist guide. Without repeating all of Topic 19, let us simply review a few of the salient points, and place the buildings in their proper periods.

The Rosario phase takes its name from the Barrio del Rosario of San Pablo Huitzo, where it was first recovered by Flannery in 1967 (Flannery and Marcus 1983a:60–62). However, it is now much better known as the result of larger samples from San José Mogote and its satellite community, Fábrica San José (Drennan 1976a). The very large sample from San José Mogote is important for the following reasons.

By the time of the Rosario phase (700–500 B.C.), Formative society in the Valley of Oaxaca had reached the level of what Wright (1984) would call a "complex chiefdom" and Carneiro (1981) would call a "maximal chiefdom." Complex chiefdoms have status differences which may be reflected in the ceramics, and the Rosario phase is no exception. Rosario has both utilitarian ceramics, which occur in smaller hamlets and in the lower-status residential areas of large communities, and much fancier elite vessels, which occur only in high-status residential areas and around important public buildings. Even at Fábrica San José, a 3-ha village, those status differences are detectable. Drennan (1976a:111–13) reports that bowls (especially decorated Socorro Fine Gray bowls) are more common around high-status households, while jars and other drab storage vessels are relatively more common around low-status households.

The contrasts are even greater between San José Mogote, a 70-ha site which was probably a paramount chief's village, and its smaller satellite communities. In high-status areas of San José Mogote there are unusual Rosario ceramics, such as the set of miniature vessels illustrated in Figure 2.6, and a much higher frequency of negative or resist white-on-gray decoration than one finds at smaller villages in the valley. Part of Winter's confusion about Rosario ceramics stems from the fact that he is familiar only with small samples like those from two bell-shaped pits at Tierras Largas (Winter 1976) — a site that was only a 3-hectare hamlet during Rosario times, and therefore did not produce the full range of types, vessels, and decoration seen at larger and more elite communities.

One of the most useful studies of Rosario phase pottery is that of Drennan (1976a, 1976b), who showed that at Fábrica San José, Rosario phase ceramics evolved into the pottery of Monte Albán Ia through a series of gradual, quantifiable steps. For example, the Socorro Fine Gray pottery of the Rosario phase is the direct ancestor of the Monte Albán Ia types G3, G5, G15, G16, and G17. Guadalupe Burnished Brown, one of the most common utilitarian wares of the Rosario phase, evolves into several of the *café* wares of Monte Albán

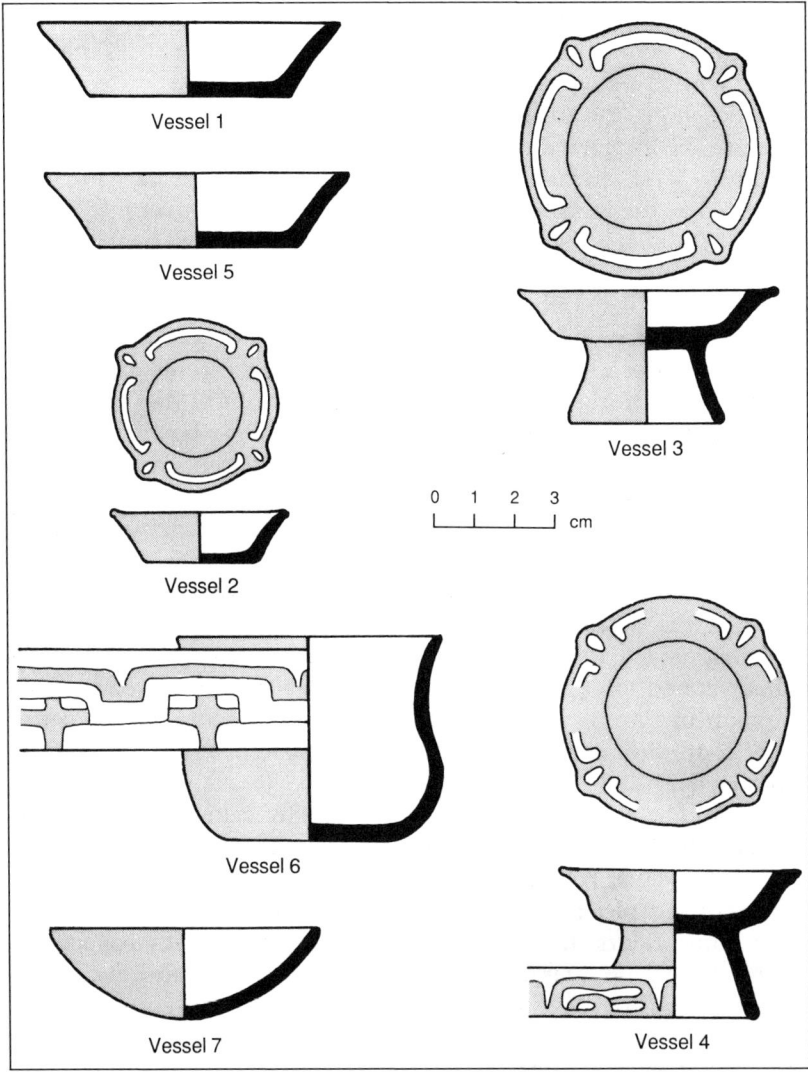

Figure 2.6. Set of seven miniature Socorro Fine Gray vessels from Burial 68, Mound 1, San José Mogote, a high-status Rosario phase interment. Vessels 2, 3, 4, and 6 have negative or resist white designs on a gray background. Note the "paw-wing" motif on the pedestal base of Vessel 4.

Ia, including types K3 and K8. Fidencio Coarse jars of the Rosario phase, with their drab maroon or brick-red wash, become lighter buff, and their wash gradually becomes a clearer red, until they have been transformed into the C2 jars of Monte Albán Ia.

Drennan (1976a, 1976b) produced a multidimensional scaling program which allows anyone to place an excavated collection of ceramics along the continuum from Rosario to Monte Albán Ia. For example, he took the flat-based Socorro Fine Gray bowls of the Rosario phase and divided them into 12 rim forms, 4 of which are restricted to the Rosario phase and 8 of which carry over into Monte Albán I grayware. He further defined 7 forms of rim eccentricities, 5 of which are restricted to the Rosario phase and 2 of which carry over (in modified form) into Monte Albán I grayware. Incised designs on the rims of these bowls show a similar series of gradual changes. Early in the Rosario phase the designs include crescents, double-line breaks, and a curious motif like a pennant or naval flag (which we now know evolved out of the earlier "diamond-in-a-box" motif of the Guadalupe phase). During Monte Albán Ia, crescents and pennants are absent; only the most elaborate versions of the double-line break survive; and swirling clouds, sine curves, and triangular areas of opposed hachure come to dominate.

Two other attributes on Socorro Fine Gray bowls which are diagnostic of the Rosario phase are the use of negative or resist white painting, and a form of pattern burnishing between incised lines called "zoned toning." Negative/resist white painting is particularly common in elite residential areas at San José Mogote, where it was used to produce crescents, double-line breaks, or even pennants on gray bowls.

It should be noted that Drennan's method of achieving chronology through multidimensional scaling of attributes, while it has worked extremely well at Fábrica San José and San José Mogote, is intended for use on samples from excavated context, such as unmixed samples from house floors. It is not intended for surface survey collections, where there is no guarantee that the sherds collected are all contemporaneous or from the same original provenience. Moreover, some of the motifs that are the most characteristic of the Rosario phase—and therefore most useful for surface survey—are some of the rarest. Not only are many versions of pennant incising and negative/resist white not particularly common, they may be far more frequent in elite residential areas than they are in low-status residential areas; a map of their occurrence, therefore, would be more of an indicator of Rosario phase elite residences and public buildings than of lower-status residences. The latter may be indicated primarily by Guadalupe Burnished Brown bowls and Fidencio Coarse jars, which are easy to overlook on surface survey, and can be hard to pin down to time period. We feel that these problems have sometimes led our colleagues on the Oaxaca Settlement Pattern Project (Kowalewski et al. 1989) to underestimate low-status Rosario populations, while overestimating Monte Albán Ia populations, at sites for which we have excavation data. We will pursue this problem further in a future article.

One of the most complex yet rewarding excavations we undertook on Mound 1 at San José Mogote was that of the stratified mound incorporating Structure 19. There were at least seven major construction levels in this mound, and it took three field seasons to excavate it completely, using not only Mesoamerican techniques but also methods used at Near Eastern *tells* such as Tepe Gawra (Tobler 1950). The lowest levels dated to the San José and Guadalupe phases and preceded the construction of Structure 19. Then came Structure 19, a public building of the Rosario phase, with many architectural modifications and additions which will be described below. Next, after Structure 19 had ceased to function as a public building, it came to be used as the platform to support an elite residence of late Rosario times (see Flannery and Marcus 1983a: Fig. 3.11). This elite residence in stratigraphic Zone B—consisting of adobe rooms around a central courtyard, two tombs (one of which had two chambers), a storage room with several ceremonial vessels, and burials with jade offerings—produced abundant ceramics, unmistakably dated to the Rosario phase on the basis of the criteria discussed above. We mention this to make it clear that Structure 19—which was stratigraphically sealed below this Rosario phase elite residence—*cannot therefore be later than Rosario in date.*

In Zone A2, stratigraphically above Zone B, we found a small platform (Structure 23) and a skeleton (Burial 53) dating to Monte Albán Ia. The burial was accompanied by two typical garnet-slipped C4 bottles which are unmistakably Period Ia. It is worth noting that this modest structure was the only Monte Albán I construction we have ever found in fifteen years of work at San José Mogote, and it is as unimpressive as the earlier Rosario public buildings are impressive.

Finally, in Zone A1, stratigraphically above A2, we found the badly-eroded remains of a Monte Albán II temple (Structure 29) with an offering box under its stucco floor. This offering box (Feature 75) yielded the large effigy *brasero* shown in Figure 2.7 (see also Flannery, Marcus, and Kowalewski 1981: Fig. 3–30), a piece now on display in the museum at San José Mogote. Unfortunately, Winter's tourist guide misdates this piece, calling it "a Period I effigy brazier" (Winter

Figure 2.7. Effigy *brasero* from Feature 75, an offering box below the floor of Structure 29. Structure 29 is a Monte Albán II temple on Mound 1 at San José Mogote. Maximum height, 55 cm.

Figure 2.8. Typical Monte Albán II bowl with mammiform supports and scratched-in *xicalcoliuhqui* motif. Such vessels can occur in either black or red.

1989:118) . In this case, Winter's misdating makes the piece too old—a deviation from his usual syndrome, which is to assign our discoveries to too recent a period. The fill in the offering box containing the *brasero* in question had prototypic Monte Albán II sherds, including G21 cane-swirled bowl bases, waxy red-on-oranges (C7), bowls with mammiform supports and scratched-in *xicalcoliuhquis* (see Fig. 2.8), and red-on-cream (A9). We would be just as pleased with the *brasero* if it were earlier, but it isn't. In fact, all the temples with subfloor offering boxes found so far at San José Mogote are Period II or later.

Now let us look in more detail at Structure 19, the centerpiece of this interesting stratigraphic sequence (Fig. 2.9). Its first stage of construction, called Structure 19B, was that of a rectangular dry-laid stone masonry platform, roughly 17 x 17 m and oriented 8 degrees west of north. This stage can be dated to the early Rosario phase by the sherds in its fill. On top of this stone-faced platform rested Structure 28, a large adobe platform with a whitewashed surface (Fig. 2.10). Structure 28 supported a massive wattle-and-daub structure which had eventually burned, converting parts of its sand floor into silica slag. Under each corner of that wattle-and-daub structure we found a large buried offering vessel; two of the vessels were Guadalupe Burnished Brown and two were Socorro Fine Gray, all typically Rosario specimens.

Later in the Rosario phase, while Structure 28 seems not to have been modified, the stone-faced platform below it was enlarged. This second stage of construction, called Structure 19A (see Fig. 2.9), was

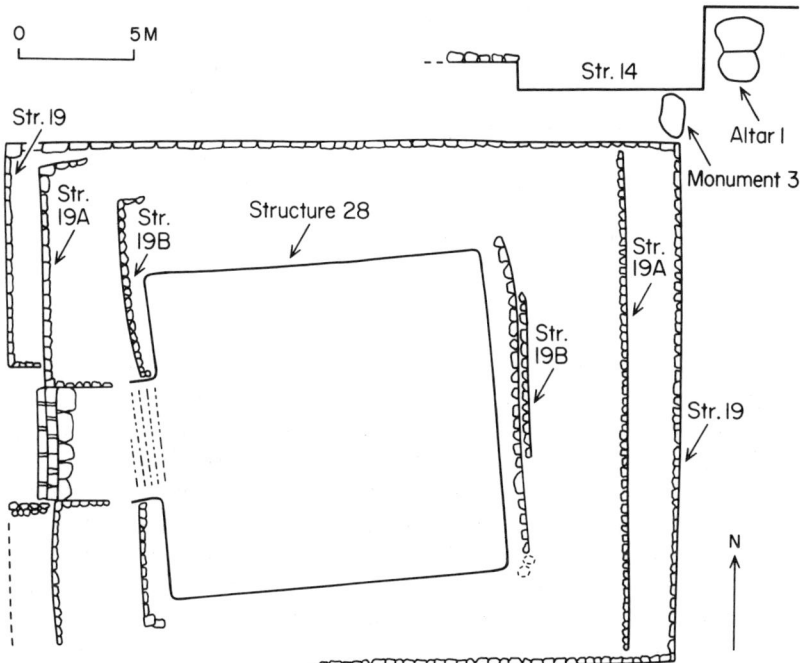

Figure 2.9. Plan of the Structure 19 area at San José Mogote, showing the relationship of Structures 19, 19A, 19B, 28, and 14, as well as Monument 3.

Figure 2.10. Structure 28, a white-washed Rosario phase adobe platform atop Structure 19 at San José Mogote, seen from the northeast.

approximately 25.5 x 20 m and oriented true north-south rather than 8 degrees west of north. It also had a stone masonry stairway on the west side (see Fig. 2.11, as well as Flannery and Marcus 1983b: Fig. 3.17a; Flannery, Marcus, and Kowalewski 1981: Fig. 3–22).

Finally, late in the Rosario phase, the stone masonry platform was enlarged for the final time, coming to measure 21.7 x 28.5 m. In building this enlargement, called Structure 19 (see Fig. 2.9), the architects used larger stones in the outer wall of the platform, but did not modify the stairway. They simply turned the later (and larger) west wall of Structure 19 in at a 90 degree angle so that it met the earlier (and less impressive) west wall of Structure 19A on both sides of the staircase (see Fig. 2.11).

Figure 2.11. Stone masonry stairway of Structure 19A, San José Mogote. Behind the workman with the stadia rod, one can see the later Structure 19 wall turn back at a right angle to meet the earlier Structure 19A facade.

Figure 2.12 will give the reader an idea of the method by which every stage of this building was dated. The photograph shows the earlier east wall of Structure 19A, exposed by removing the fill between that wall and the later enlargement called Structure 19. Every sherd in that fill was saved, washed, and analyzed by us, with the most recent sherds in the fill giving us a *terminus ad quem* for the Structure 19 enlargement. Over the course of three field seasons, Structures 19, 19A, and 19B were hollowed out to a point well below

Figure 2.12. Structure 19 seen from the northeast, showing how its various building stages were dated. At this point, the north half of the fill between the east wall of Structure 19A and the east wall of Structure 19 had been removed and the sherds saved. The workman with the stadia rod stands in the area between the Structure 19 wall (*left*) and the Structure 19A wall (*right*). The talud-like stone foundations of the Structure 19A wall can be seen just to the right of the stadia rod. After this photo was taken, the south half of the fill (immediately behind the workman) was removed and the sherds saved; then the entire area was backfilled. The sherds indicated a late Rosario phase date for the Structure 19 enlargement of the building.

their foundations, one architectural stage at a time, until there could be no doubt about the date of every building stage (Fig. 2.13). After that, each wall was consolidated with cement and the excavated areas were backfilled, with modern soft drink bottles included in the backfill dirt to indicate that each area had been completely excavated. Because of this slow and painstaking dissection of Structure 19—as

Figure 2.13. Structure 19 seen from the northwest. At this point in the excavation, the fill had been removed from between the Structure 19 facade and the Structure 19A facade, and removal of the fill from between the Structure 19A facade and the Structure 19B facade was just beginning. The workman with the stadia rod stands beside Structure 28 (see Fig. 2.10).

well as our excavation of the Guadalupe levels below it, and the late Rosario levels above it—there is no question about the date of the building. It was built in three stages, beginning in early Rosario and ending in late Rosario.

We believe that one reason the orientation of the stone platform changed from 8 degrees west of north to true north in its later stages was so that its north wall would run parallel to the south wall of another building, Structure 14, which lay just to the north (see Fig. 2.9). Structure 14 was also begun in the Rosario phase, but we know less about it because it was greatly modified, altered, and enlarged during Monte Albán II times. Alterations included raising the height of the wall, "borrowing" stones from a massive staircase on the east side of the building to use elsewhere, and ripping out the original west wall of the earlier Rosario building in order to put in a Monte Albán II staircase.

These later modifications need not concern us here. The point is that during late Rosario times, there was a corridor running east-west between the north wall of Structure 19 and the south wall of Structure 14. Serving as the threshold for this corridor was a large carved stone, Monument 3 (see Fig. 2.9). As will be clear from Figure 2.14, that stone was carefully laid flat on a bed of *lajas* or flagstones, which served to level it and prevent it from moving. Both the monument and the *lajas* are of non-local stone brought in for that purpose.

As Marcus (1974, 1976a, 1980) has argued in more detail elsewhere, the upper surface of the stone depicts a slain or sacrificed captive with the calendric name "1 Earthquake" between his feet (Fig. 2.15). He is shown naked but with a complex scroll covering his chest, possibly depicting blood issuing from an open wound like that made for the removal of the heart during sacrifice; a ribbon-like stream extends from this scroll to the edge of the stone, where two motifs (probably representing stylized drops of blood) run down the east edge of the monument. Identical motifs occur on shell ornaments of the Guadalupe phase (Drennan 1976a: Fig. 78d).

There are undoubtedly several reasons why this stone is laid flat. First of all, the viewer is meant to look down on the figure, as he would look down on a victim lying flat on a sacrificial altar. Second, the streamer of blood flows horizontally over the stone and down the edge, just as blood would behave on an actual altar. Third, by placing the stone as a threshold for the corridor, the architects ensured that anyone entering or leaving the corridor would tread on the body of the slain captive—a symbolic act akin to the Maya custom of incorporating prisoner slabs into stairways, or depicting rulers standing on the bodies of captives (see below).

Let us now discuss the stratigraphy and dating of Monument 3. First of all, it was found stratigraphically beneath an old land surface with Rosario sherds *in situ* on it. This old land surface was later buried under not one, but two, superimposed stucco floors of the Monte Albán II period. In other words, during Monte Albán II it would have been invisible, buried without a trace below plaster floors. Second, the monument's stratigraphic level clearly associates it with the foundations of Structure 19, which we already know are late Rosario. However, the final evidence for its date must rest with the sherds found sealed below it.

Figure 2.14. Monument 3 seen from the east, showing the layer of flagstones which were laid below it to level it. At this stage of excavation, the associated Rosario phase corridor floor had been removed, in order to expose both the Monument 3 flagstones and the foundations of Structures 19 (*left*) and 14 (*right*).

44 DEBATING OAXACA ARCHAEOLOGY

Figure 2.15. Top view (*right*) and side view (*left*) of Monument 3. [Drawing by Mark Orsen.]

Because we did not want to risk breaking Monument 3, or causing it to slump, it took us three field seasons to remove all the sherds from beneath it. What we did was to tunnel under the stone, removing a third of the earth from beneath it, while leaving the other two-thirds to support the stone. After removing the sherds from that section of earth, we backfilled, leaving the fill dirt to become firmer between field seasons. During the next season we tunneled under the stone again, removing the second third of the earth beneath it, and once again backfilling after we had removed the sherds. Finally, during the

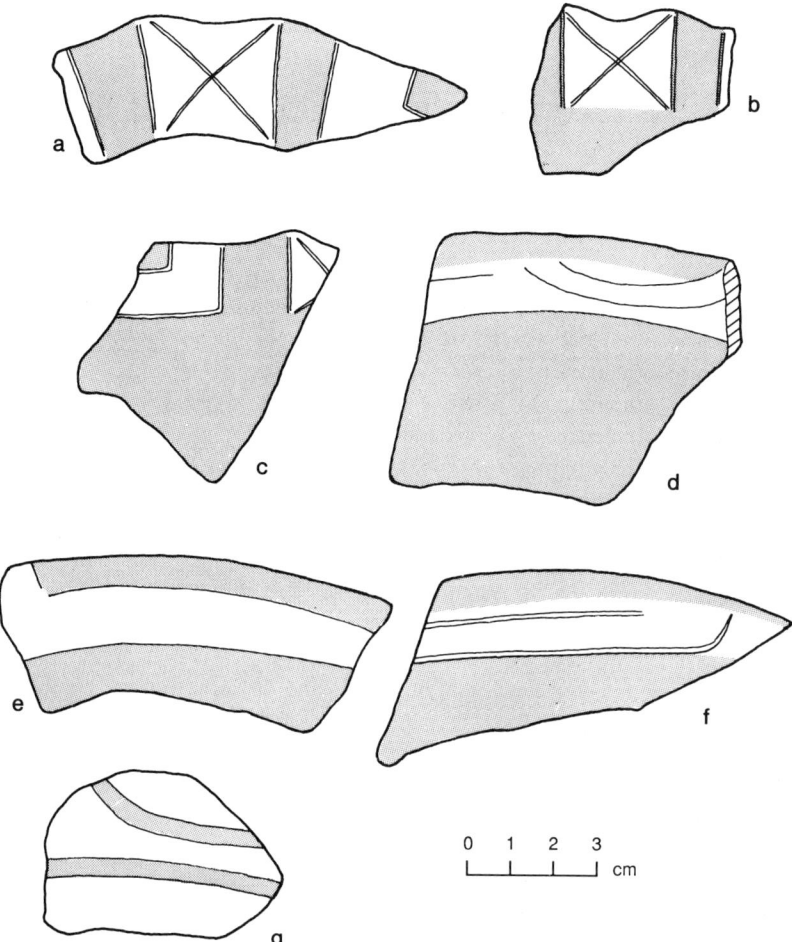

Figure 2.16. Decorated Socorro Fine Gray bowl sherds from below Monument 3. *a-c*, rims of bowls with Rim Form 5, Eccentricity 7(?), featuring incised lines with line breaks, X motif, and zoned toning (matte areas are shown as white). *d-e*, rims of Rim Form 5 with zoned toning (matte areas are shown as white). The incising on *d* is Drennan's "Type a scallop," while *e* is a double-line break. *f*, Rim Form 4 with zoned toning. *g*, Rim Form 5 with wide-line grooves.

third season we removed the last of the earth from beneath the stone to complete our collection of sherds. We then did everything we could to firm up and tightly pack the backfill, cement the *lajas* in place, and construct a protective roof over the monument.

TABLE 2.1

Sherds from below Monument 3, Mound 1, San José Mogote

Socorro Fine Gray
(1) Composite silhouette bowls with sharp carinations
   Plain-2 rims
   Negative white above carination-3 rims
   Negative white above carination and pattern burnishing below-1 rim
(2) Composite silhouette bowls with patterned burnishing/zoned toning-2 rims
(3) Composite silhouette bowls with exterior incising-3 rims
(4) Composite silhouette bowls with exterior incising + negative white-1 rim
(5) Composite silhouette bowls, body sherds
   With pattern burnishing-2 sherds
   With negative white-1 sherd
   With incising and negative white-1 sherd
(6) Miniature composite silhouette bowl-1 sherd
(7) Outleaned wall bowls-38 rims (see inventory in Table 2.2)

Josefina Fine Gray
(1) Composite silhouette bowl, incised outside and negative white-2 rims
(2) Beakers
   Plain-1 sherd
   Incised-1 sherd
(3) Outleaned wall bowl-1 sherd

Guadalupe Burnished Brown
   Outleaned wall bowls-5 rims

Coatepec White
(1) Composite silhouette bowls, incised on exterior-1 rim sherd, 1 body sherd
(2) Composite silhouette bowls-1 plain body sherd

Fidencio Coarse
(1) Jars with flaring necks-11 rims
(2) *Olla* or *tecomate* sherd with zoned slashes/jabs-1 sherd

Lupita Heavy Plain
(1) Outleaned wall bowl-1 rim
(2) *Tecomate* with zoned sloppy jabs-1 body sherd
(3) Undecorated Suchilquitongo tripod dishes-2 rims, 1 foot

TABLE 2.1 CONTINUED

Atoyac Yellow-white
(1) Outleaned wall bowls
   Plain-1 rim
   2 lines incised at rim-4 rims
   3 lines incised at rim-2 rims
   Motif 35 of Plog (1976)-1 rim
(2) Cylinders
   Plain-2 rims
   3 lines incised at rim-2 rims
   Motif 4 of Plog (1976)-1 rim
   Fine-line hachure-1 rim
(3) Bowl, oval with pinched-in sides, incised outside-1 rim
(4) Jar, tall vertical neck, incised with 2 lines-1 rim
(5) *Tecomate*, zoned, perforated for suspension-1 rim

Leandro Gray
(1) Cylinders
   Plain-1 rim
(2) Bowl, incised on outside-1 base

San José Red-on-white
Bowl, bolstered rim, slipped white inside, red band on rim, unslipped outside but incised-1 rim

Avelina Red-on-buff
Hemispherical bowls, red band on rim inside and outside-3 rims

Tierras Largas Burnished Plain
(1) Hemispherical bowls-5 rims
(2) *Olla*-1 rim

Matadamas Orange
Jars-2 rims

Figurines
(1) Guadalupe phase figurine-1 head
(2) San José phase figurines-2 heads
(3) Figurine bodies-3 fragments

TABLE 2.2

Total Inventory of Socorro Fine Gray outleaned wall bowls associated with Monument 3, San José Mogote. All rims coded following Drennan 1976a.

Rim Form	Eccentricity	Zoned Toning	Negative Painting	Incising	Motif
2					
2			yes		single crescent
2					
1					
2					
3					
3			yes		crescent
3			yes		crescent and blob
5		yes			pattern burnished band at rim
5		yes			pattern burnished band at rim
5		yes			pattern burnished band at rim
5		no			
5		yes			band at rim
2				yes	motif g, wide incising, line break
2				yes	single wide line
?				yes	motif h, fine incising, line break
?				yes	motif h, fine incising, line break
2				yes	pennant, fine incising
2				yes	motif g, wide incising, line break
3				yes	2 parallel lines, fine incising
5		yes		yes	matte between 2 parallel lines
5		no		yes	2 parallel lines, fine incising
4		yes		yes	matte between 2 parallel lines, fine
5		yes		yes	matte between incised line break
4		yes		yes	motif g, matte between lines
2				yes	motif g
5		yes		yes	scallop motif a, matte bet. lines
?		yes		yes	scallop motif b, matte bet. lines
5				yes	motif g, wide, line break
?	3			yes	motif g, fine, line break
5				yes	pennant, fine-line incising
3				yes	pennant, fine-line incising
2				yes	pennant, fine-line incising
2				yes	pennant, fine-line incising
5	7	yes		yes	bowtie and double-line break
5	7	yes		yes	bowtie and double-line break
5	7	yes		yes	bowtie and double-line break
5	1	yes		yes	fine, double-line break

SETTING THE RECORD STRAIGHT 49

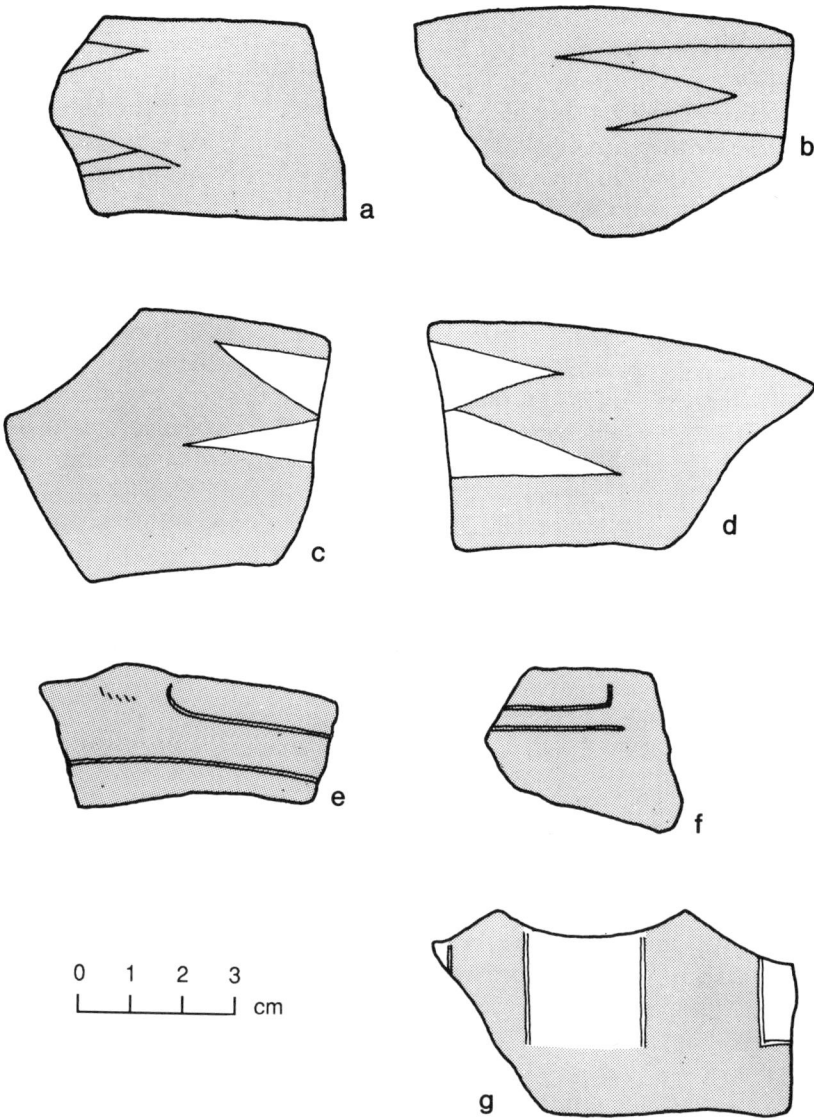

Figure 2.17. Decorated Socorro Fine Gray bowl sherds from below Monument 3. *a-b*, rims with incised pennant motif (*a* is Rim Form 3, *b* is Rim Form 5). *c-d*, rims of Rim Form 2 with pennant motif in zoned toning (matte areas are shown as white). *e*, rim with Eccentricity 3 and incised double-line break. *f*, Rim Form 2 with incised double-line break. *g*, rim of Rim Form 5, Eccentricity 1, with zoned toning and apparent line break motif (matte areas are shown as white).

The complete list of sherds found beneath Monument 3 is given in Table 2.1, and the decorated Socorro Fine Gray sherds are listed in Table 2.2 and illustrated in Figures 2.16 and 2.17. It will be clear not only from Table 2.1, but also from the illustrations, that the *terminus ad quem* for this monument is Rosario phase. In fact, the earth beneath the stone seems to have been an extension of the same Rosario level that we found under Structures 19 and 14.

We believe that the finding of such a monument (probably dating somewhere between 600 and 500 B.C.) should not be surprising, in view of the fact that there are numerous contemporary stone monuments from sites like Chalcatzingo (Grove 1984, 1987). There is also a much larger corpus of monuments from 500–400 B.C. at Monte Albán. However, we have taken time here to explain the stratigraphic position of Monument 3 and its associated ceramics because the statements made about it in Winter's tourist guide are not only inaccurate but very strange indeed.

According to Winter (1989:118): "Stylistically, the carving is similar to the [Monte Albán] Period I *danzantes,* and Late Period I pottery occurred in the area where the stone was found. The carved figure covers one broad surface and continues around on one narrow side. This suggests the stone was originally displayed in upright position in the corner of a building with one wide and one narrow face exposed. It seems likely that the stone was carved and the building constructed in Period I." He further says that the stone "was later removed and reused in the fill between two structures."

It is hard to imagine where Winter got such misinformation, especially since he was not remotely involved in the discovery or excavation of the stone, the stratigraphic work which preceded and followed its discovery, or the analysis of the ceramics associated with it. First of all, as we have just seen, the most recent ceramics associated with both Structure 19 and Monument 3 are indisputably Rosario phase in date; Monument 3 was sealed beneath an old Rosario phase land surface, and Structure 19 was sealed beneath a later Rosario residence.

Winter's statement that Late Monte Albán I pottery was found "in the area" is particularly strange, since no Late Monte Albán I pottery has *ever* been recovered in any excavation at San José Mogote! Our project has recovered many interesting Late I structures, burials, and features at sites like Abasolo, Tomaltepec, and Mitla (see Fig. 2.18), but none at San José Mogote—not on Mound 1, not in Areas A, B, C, and D, and not on Mounds 3, 7, 8, or 9. Thus Winter could hardly have picked a less probable period to which to attribute the stone—and this leaves aside the question of why he did not simply consult

SETTING THE RECORD STRAIGHT 51

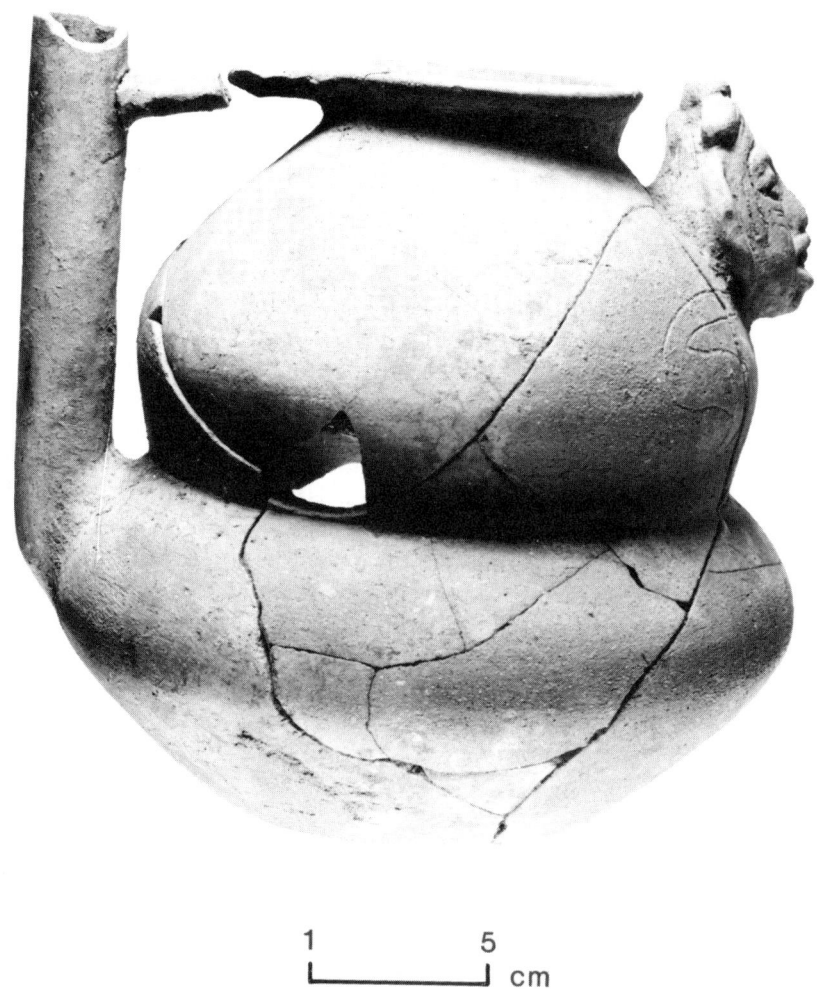

Figure 2.18. Typical effigy bridgespout vessel of Monte Albán Ic. (San Sebastián Abasolo, Burial 5).

our publications on the subject. (If he thought we were just guessing at the date, he was certainly mistaken).

The only explanation we can think of is this: to the east of Monument 3 was an area where the temple staff of Structures 13, 35, and 36 (three Monte Albán II temples, later superimposed on Structure 14) appear to have dug a series of immense trash pits, into which they swept thousands of broken urn and *brasero* fragments from the temples. The deepest of these trash pits were intrusive through both of the stucco floors above Monument 3, as well as the old Rosario land surface and some of the underlying Guadalupe deposits. We might have mentioned these pits to Winter, or even shown him a few Early Monte Albán II sherds from them, and with the passage of time his memory might have become hazy as to whether the sherds were Early II or Late I. For the record, the pits were Period II (and later) and had nothing to do with Monument 3.

As for Winter's notion that Monument 3 was once set upright in another building and later "reused in the fill" of the corridor, we could hardly imagine anything for which there is less evidence. In the first place, as Figure 2.14 shows, the stone was deliberately laid flat on a set of leveling slabs—hardly something you would do to a stone reused in the fill. Second, the stone was associated with a Rosario phase corridor floor. Third, it should not be at all surprising that the stone was laid horizontally; after all, it is supposed to represent a person lying flat on a sacrificial altar. Strangest of all is Winter's confident assertion that the stone had once been in an earlier wall. What earlier wall? Does Winter know of a wall anywhere with a stone missing, leaving a gap just the right size and shape to accommodate Monument 3? For that, after all, would be the kind of evidence you'd need before making such a statement.

V

At the end of the Rosario phase, San José Mogote suffered a rapid population loss, accompanied by a virtual cessation of monumental construction. Residential areas A, B, and C were all abandoned; in fact, in fifteen years of research at the site, the only evidence for Monte Albán Ia occupation we have found comes from stratigraphic zone A2 above Structure 19 on Mound 1 (see above). By Monte Albán Ic, the loss of population was so severe that during the entire time we have worked at San José Mogote, we have not found a single residence, a single burial, a single feature, or a single public building of Monte Albán Ic. San José Mogote was not the only site in the Etla subvalley to experience such population losses at this time (Flannery and Marcus 1983b:75), since the demographic center of gravity of the Valley of Oaxaca was in the process of shifting south to the area around Monte Albán (Kowalewski 1983).

In many regions of Mesoamerica such population losses are puzzling to archaeologists, but in the Valley of Oaxaca it is not difficult to figure out where everyone went: this was the moment during which the city of Monte Albán was being founded. Even during Period Ia there were too many people at Monte Albán to be accounted for by immigration from a single community, even a community as large as San José Mogote. We have to assume that many villages on the valley floor contributed population to Monte Albán, a place which in a rather short time went from an unoccupied mountaintop to the largest settlement in the valley. Fortunately, because of the continuities in ceramics and architecture from the Rosario phase, there is no longer any reason to look farther than the nearby villages of the Valley of Oaxaca to account for the founders of Monte Albán.

While we will never know the details of the founding of Monte Albán (including the role that any individual political leaders may have played in its selection and founding), a few facts seem worth considering. First of all, agriculture had been going on in the Valley of Oaxaca since at least 7000–6000 B.C., and during all those millennia no one had ever before shown any interest in Monte Albán. In fact, according to Michael and Anne Kirkby's land use studies, many of the villages of the period 1500–1000 B.C. were located on some of the best agricultural land in the valley: San José Mogote, Zaachila, Santa Ana Tlapacoyan, Huitzo, Tierras Largas, Abasolo, Hacienda Blanca, and San Lorenzo Cacaotepec are a few examples. All those localities were close to good alluvium, abundant surface water, and piedmont and mountain resource areas from which villagers could obtain a range of animal, vegetable, and mineral products. Had good farm land been the number one consideration for the occupants of Oaxaca's first city, it would probably have arisen at San José Mogote.

Instead, the founders of Monte Albán chose an unoccupied 400-meter-high mountaintop at the point where all three arms of the Valley of Oaxaca converge. Today, at least, that mountaintop is short on surface water and has almost no level land. By the end of Period I and the start of Period II, the occupants of Monte Albán had built three kilometers of defensive walls along the gentler slopes of the mountaintop, and we believe that between 300 and 400 of the first stone monuments they carved dealt with militaristic themes: slain captives, lists of conquered or tribute-paying places, Zapotec rulers thrusting a spear into a "hill sign," elite prisoners with their arms tied behind their back (Marcus 1976b, 1983). In fact, no early city in Mesoamerica shows as clear a concern for militarism in its art and architecture as Monte Albán. In addition, at least twenty temples were eventually constructed in and around Monte Albán's Main Plaza, indicating that the site was a major religious center (and perhaps a regional pilgrimage center as well). We do not believe that

Monte Albán can be explained without taking into account its clear religious focus, its defensible location, its fortification walls, and its iconographic preoccupation with conquest.

Like our colleagues Feinman and Nicholas (this volume), Blanton (1980), Kowalewski (1980), and Kowalewski and Finsten (1988), we are therefore puzzled by the relentless efforts of Sanders (1979), Sanders and Nichols (1988), Sanders and Santley (1978), and Santley (1980, 1983) to explain Monte Albán in agricultural terms. The mountain itself is not good farm land, the piedmont surrounding it is not good farm land, and anyone living on its summit would be farther from good farm land than anyone living at San José Mogote, Abasolo, Zaachila, or Santa Ana Tlapacoyan. The idea that it took Zapotec farmers more than 6000 years (from 7000 B.C. to 500 B.C.) to find the best farm land in the valley seems absurd to us, and it is not supported by the Kirkbys' land use studies. It seems to us a rather desperate effort by Sanders and his students to defend the anachronistic notion that important sites are always on or near the best farm land.

For Sanders's amusement we offer Figure 2.19, which shows an architectural complex named "Roussanou," near Meteora, Greece. Like Monte Albán, it is perched on a promontory 400 m above the valley floor. Like Monte Albán, it lies within 10 km of first-class alluvial soil. Does this mean, following Sanders and Nichols (1988), that its location can best be explained by access to good farm land? Or is it possible that its founders sought to remove it from the secular valley floor and put it in a place that was prominent and visible, but of limited accessibility? (Hint: it's a monastery.)

Setting aside the "best farm land" theory, we see evidence that Monte Albán I was a period when defense from armed conflict was so great a consideration that it resulted in a partial shift away from the previous, valley floor–based Formative settlement pattern. After all, Monte Albán was not the only hilltop or mountaintop site founded during Period I; from Cerro de la Campana and Peña de los Corrales in the north, to Santa María Ayoquezco in the south, and Yagul in the east, many communities relocated on mesas, hills, and mountains during this period (Elam 1989). During later periods, fortified sites were widespread (Fig. 2.20).

Easily the most amusing theory for the founding of Monte Albán, however, appears in Winter's tourist guide: According to Winter (1989:35), Monte Albán's attraction was "firewood," "space for house construction," "springs for water," "clay suitable for pottery," and "chert for stone tools." In other words, we are asked to believe that villagers who for 1000 years had been cutting pine trees in the forests of Cerro San Felipe, drinking water from the main Atoyac River,

SETTING THE RECORD STRAIGHT 55

Figure 2.19. "Roussanou," near Meteora, Greece. Hey, Bill Sanders! Explain to us again how access to good farm land is the most important variable determining settlement location.

using the clay sources of the Cacaotepec piedmont, and getting their chert from Matadamas and San Lázaro Etla, suddenly decided to put several more hours of travel time between themselves and those resources by moving up onto a 400-meter mountaintop. Moreover, we are asked to believe that villagers, who already had 700 km^2 of flat land available to them for house construction, decided it would be

Figure 2.20. Concentric defensive walls identify "La Corona Grande," a fortified hilltop site in the Etla Valley.

lots more fun to carve out architectural terraces on a steep-sided mountain, much farther from the valley's alluvium.

Winter goes on to compound this silliness by adding something for which there is literally no evidence: "Monte Albán was the logical place to establish a market. . . . Once the market was established, Monte Albán's growth was exponential" (1989:36). We're sorry, but there is no evidence whatsoever for markets in the Formative and Classic Valley of Oaxaca. Indeed, markets are one of the most difficult institutions on which to recover archaeological data; we really have no solid evidence for them in the Valley of Oaxaca until the documents of the Spanish Colonial period speak of markets, and even then it is difficult to separate what is prehispanic from what is European influence. In the case of Monte Albán, it is most certainly *not* a logical place for a market: it's a 400-meter mountain. Markets are supposed to be in readily accessible areas, and the Main Plaza at Monte Albán (which Winter thinks was the market place) has been shown by Blanton's ekistic study to have been in one of the least accessible parts of the city, a place not served by any of the main roads (Blanton 1978). In fact, the Main Plaza is an area of very restricted access, reached only by small openings at the corners which could be blocked or opened by the administrators of the site. In traffic flow terms, it appears to be a place where access to religious or

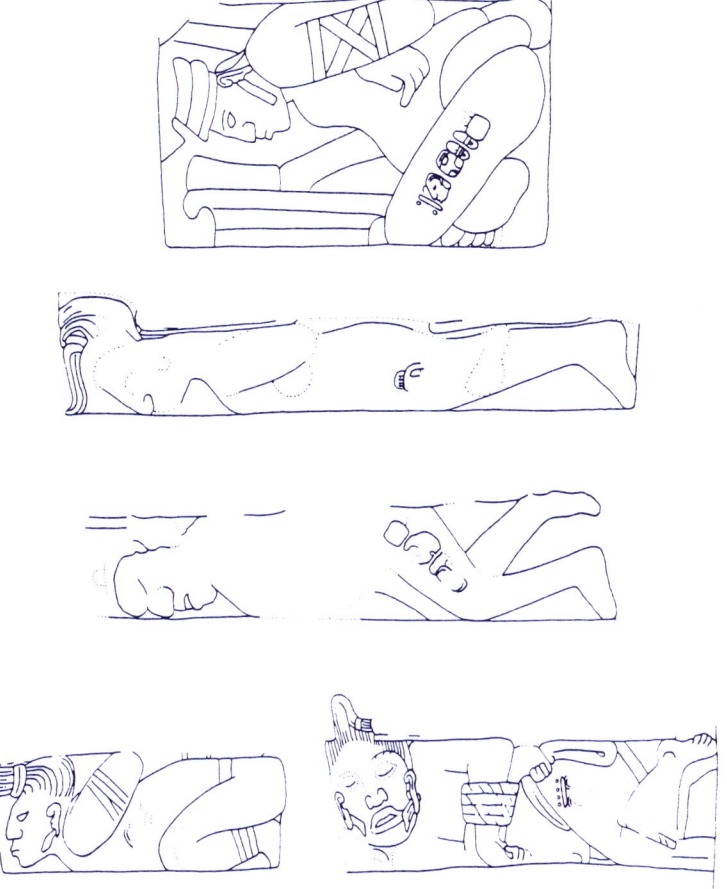

Figure 2.21. Depictions of captives on monuments at the Maya site of Naranjo, Guatemala. The figure at lower right resembles a number of Monte Albán *danzantes* (for example, Fig. 2.22 top).

political events could be easily controlled by the rulers. This is in striking contrast to the Great Compound, at the intersection of the Avenue of the Dead and the main East-West Avenue at Teotihuacán, a highly accessible locality which Millon (1981:229) feels (admittedly, without conclusive evidence) to have been the principal marketplace. At least the ekistic data do not undermine Millon's hypothesis as they undermine Winter's.

We believe that the evidence for militarism and defense at Monte Albán—combined with the site's obvious role as a ritual and adminis-

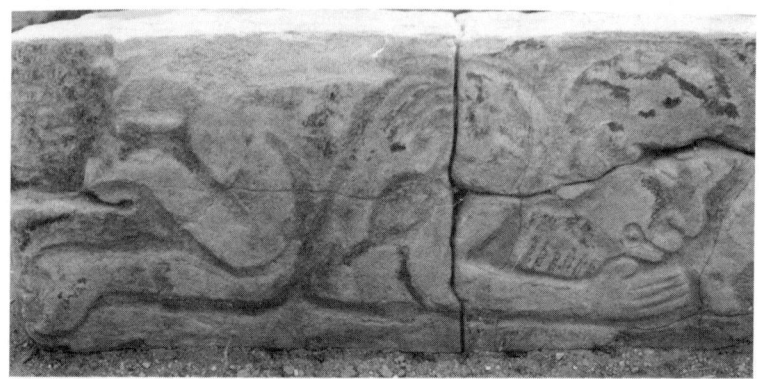

Figure 2.22. Examples of so-called *danzante* monuments at Monte Albán. *Top:* Is he dancing the lambada? Doing the Australian crawl? We say he's as dead as a carp. *Bottom:* Nude prisoner carving incorporated in the stairway of Building L, Monte Albán. (Unfortunately, this monument has been badly damaged by tourists.)

trative center, deliberately removed from the secular valley floor—help to shed light on many previously enigmatic features of the site. For example, let us consider the monuments once called *danzantes*, to see how our views today would differ from those of the 1940s and 50s.

There is reason to believe that all these interesting carvings (over 300 of them) originally occurred in a single wall on the east face of Building L at Monte Albán. Caso dated this wall to Monte Albán Ia by its associated pottery, making it one of the earliest monumental works at the site. For years, every conceivable type of fanciful explanation was set forth for these monuments. In 1962, Michael Coe, who was familiar with the very large corpus of prisoner representations on carved monuments of the Maya area, instantly recognized that the so-called *danzantes* were the same type of representation. Coe (1962:95-96) pointed out that the *danzantes* were all nude, dead, and in awkward positions, like those seen in depictions of prisoners being trampled by Maya rulers (see examples in Fig. 2.21). Coe knew that important persons are never displayed nude in Mesoamerican art, nor are they shown in grotesque and awkward positions. Respected persons, such as priests or members of the nobility, are shown in full regalia and in stereotyped, graceful positions that communicate their importance. On the other hand, slain enemies or captives brought back for sacrifice were humiliated by being shown nude and in awkward positions.

When people are shown dancing in Mesoamerican art, they are shown in elaborate costumes and headdresses, not nude. Moreover, like the example shown at the top of Figure 2.22, most *danzantes* clearly depict dead people. Occasionally, they were even used (or reused) in the stairways of buildings, as shown in the bottom of Figure 2.22, so that anyone ascending the staircase would tread on their bodies (Marcus 1974, 1980). This is a very common device in the Maya area as well; see, for example, the prisoner staircases at the sites of Tamarindito and Dos Pilas.

In 1974, Marcus expressed agreement with Coe's interpretation, and concluded that all 300-plus *danzantes* probably once constituted a huge display of slain or sacrificed captives erected by the founders of Monte Albán (Marcus 1974: Fig. 26). Anyone familiar with the depictions of prisoners in the much larger corpus of Maya monuments needs no persuasion to see the appropriateness of this interpretation, and in his recent official guide to the Oaxaca Valley, Bernal (1985:61), while keeping an open mind, states that "the most probable explanation . . . is that they represent prisoners who were going to be sacrificed, thus initiating the imperial course of Monte Albán."

Sadly, Winter has missed this reanalysis of the Building L monuments, continuing to refer to them as "dancers" and "swimmers" (Winter 1989:52). For him they show "the founders of Monte Albán" engaged in events from "the early history of the site." While Winter does not provide us with a hypothesis as to why the occupants of Monte Albán (in contrast to all other Mesoamerican people) would depict their revered founding fathers in the nude, maybe we can construct such a hypothesis for him, based on the statements in his tourist guide. Perhaps, in his view, the *nadadores* show the early founders of the site swimming to Monte Albán across the waters of the giant lake, while the *danzantes* show them after they had taken off their wet clothes and were running around the slopes naked, collecting firewood. The sexually mutilated *danzantes* might then be people who accidentally ran into a *mala mujer* (*Jatropha urens*) and had to do something about the maddening itch.

At the risk of sounding like arch conservatives, we will sidestep this hypothesis. To us, the Building L wall represents a gallery of simplified, conventionalized, slain or sacrificed captives, consistent with similar galleries in later Maya art. The Period Ia date of this large gallery makes it not at all surprising that a single depiction of a Rosario phase slain or sacrificed captive should have occurred one ceramic phase earlier at San José Mogote, one of the sites from which the founders of Monte Albán almost certainly came. Moreover, although the Building L figures are set in a vertical wall, we believe they are meant to be viewed as if they were lying sprawled on the ground, the same position in which the figure on Monument 3 at San José Mogote is shown.

VI

It is unfortunate that we have recovered so little Monte Albán I material at San José Mogote, because that is one of the periods for which we most urgently need data. Although Monte Albán itself has abundant remains from Period I, some of the most important structures of that period lie buried under later overburden which cannot be conveniently removed. For example, important buildings of Period I are buried under the North Platform, Mound K, and Building L at Monte Albán (Flannery and Marcus 1983c: Fig. 4.3). To give just two examples of the data we are missing, we do not know what the residence of the highest-ranking family during Monte Albán I looked like, nor do we know whether the typical Zapotec colonnaded temple existed during this period.

Did the highest-ranking person in Monte Albán I live in a palace, as was the case in Monte Albán II, or did he simply live in a large adobe house with an interior patio, as was the case at San José Mogote in the Rosario phase? We don't know.

How early did the two-room temple with columns to either side of the doorway appear? Inside Mound K of Monte Albán's System IV lie the buried remains of a structure with a 6-meter-high sloping wall of huge stones and a pair of rubble masonry columns. The construction seems to date to Monte Albán I and has features reminiscent of public buildings at the site of Monte Negro; but because the building is buried under Mound K, we do not know its shape, its dimensions, its number of rooms, or its function. We had hoped that we would find a comparable building at San José Mogote, but we did not, although we searched very hard. We found a definite hiatus in public construction between the Rosario phase and Monte Albán II, which disappointed us because it left us with a discontinuity in our study of the evolution of the public building in Formative Oaxaca (Flannery and Marcus 1976b). This hiatus cannot be filled simply by misdating some of our public buildings, as Winter has done repeatedly in his tourist guide.

Future work on Monte Albán I is crucial for the following reasons. For the Rosario phase (700–500 B.C.), there is no archaeological evidence for the institutions of the Zapotec state. For Monte Albán II (200 B.C.–A.D. 100), we consider the evidence for statehood well documented. There was an administrative hierarchy with at least four tiers of sites; there were rulers who lived in palaces at the top two tiers of the hierarchy; there were standardized two-room temples at the top three tiers of the hierarchy; there were royal tombs with ceramic effigies of apotheosized royal ancestors; there were monuments indicating territorial conquests; and there was evidence for Zapotec military expansion into areas such as Cuicatlán, Miahuatlán, and Tututepec (Flannery and Marcus 1983d:79–83). This makes Monte Albán I (500–200 B.C.) a crucial 300-year period for our understanding of the evolution from complex chiefdom to early state.

Once again, our previous writing on this subject has been misunderstood by some of our colleagues. For example, Whalen (1988:292) says: "Going farther, Flannery and his co-authors assert that the Monte Albán I period saw the emergence of a 'class-endogamous professional ruling stratum of valley-wide significance' (Flannery, Marcus, and Kowalewski 1981:92)." Whalen then builds on this to claim that the village of Tomaltepec had households belonging to a "valley-wide ruling stratum" (Whalen 1988:291).

We're sorry Whalen misunderstood what we were saying, and are happy to have this chance to clarify it. We were trying to say that since Rosario has no evidence for state institutions—and Monte Albán II does—then the processes leading to those institutions must have been set in motion during Monte Albán I. We did not mean to imply that those processes were carried to completion, and the state fully formed, as early as Monte Albán I. On the contrary, we stated our position previously: "the evidence from Monte Albán I is so fragmentary as to be ambiguous" (Flannery and Marcus 1983d:80) and "the full-fledged state" appeared by Monte Albán II (Flannery, Marcus, and Kowalewski 1981:92). While significant processes were probably underway during Period I, it remains to be shown what the sociopolitical organization of that period was. In fact, there may even turn out to be significant differences between Early Monte Albán I (Ia) and Late Monte Albán (Ic).

Even if we had evidence for a state in Monte Albán I, it is by no means certain that a village of 5 to 8 ha, like Tomaltepec, would have been important enough to have members of an elite "of valley-wide significance". In Monte Albán II, when Monte Albán was a 416 ha capital with an estimated 9,650–19,300 persons, San José Mogote was a 70 ha secondary center with a palace, a ballcourt, and perhaps as many as ten temples. Tomaltepec at that time was a 5 to 8 ha site with only one temple, no ballcourt, and no evidence for a palace that might have housed a member of the major nobility. While there were undoubtedly differences in status among the households at Tomaltepec, it is likely that the highest-ranking persons there were of local, rather than valley-wide, significance. Almost certainly, Tomaltepec was administratively below one of the larger nearby secondary centers.

This seems an appropriate place to correct two recent errors in the literature on Monte Albán I and II. Let us deal first with canal irrigation. The sociopolitical changes of Monte Albán I and II seem to have been accompanied by an increase in canal irrigation, and while no single one of these systems was large, they were significant nonetheless. For example, a system consisting of a dam and a 2 km canal, dating to Monte Albán I-II, lies in the piedmont on the southeast flank of Monte Albán (Mason et al. 1977). Another canal and terrace system was found by Neely (1967) at Hierve el Agua in the mountains east of Mitla. Here, 168 ha of artificially terraced hillside was served by a complex series of canals which descend from a mineral spring. Recently, it was erroneously reported by Hewitt, Peterson, and Winter (1987) (see also Peterson, Winter, and Hewitt 1989) that the water at Hierve el Agua is unsuitable for irrigation, and that the site must therefore have been a "saltworks." As demonstrated by Neely, Caran, and Winsborough in Chapter 4 of this volume, those conclusions were based on a flawed analysis of the water and a mistaken comparison of Hierve el Agua with Salinas Zapotitlán near Tehuacán. As Chapter 4 indicates, more carefully collected and studied samples of the water show it to be suitable for irrigation, and diatom analysis of the terrace soils shows no evidence of salt-tolerant species. Moreover, the terraces do not resemble those of Salinas Zapotitlán, which are broad, shallow, evaporating pans; Hierve el Agua's terraces are narrow, deep, and filled with organic soil containing ancient maize pollen.

A second correctable error in the literature has to do with the first appearance of the ballcourt in ancient Oaxaca. While we do not know exactly when the ballgame originated, Bernal and Oliveros (1988) consider it possible that the game was played on a simple rectangular court at Dainzú, near Tlacolula, as early as Late Formative times. By Monte Albán II, standardized "I"-shaped ballcourts had appeared at major sites like Monte Albán and San José Mogote. The ballcourt at San José Mogote (which had undergone two or three building stages) was excavated in 1974 by Chris L. Moser, who found it to have been laid out originally in Period II and rebuilt in Period IIIa. We quote from his report:

> ... it is clear that the two lower construction phases evident as stucco taludes, or aprons 2 and 3, in the east and west side mounds are earlier; and the absence of associated Monte Albán IIIa sherds or artifacts further suggests that the ballcourt was planned and originally built in Monte Albán II (200 B.C.-A.D. 100), with its final rebuilding, with the addition of the benches, stone and plaster floors, and enlarged east and west temple platforms occurring in early Monte Albán IIIa. [Moser n.d.]

Unfortunately, Winter's tourist guide is once again in error here, as it states: "A large ballcourt just to the west of the plaza was constructed in Period III; a Period IIIa tomb, found beneath the stucco floor, presumably predates the construction" (1989:118). This is not true. The tomb in question, Tomb 6, was not sealed beneath stucco flooring, but was found in an area where the stucco had eroded away and only a layer of cobblestones remained. The brown fill beneath those cobbles had only Monte Albán II (and earlier) sherds in it, while the vessels in the tomb were clearly Monte Albán IIIa.

Several lines of evidence make it likely that Tomb 6, far from predating the construction of the ballcourt, was a later intrusion. First of all, its orientation (true north-south) did not conform to that of the ballcourt, which was 5-7 degrees west of north. Second, Moser found that the tomb had been used at least twice, having been reopened so that additional bodies could be added. It is unlikely that this opening and reopening went on while the building was actively being used as a ballcourt; more likely, the tomb was placed there after the court had ceased to function.

The ballcourt had a complex history of repairs and renovations, and Moser (n.d.) felt that "the earlier ballcourt may have had a slightly different orientation." Between the earlier and later stucco surfaces (which in places were separated by 145-150 cm of construction fill), the sherds were only Monte Albán II and earlier. Thus, Tomb 6 had to have been added either (1) during a later, Period IIIa renovation, or (2) shortly after the ballcourt fell into disuse. At San José Mogote, it was not unusual for later tombs or burials to be placed in the ruins of earlier buildings.

We hope that this brief discussion of the earlier periods of Oaxaca prehistory has cleared up some of the confusion in the secondary literature. As we said at the outset of this chapter, it is becoming increasingly necessary for archaeologists to spend time correcting the errors of colleagues who misquoted them or made factual misstatements about their work. Nine out of ten of your fellow archaeologists will get it right, but there will be always be one turkey who describes your single-room, wattle-and-daub, astronomically oriented public building as "an adobe residence with a courtyard."

To be sure, we would never be so ungracious as to classify Winter as one of those turkeys. We do notice, however, that he gets very nervous every year just before Thanksgiving.

References Cited

Bernal, Ignacio
1946   La cerámica preclásica de Monte Albán. Master's thesis. Escuela Nacional de Antropología e Historia, México.
1949a   La cerámica de Monte Albán IIIa. Ph.D dissertation. Universidad Nacional de México, Mexico City.
1949b   La cerámica grabada de Monte Albán. Anales del Instituto Nacional de Antropología e Historia 3:59-77. Mexico City.
1965   Archaeological synthesis of Oaxaca. In: Handbook of Middle American Indians, Vol. 3 (Archaeology of Southern Mesoamerica), Part 2, edited by Robert Wauchope and Gordon R. Willey, pp. 788-813. Austin: University of Texas Press.
1985   Offical Guide: Oaxaca Valley. Mexico: Salvat Mexicana de Ediciones, S.A. de C.V.

Bernal, Ignacio and Arturo Oliveros
1988   Exploraciones arqueológicas en Dainzú. Colección Científica, Serie Arqueología, Instituto Nacional de Antropología e Historia, México.

Blanton, Richard E.
1978   Monte Albán: Settlement Patterns at the Ancient Zapotec Capital. New York: Academic Press.
1980   Cultural ecology reconsidered. American Antiquity, 45:145-51.

Caso, Alfonso, Ignacio Bernal, and Jorge R. Acosta
1967   La cerámica de Monte Albán. Memorias del Instituto Nacional de Antropología e Historia, 13. Mexico: Instituto Nacional de Antropología.

Coe, Michael D.
1962   Mexico. New York: Frederick A. Praeger.

Drennan, Robert D.
1976a Fábrica San José and Middle Formative Society in the Valley of Oaxaca. Prehistory and Human Ecology of the Valley of Oaxaca, Vol. 4. Memoirs, 8. Museum of Anthropology, University of Michigan. Ann Arbor.
1976b A refinement of chronological seriation using nonmetric multidimensional scaling. American Antiquity, 41(3):290–302.

Dupaix, Guillermo
1969   Expediciones acerca de los antiguos monumentos de la Nueva España, 1805–1808. Edición, introducción, y notas por José Alcina Franch, 2 volumes. Madrid: José Porrúa Turanzas.

Elam, Michael
1989   Defensible and fortified sites. In: Monte Albán's Hinterland, Part II. Prehispanic Settlement Patterns in Tlacolula, Etla, and Ocotlán, the Valley of Oaxaca, Mexico, Vol. 1, by Stephen A. Kowalewski et al., pp. 385–407. Memoirs, 23. Museum of Anthropology, University of Michigan. Ann Arbor.

Finsten, Laura, Kent V. Flannery, and Barbara Macnider
1989   Preceramic and cave occupations. In: Monte Albán's Hinterland, Part II. Prehispanic Settlement Patterns in Tlacolula, Etla, and Ocotlán, the Valley of Oaxaca, Mexico, Vol. 1, by Stephen A. Kowaleski et al., pp. 39–53. Memoirs, 23. Museum of Anthropology, University of Michigan. Ann Arbor.

Flannery, Kent V.
1983   Pleistocene fauna of Early Ajuereado type from Cueva Blanca, Oaxaca. In: The Cloud People: Divergent Evolution of the Zapotec and Mixtec Civilizations, edited by Kent V. Flannery and Joyce Marcus, pp. 18–20. Orlando: Academic Press.

Flannery, Kent V. (ed.)
1986   Guilá Naquitz: Archaic Foraging and Early Agriculture in Oaxaca, Mexico. Orlando: Academic Press.

Flannery, Kent V., and Joyce Marcus
1976a Formative Oaxaca and the Zapotec cosmos. American Scientist, 64(4):374–83.
1976b Evolution of the public building in Formative Oaxaca. In: Cultural Change and Continuity: Essays in Honor of James Bennett Griffin,

    edited by Charles Cleland, pp. 205-21. New York: Academic Press.
1983a The growth of site hierarchies in the Valley of Oaxaca: Part I. In: The Cloud People: Divergent Evolution of the Zapotec and Mixtec Civilizations, edited by Kent V. Flannery and Joyce Marcus, pp. 53-64. Orlando: Academic Press.
1983b The Rosario phase and the origins of Monte Albán I. In: The Cloud People: Divergent Evolution of the Zapotec and Mixtec Civilizations, edited by Kent V. Flannery and Joyce Marcus, pp. 74-77. Orlando: Academic Press.
1983c The earliest public buildings, tombs, and monuments at Monte Albán, with notes on the internal chronology of Period I. In: The Cloud People: Divergent Evolution of the Zapotec and Mixtec Civilizations, edited by Kent V. Flannery and Joyce Marcus, pp. 87-91. Orlando: Academic Press.
1983d Editors' introduction to "The origins of the state in Oaxaca." In: The Cloud People: Divergent Evolution of the Zapotec and Mixtec Civilizations, edited by Kent V. Flannery and Joyce Marcus, pp. 79-83. Orlando: Academic Press.

Flannery, Kent V., and Joyce Marcus (eds.)
1983 The Cloud People: Divergent Evolution of the Zapotec and Mixtec Civilizations. Orlando: Academic Press.

Flannery, Kent V., Joyce Marcus, and Stephen A. Kowalewski
1981 The Preceramic and Formative in the Valley of Oaxaca. In: Handbook of Middle American Indians, Supplement 1: Archaeology, edited by Jeremy A. Sabloff, pp. 48-93. Victoria R. Bricker, general editor. Austin: University of Texas Press.

Grove, David C.
1984 Chalcatzingo: Excavations on the Olmec Frontier. London: Thames and Hudson.

Grove, David C. (ed.)
1987 Ancient Chalcatzingo. Austin: University of Texas Press.

Hewitt, William P., Marcus C. Winter, and David A. Peterson
1987 Salt production at Hierve el Agua, Oaxaca. American Antiquity, 52(4):799-816.

Kidder, Alfred V., J. D. Jennings, and E. M. Shook
1946 Excavations at Kaminaljuyú, Guatemala. Carnegie Institution of Washington, Publication 561. Washington, D.C.

Kowalewski, Stephen A.
1983 Valley-floor settlement patterns during Monte Albán I. In: The Cloud People: Divergent Evolution of the Zapotec and Mixtec Civilizations, edited by Kent V. Flannery and Joyce Marcus, pp. 96-97. Orlando: Academic Press.

Kowalewski, Stephen A., and Laura Finsten
1988   Comment on Sanders and Nichols' 1988 article. Current Anthropology, 29(1):59-60.

Kowalewski, Stepehen A., Gary M. Feinman, Laura Finsten, Richard E. Blanton, and Linda M. Nicholas
1989   Monte Albán's Hinterland, Part II. Prehispanic Settlement Patterns in Tlacolula, Etla, and Ocotlán, the Valley of Oaxaca, Mexico. Memoirs of the Museum of Anthropology, 23. Museum of Anthropology, University of Michigan. Ann Arbor.

Lothrop, Samuel K.
1937   Coclé: An archaeological study of Central Panama. Part I: Historical Background, Excavations at the Sitio Conte, Artifacts and Ornaments. Memoirs of the Peabody Museum, 7. Harvard University. Cambridge.

Marcus, Joyce
1974   The iconography of power among the Classic Maya. World Archaeology, 6(1):83-94.
1976a   The origins of Mesoamerican writing. Annual Review of Anthropology, 5:35-67.
1976b   The iconography of militarism at Monte Albán and neighboring sites in the Valley of Oaxaca. In: Origins of Religious Art and Iconography in Preclassic Mesoamerica, edited by Henry B. Nicholson. Latin American Studies Series, 31. Los Angeles: UCLA Latin American Center.
1980   Zapotec writing. Scientific American, 242:50-64.
1983   Stone monuments and tomb murals of Monte Albán IIIa. In: The Cloud People: Divergent Evolution of the Zapotec and Mixtec Civilizations, edited by Kent V. Flannery and Joyce Marcus, pp. 137-43. Orlando: Academic Press.
1989   Zapotec chiefdoms and the nature of formative religions. In: Regional Perspectives on the Olmec, edited by Robert J. Sharer and David C. Grove, pp. 148-97. Cambridge: Cambridge University Press.

Mason, Roger D., Dennis E. Lewarch, Michael J. O'Brien, and James A. Neely
1977   An archaeological survey on the Xoxocotlán piedmont, Oaxaca, Mexico. American Antiquity, 42(4):567-75.

Millon, Rene
1981   Teotihuacan: City, state, and civilization. In: Handbook of Middle American Indians, Supplement 1: Archaeology, edited by Jeremy A. Sabloff, pp. 198-243. Victoria R. Bricker, general editor. Austin: University of Texas Press.

Moser, Chris
n.d.   The San José Mogote Ballcourt. Manuscript.

Neely, James A.
1967   Organización hidráulica y sistemas de irrigación prehistóricos en el Valle de Oaxaca. Boletín del Instituto Nacional de Antropología e Historia, 27:15–17. México, D.F.

Peterson, David A., Marcus C. Winter, and William P. Hewitt
1989   Reply to Doolittle. American Antiquity, 54(4):847–50.

Plog, Stephen
1976   Measurement of prehistoric interaction between communities. In: The Early Mesoamerican Village, edited by Kent V. Flannery, pp. 255–72. New York: Academic Press.

Sanders, William T.
1979   Review of Monte Albán: Settlement Patterns at the Ancient Zapotec Capital (Blanton). American Scientist, 67:617.

Sanders, William T., and Deborah L. Nichols
1988   Ecological theory and cultural evolution in the Valley of Oaxaca. Current Anthropology, 29(1):33–80.

Sanders, William T., and Robert S. Santley
1978   Review of Monte Albán: Settlement Patterns at the Ancient Zapotec Capital (Blanton). Science, 202(4365):303–4.

Santley, Robert S.
1980   Disembedded capitals reconsidered. American Antiquity, 45(1):132–45.
1983   Ancient population at Monte Albán: A reconsideration of methodology and culture history. Haliksa'i: University of New Mexico Contributions to Anthropology, 2:64–84.

Tobler, Arthur J.
1950   Excavations at Tepe Gawra, Vol. 2. Philadelphia: University of Pennsylvania Press.

Tolstoy, Paul
1989   Coapexco and Tlatilco: Sites with Olmec materials in the Basin of Mexico. In: Regional Perspectives on the Olmec, edited by Robert J. Sharer and David C. Grove, pp. 85–121. Cambridge: Cambridge University Press.

Vaillant, George C.
1931   Excavations at Ticomán. Anthropological Papers of the American Museum of Natural History, 32(2). New York: American Museum of Natural History.

Voorhies, Barbara
1984   Review of The Cloud People: Divergent Evolution of the Zapotec and Mixtec Civilizations (Flannery and Marcus). American Anthropologist, 86:760–62.

Whalen, Michael E.
1981   Excavations at Santo Domingo Tomaltepec: Evolution of a Formative Community in the Valley of Oaxaca, Mexico. Prehistory and Human Ecology of the Valley of Oaxaca, edited by Kent V. Flannery, Vol. 6. Memoirs, 12. Museum of Anthropology, University of Michigan. Ann Arbor.
1988   Small community organization during the Late Formative Period in Oaxaca, Mexico. Journal of Field Archaeology, 15:291–306.

Winter, Marcus C.
1976   Cerámica de la Fase Rosario encontrada en dos Pozos Tronco-Cónicos en el Sitio de Tierras Largas, Valle de Oaxaca, México. Centro Regional de Oaxaca. (Pamphlet.)
1989   Oaxaca: The Archaeological Record. Mexico, D.F.: Trivia Mexicana.

Wright, Henry T.
1984   Prestate political formations. In: On the Evolution of Complex Societies: Essays in Honor of Harry Hoijer, 1982, edited by Timothy Earle, pp. 41–77. Los Angeles: Undena Publications [for the UCLA Department of Anthropology].

3

SETTLEMENT AND LAND USE IN ANCIENT OAXACA

Gary M. Feinman and Linda M. Nicholas,
University of Wisconsin

Four decades have now passed since a more economic-ecological approach to highland Mesoamerica was introduced and advanced through the writings of Armillas (1948), Wolf (1959; Wolf and Palerm 1955), Palerm (1955; Palerm and Wolf 1957), and others (Meggers 1954). Since those early years a variety of economic approaches have been offered. Also, the significance attributed to the role of the environment as a determinant of cultural change has varied. Since the 1960s anthropological work in Oaxaca has examined prehispanic human/environmental relationships (Flannery et al. 1967). We have continued this work, with our regional surveys of the valleys of Oaxaca (Blanton *et al.* 1982; Kowalewski *et al.* 1989) and Ejutla (Feinman 1985; Feinman and Nicholas 1988). The data collected enable us to address questions of demographic trends, the roles of population and land quality, the process of colonization, and (to some extent) the production of surplus.

To place our settlement pattern studies within a more diachronic context, we will first briefly review these shifting theoretical frameworks. Then we will focus on the principal results of our investigations in which we examined the diachronic relationship between population, land, and settlement in ancient Oaxaca.

THEORETICAL FRAMEWORKS

After World War II, influenced by the more general works of Wittfogel (1957), Childe (1950), and Steward (1949), a series of scholars reacted to the existing emphases on artifact-focused culture history and trait-based diffusion by adopting a more materialist approach to prehispanic Mesoamerica. Significantly, in these seminal papers, the authors generally recognized that the relationships among the environment, agricultural technology, population, and social relations were neither simple nor deterministic. For example, Palerm and Wolf began their 1957 article by noting:

> we shall limit ourselves to a discussion of the *complex and changing relationships* between the natural environment and the cultural equipment at the roots of Mesoamerican development. [Palerm and Wolf 1957:1, emphasis added]

An illustration of this interpretive flexibility is their opening definition of Mesoamerica's northern frontier that concludes:

> [t]he cultural frontier did not always coincide with the ecological divide. Its displacement to either north or south was not caused by climatic changes, nor was it caused wholly by technological innovations. Its location depended also on the *ever-changing balance in socio-political integration and military power*. [1957:5, emphasis added]

To summarize the article, they reiterated:

> we feel that the relative intensity and geographic extension of each stage of cultural development in Mesoamerica is closely related to the variety of environmental conditions found in the area, to the agricultural techniques used in their exploitation, *and to institutions which furthered or hampered the growth and efficiency of such new technologies*. [1957:37; emphasis added]

This new more materially based perspective on ancient Mesoamerica was extremely influential, generating new research topics and approaches to the region's archaeology. Yet, as Wolf later recalled in a review of this earlier period:

> as the new interest in the interrelationships of environment, technology, settlement pattern, and sociopolitical organization gained ground, new questions were raised for which the extant data were clearly insufficient. [Wolf 1976:3-4]

In 1965, the economist Ester Boserup published *The Conditions of Agricultural Growth*. The main thesis of the book is that the pressure of increasing population leads to technological change, specifically agricultural intensification. Boserup regards population growth as a *given*. She maintains that intensive agricultural systems are less productive per unit of labor input than extensive ones, and that people will not switch to more intensive methods without pressure to do so. Based on the frequency of cropping, Boserup describes a continuum of farming strategies, from forest fallow to annual cropping to multi-cropping. She argues that the reduction of fallow under conditions of population pressure, in spite of declining per-hour returns on labor, is *the* central issue in the evolution of intensified agricultural strategies.

While Boserup's volume had considerable initial influence in anthropology and archaeology (Spooner [ed.] 1972; Spooner and Netting 1972), the reception in economics was not uniformly warm. For example, in a review in the *Journal of Farm Economics*, Theodore Schultz of the University of Chicago recognized Boserup's thesis as a "new angle"; however, he added:

> I see no point in belaboring Mrs. Boserup's central thesis and thus spoiling the reader's pleasure in discovering the gaps in the underlying economic logic. [T]he book is worth reading in spite of the fact that the thesis is in general wrong. [1966:487]

Likewise, W. O. Jones wrote in the *American Economic Review*:

> The argument is attractive, and there is much in it that seems to correspond with history; if it were advanced as one of the possible lines of causation in agricultural change it would probably meet little serious opposition. But Mrs. Boserup means it to be *the* line of causation, and supports that thesis by a mass of assertions, mostly undocumented, about the nature of agriculture around the world and through history. Many of her assertions of fact are open to question . . . [1967:679–80]

Referring to Boserup's proposed relationship between population pressure and agricultural intensification, a third critic, Edward Nell (1972:39), wrote in the *Peasant Studies Newsletter* that "just where she is most original, her argument is most questionable."

A series of additional reviews of *The Conditions of Agricultural Growth* by geographers, economists, and social historians (Adams 1966; Blitz 1967; *Choice* 1966; de Vries 1972; Diebold 1967; Dovring 1966; Grigg 1979; *International Labour Review* 1965; Olmstead 1970; Rubin 1972; *Times Literary Supplement* 1965) have been published since 1965. While many reviewers consider Boserup's arguments to be stimulating and thought-provoking (Adams 1966; Blitz 1967; Olmstead 1970), most are not very supportive of her major thesis. Obvious weaknesses have been enumerated, especially regarding her population theory (Dovring 1966; Nell 1972; Sheffer 1971), her proposed uniform and linear trajectory of change (Diebold 1967; Rubin 1972), and the slight consideration she gives to the role of the market on agricultural transitions (Blitz 1967; de Vries 1972). Adams (1966) argued that, in comparison to Boserup's views, the original Malthusian assumptions appeared more satisfactory, while Sheffer (1971:378) stated:

> Boserup's theory applies in a limited number of historical instances, probably far fewer than she implies. . . . Her theory should not be interpreted as evolutionary, since it does not apply to many of the occurrences of the phenomenon under study.

Nevertheless, stimulated by Boserup, and perhaps also by the increasing broad-based concern with world ecology *vis à vis* the twentieth-century population explosion, a more demographically deterministic approach to highland Mesoamerica (e.g. Sanders 1972; Sanders and Nichols 1988; Sanders et al. 1979; Sanders and Price 1968) and other areas (e.g. Cohen 1975, 1977; Smith and Young 1972) crystallized during the late 1960s and early 70s. This ongoing framework, which had roots in earlier environmentalist models, presumes population growth is a given and assumes that population pressure precedes major episodes of societal change. Borrowing Boserup's thesis as a tool for interpreting data, these researchers assume that regional colonization, settlement and demographic distributions, and population nucleation correspond in an efficient and rather mechanical way to environmental and agricultural considerations. In general, the diachronic interplay between demographic-resource ratios and sociocultural factors is considered to be less causally systemic and more uniform and linear than previously proposed. However, in contrast to a recent assertion (Boserup 1981), for which Boserup cites several archaeological studies (Adams and Nissen 1976; Butzer 1976; Sanders 1972; Smith and Young 1972) as *confirming* her model in historical context, no such independent support has yet been offered. Rather, to date, archaeologists who are advocates of Boserup's views have only borrowed her perspective as an interpretive analogy, or have constructed trial models that still remain to be tested with independent archaeological data.

Given the nature of the archaeological record and the established traditions of archaeological inquiry, a concentration on the primacy of demographic and environmental factors seems understandable. Nevertheless, as Richard Bradley (1984:2) reminded us in his recent book on ancient Britain:

> economic patterns were amenable to archaeological analysis, and in time they came to dominate the research of a whole generation, but the fact that this evidence seemed increasingly easy to analyse did not mean that it was sufficient to *explain* the character of the prehistoric sequence.

THE ECOLOGICAL APPROACH IN THE VALLEY OF OAXACA

The initiation in 1966 of Kent Flannery's Prehistory and Human Ecology Project (Flannery et al. 1967, 1970) signaled a heightened ecological interest in Valley of Oaxaca research. Yet, the theoretical perspective of the Prehistory and Human Ecology Project was less deterministic than the approach that had been advanced by those researchers influenced by the work of Ester Boserup. In that way, the Oaxaca research remained more in line with the framework advanced in the more synthetic, but less specific, materialist works of the 1950s. In the Introduction to Anne Kirkby's landmark study, *The Use of Land and Water Resources in the Past and Present Valley of Oaxaca, Mexico*, Flannery stated:

> Although the overall framework for the Oaxaca project could be described as "ecological" and "evolutionary," we have perhaps defined those terms more broadly than some previous projects in Mesoamerica. We do not believe in linear causality or in prime movers, and we do not view such generalized phenomena as population pressure, trade, or regional symbiosis as sufficient explanations for the course of cultural evolution in Oaxaca. [Flannery 1973:v]

During the last three decades, participants of both the Valley of Oaxaca Prehistory and Human Ecology Project and the Valley of Oaxaca Settlement Pattern Project have continued to recognize and focus on the importance of human relationships with their physical and social environment. As an important part of her regional study of agricultural practices in the Valley of Oaxaca, Kirkby (1973) extrapolated her contemporary findings to the past. Based on the distribution of land and water resources, she derived expectations for regional colonization and prehispanic site location that were then compared to the available archaeological settlement information—274 sites that had been recorded during Ignacio Bernal's extensive reconnaissance. Although Kirkby acknowledged that these findings were preliminary, several of her results subsequently have been supported. These include her observations that agricultural productivity became a less adequate predictor of site location during the last millennium B.C. when Monte Albán was founded, and that such distributional deviations from environmental expectations were even more marked toward the end of the prehispanic sequence.

Since the 1973 publication of Kirkby's study, systematic settlement pattern surveys have been conducted across more than 2500 km^2, encompassing the entire Valley of Oaxaca (Blanton et al. 1979, 1982; Feinman et al. 1985; Kowalewski et al. 1989), as well as the adjacent Ejutla Valley to the south (Feinman 1985; Feinman and Nicholas 1988; see Fig. 3.1, this volume). The new prehispanic settlement data have permitted us to update, expand, and modify Kirkby's investigations of the diachronic relations between ancient Oaxacans and their land and water resources. In addition, we now have the empirical information to begin to answer some of the questions—such as how ancient centers were provisioned—that could barely be asked three decades ago.

While we have generated the data to address long-held, but still crucially important questions, we also have made unexpected findings that have served to initiate additional questions. Although the last three decades have seen a continual give and take between new empirical findings and theoretical positions, we continue to see wisdom in the broader approach to causality that Flannery outlined:

> human ecology is the study of the subtle and intricate interrelationships of man's exchanges of matter, energy, and information. To concentrate only on matter and energy exchanges . . . is to present an unbalanced approach to ecology. [1973:v]

METHODOLOGY

Several major goals of the settlement pattern projects in Oaxaca (Blanton et al. 1979, 1982; Feinman et al. 1985; Kowalewski et al. 1989) have been to examine questions of population growth, settlement location, and land use. Because of the semi-arid nature of the region, its suitability to surface survey (Feinman et al. 1985:336; Nicholas et al. 1986:134), and the quantity of archaeological material visible on the surface, systematic archaeological survey in the Valley of Oaxaca has provided an ideal situation for collecting such information. As Ignacio Bernal said of his work in the valley:

> In collaboration with Lorenzo Gamio, I began the work by trying in all innocence to collect pottery wherever it lay and to mark the sites on the map. I soon found that it was easier to mark places where there was nothing, since the valley is literally covered with remains of all sorts, especially potsherds. [1965:795]

With the completion of the regional settlement pattern projects, the Valley of Oaxaca is now one of the largest contiguous regions investigated by an intensive pedestrian survey. Every field, ridge, knoll, and street has been walked, and all visible archaeological remains have been mapped on aerial photographs carried into the field. For each site, information on size, periods of occupation, surface ceramic densities, architectural features, distance to water, present land use, and other environmental variables was collected. While the information recorded for each site is not as detailed nor complete as some might like, the large corpus of sites and the broad regional coverage provide other advantages.

On the one hand, the value of a set of data depends in part on the questions asked, and some archaeological issues (i.e., demographic change, settlement location, regional patterns of land use) simply cannot be addressed with information from only a few sites, no matter how well excavated or studied those sites are. On the other hand, we recognize that other questions require detailed information that regional surveys cannot provide.

Population

To examine demographic change, we employed procedures for estimating populations that are modeled after and thus very similar to those developed by Sanders (1965:50) and Parsons (1971:23) in their settlement pattern surveys of the Basin of Mexico. As in those studies, we proceeded on the assumption that population size is largely a function of site size. We have employed a range of figures—based on the density of surface ceramics and which were derived from sixteenth and twentieth century settlement densities in highland Mesoamerica—for converting site size into population estimates. Unlike the Basin of Mexico results, however, we found relatively little variation in surface artifact density. Consequently, though specific adjustments were made in our estimates for extremely light or unusually heavy artifact concentrations, most settlements in the Valley of Oaxaca were estimated at a uniform population range of 10–25 persons per hectare of occupied area. An alternative set of procedures was used to estimate the populations of the hilltop terraced sites, because the large sample of residential terraces at many sites provided an opportunity to make more accurate population estimates. At such sites it was possible to estimate the number of households rather than just the density of occupation. A more complete presentation of the methodology is presented in Blanton et al. (1982:10–11) and Feinman et al. (1985:336–37).

These procedures yield a range of population estimates, of which, for ease of discussion, we usually refer to the mean values. We do not apply correction factors to our population estimates, as Sanders (Sanders and Nichols 1988) and Tolstoy (1982–1983, 1988) suggest, because it is unclear what values should be used for Oaxaca, how they should be employed for different temporal episodes, and whether they are even necessary. Sanders (Sanders et al. 1979) raised some of his prehispanic population estimates for the Basin of Mexico by 20 percent so that they *appear* more in line with ethnohistoric figures, and he used the same rationale for raising the estimates for the Postclassic period in the Valley of Oaxaca (Sanders and Nichols 1988). However, in both areas, the boundaries of the archaeological survey region and the ethnohistorically defined area almost certainly are not the same. In fact, we know that in Oaxaca Monte Albán V settlement continues up into the mountains and beyond (e.g. Drennan 1989), outside the limits of the surveyed area (but within the contemporary *distrito* boundaries of valley-based communities). Thus, the documentary population estimates may well pertain to a larger area. Our archaeological estimates apply only to the area actually surveyed, which in other phases does encompass most of the settlement system.

Furthermore, differences in recent urbanization, modern farming techniques, and other factors do not justify an arbitrary and unsubstantiated adjustment of the archaeologically derived Valley of Oaxaca population figures. While the use of maxima (rather than mean) population figures may make sense for the Basin of Mexico due to the magnitude of the Colonial and modern destruction of prehistoric sites, Oaxaca had been less affected by these processes when we carried out our surveys. In addition, a larger proportion of the Valley of Oaxaca (95%) has been surveyed systematically.

Settlement Location and Land Use

Kirkby's (1973) study enables us to conduct various specific analyses comparing settlement location (derived from the regional surveys) in relation to land quality and agricultural productivity.

Recognizing that water is the critical resource for agriculture in the valley, and therefore a principal determinant of agricultural yield, Kirkby mapped the distribution of different agricultural conditions across the region. Kowalewski (1982:151) simplified Kirkby's land classification scheme, grouping classes which have similar yield profiles, and we adhere to his tripartite classification of arable land. Class I land consists of "canal-irrigable" and "water-table" land and produces the highest yields. Class II combines "marginal water-table" and "good floodwater-farming" land, where harvests may be as high as on Class I land but generally are more variable. Class III consists of "poor floodwater" and "dry-farming" land, which in dry years may produce little or nothing.

Following Kirkby (1973), we assume that present conditions can be used as a reasonable guideline to project the distribution of land classes over the past 3500 years. We have no evidence to contradict this (Byers 1967; Flannery and Schoenwetter 1970; Schoenwetter 1974). However, we do take into account the effect of modern technology, such as motorized pumps, which have increased the availability of water in some areas, most notably around modern Oaxaca City. Based on Kirkby's (1973:124–26) study of prehistoric maize cobs through time—in which she plotted an increase in mean cob length, and hence productivity—we extrapolated yield figures for the past for the different land classes (Kowalewski 1980:154, 1982:156; Nicholas 1989). While maize clearly was not the only crop cultivated in prehispanic Oaxaca, it was the most important. Since we lack information on prehispanic crop mixes that would allow a precise accounting of land sown with each crop, we use maize yields as a proxy for total crop yields. The range of potential yields also has been adjusted to reflect spatial variation in rainfall. Even though these yield figures are extrapolations, they have an empirical basis in the Valley of Oaxaca. Consequently, it is frankly absurd for Tolstoy (1988:66) to argue that the estimates of agricultural fertility in Oaxaca should be brought into line with estimates for the Basin of Mexico. While the Valley of Oaxaca and the Basin of Mexico are topographically similar, the latter region is 2000 feet higher in elevation, it experiences a much greater frequency of frosts, and it is more than 300 miles to the north. Furthermore, lacking a study comparable to Kirkby's, Sanders (1976:146) acknowledges that his prehispanic yield estimates for the Basin were derived in "the absence of empirical data."

Taking into account the amount of each land class present in the surveyed area, we have estimated the total potential corn yield for the Valley of Oaxaca during each prehispanic phase. In these calculations, separate adjustments for fallow (as suggested by Sanders and Nichols 1988:43) were not necessary (Tolstoy 1988), since Kirkby (1973:127) had already built an average of 30 percent fallow into her assumptions regarding land use. We express these potential yields in ranges, as we did for our archaeological population figures. These estimates of potential corn production are based on resources alone, not labor, and therefore, are explicitly not considered to be estimates of the amount of maize that actually was produced.

To compare potential agricultural productivity to the distribution of prehispanic populations, we have converted the valley yield figures into levels of potential population by taking into account a range of consumption figures (.16–.29 metric tons/person/year) that have been drawn from ethnographic studies of communities in the Valley of Oaxaca, as well as other parts of Mesoamerica (see Kowalewski 1982:158 for a fuller discussion and Williams 1989:725 for an alternative approach that shows similar findings). Clearly, these potential population figures are rough approximations, and while they cover a fairly wide range, they represent reasonable baselines with which to compare the observed archaeological populations. For potential population we generally use the mean figures (as we did for the archaeological population estimates), but we have not restricted our analyses to them (see Nicholas 1989).

These absolute potential population figures represent maximum numbers of people that the valley could have supported (with *land*, not labor, the limiting factor) under existing available technologies, and they provide a means of comparison (against estimated archaeological populations) among valley subregions and at smaller analytical scales. However, they are not intended to provide much insight into *actual* prehispanic land use. To examine that, it is necessary to consider labor. Hence, in other analyses we use the same yield and consumption figures as above, but also factor in the amount of land that a prehispanic farmer could have cultivated. In doing so, we follow Kirkby (1973:73) who estimates that a prehispanic farmer, using the traditional Mesoamerican hoe, the *coa*, could farm 2 ha (see also Tolstoy 1988). Sanders and Nichols (1988:71; see also Nichols 1989:1023) assert that "we are reasonably sure that she is talking about *family* labor costs . . . ". Yet they offer absolutely no rationale for their view. Despite their protestations, Kirkby (1973:127) clearly is referring to labor costs per *individual* when she assumes that a family of five (using a *coa*) could have cultivated a maximum of 8 ha.

Based on Kowalewski's (1980:156) interpretation of Wayne Kappel's (1977) present and historic population profiles in four communities in the eastern arm of the valley, we estimate that the prehispanic labor force was approximately half of the archaeological population (lower than Kirkby's estimate, but considerably higher than Sanders' and Nichols' [1988]). The resulting maximum production figures represent reasonable approximations of the population that the prehispanic labor force could have supported in the valley. These figures also should not be used as specific representations of the past. Rather, they are meant to reflect general patterns of past land use and to be examined in relation to ideal models and expectations. More detailed accounts of the methodology used in the land use analyses are presented in Kowalewski 1982 and Nicholas 1989.

A 4 x 4 km grid system has been superimposed over a map of the surveyed area to facilitate analysis and comparison. Amounts of each land class, the total potential yields, yields based on labor requirements, potential populations, and the total population have been recorded for each of 190 grid squares. Much of our land use analysis has been carried out at the level of the grid square, but we also have varied the scale of analysis from that of individual sites to valley subregions and beyond. While the large number of sites in many phases (over 2400 in Period V) make traditional site catchment studies (which measure circular catchments of a defined radii from each site) very cumbersome for projects as large as the Oaxaca settlement studies, we have completed such site-based catchment analyses for some phases (when the number of sites or points was manageable) and for the largest sites in all phases (Fisch 1982; Nicholas 1989). Regardless of the scale of analysis or the means of catchment definition employed, our overall findings have been consistent. The greatest utility of the grid-square analyses is that they provide constant units through time that can be examined relative to other variables. Alternatively, traditional, circular site catchments change as settlements are established, grow, and are abandoned. For some analyses, especially when trying to assess environmentally based predictions of human behavior or settlement location, it is more appropriate to begin with land-based information on agriculture and the environment, not site-based information. Potentially, the use of site catchments as the starting point for predicting site location may introduce circularity into any resultant explanation because the catchments are initially defined by site location. Although certain patterns or relationships might be masked by analyzing information at the grid-square level, we do employ a large number of units (190) and their size is relatively small (16 km^2 each, relative to 12.5 km^2 for a 2-km-radius catchment circle). In fact, rather than being too large, the grid square as a unit of analysis may be overly restrictive for labor-based analyses in some cases, especially for large sites such as Monte Albán that may be expected to have somewhat larger catchment areas than other sites in the valley. We are convinced that the grid-square-based analysis is one appropriate and manageable procedure for examining man-land relationships.

RESEARCH FINDINGS

The results of our settlement and land use analyses relate to a series of important issues, including demographic trends, the relationship between land quality and settlement location, prehispanic colonization of the valley, the role of surplus production in societal change, and the utility of Boserup's thesis for examining prehispanic agriculture. Now we will review our principal findings.

Demographic Trends

It has become clear that long-term demographic change in the Valley of Oaxaca did not follow a simple trajectory nor unidirectional progression (Fig. 3.2). However, the description of the change depends to a large degree on the time frame that is used. If we examine the sequence from the Tierras Largas phase (1400–1150 B.C.) through Monte Albán V (A.D. 900–1520) as a single episode, we calculate that the regional population grew at a rate slightly higher than 0.2% per year, which implies the population doubled every 300 years (Feinman et al. 1985:361). Yet if we divide that episode into phases, we note that the transitions were marked by both rapid growth (Rosario to Early I; Early I to Late I; II to IIIa; IV to V) and declines (Late I to II; IIIa to IIIb; and IIIb to IV), with phase-to-phase rates varying between -0.17% and +1.4% per year (Fig. 3.3). These demographic changes cannot be explained simply as the consequences of environmental variables, such as increasing maize productivity. While the number of people potentially supported by the valley's agricultural resources grew by roughly a factor of five between the Tierras Largas phase and Monte Albán V, the region's population grew by 500 times over the same period (Feinman et al. 1985:361). The most rapid population increases were observed for the transition to, and the period just after, the establishment of Monte Albán and the development of state-level political complexity in the region. A relationship between these latter organizational changes, their effects on households, and the demographic increases is suggested by the particular rapidity of growth at that time both in and immediately around Monte Albán, an area that had been occupied only sparsely in prior phases (Feinman et al. 1985:345–346; Kowalewski et al. 1989).

The population dynamics observed for the valley as a whole did not simply determine the patterns of change within smaller valley subunits. In fact, subregional-scale demographic shifts were generally even more complicated and less uniform (Fig. 3.4). Within the valley, different areas grew and declined at different times, and regional trends were rarely mirrored in all subregions. During only four of ten phase transitions (Tierras Largas to San José; Rosario to Early I; Early I to Late I; and IV to V) did all six subregions change in the same direction, though in each of these transitions the rates of growth were not uniform (Feinman et al. 1985:362). No subregion was the most densely occupied in all phases. Generally the Central area was the most intensively occupied, even though it is agriculturally one of the least productive portions of the valley (Nicholas 1989:460–62). At times, however, the Central area was only sparsely settled. Even the

SETTLEMENT AND LAND USE   83

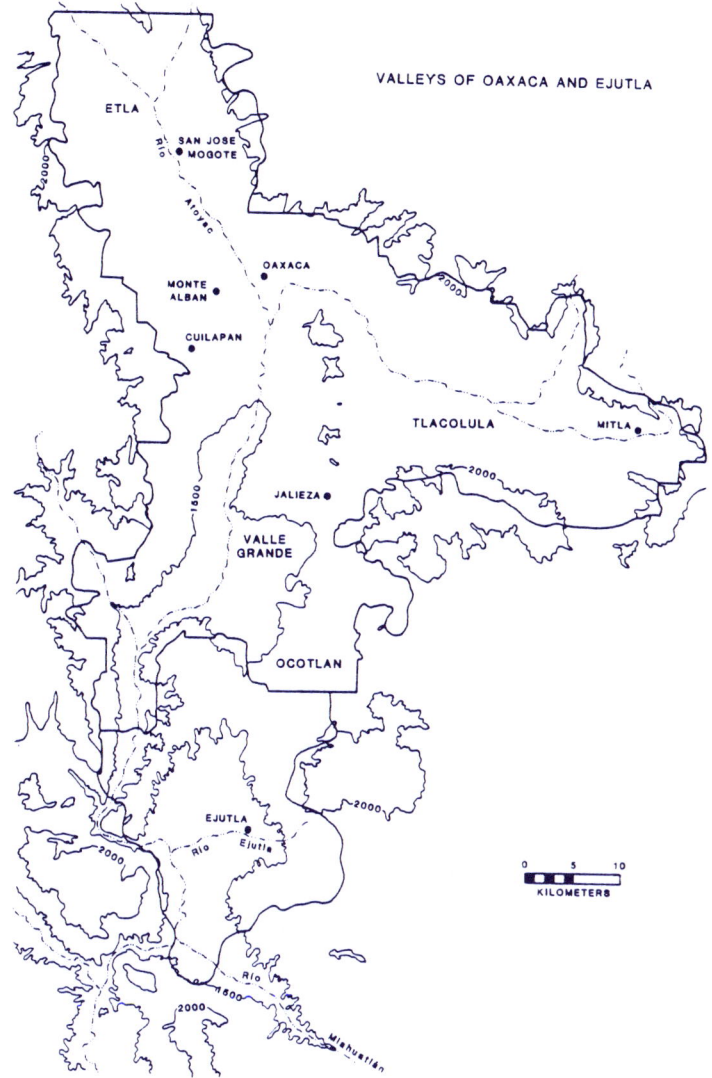

Figure 3.1. Valley of Oaxaca and Ejutla survey areas.

dry eastern end of the Tlacolula subvalley, the least productive area, was densely populated late in the prehispanic sequence.

The most recently surveyed area, the Ejutla Valley (Feinman 1985; Feinman and Nicholas 1988), has a demographic profile that differs from that of the Valley of Oaxaca (Fig. 3.2). Ejutla's growth episodes

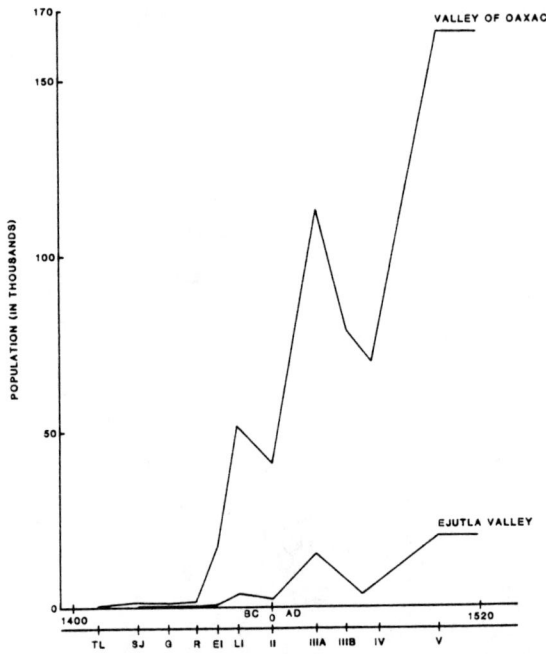

Figure 3.2. Population trends in Oaxaca and Ejutla.

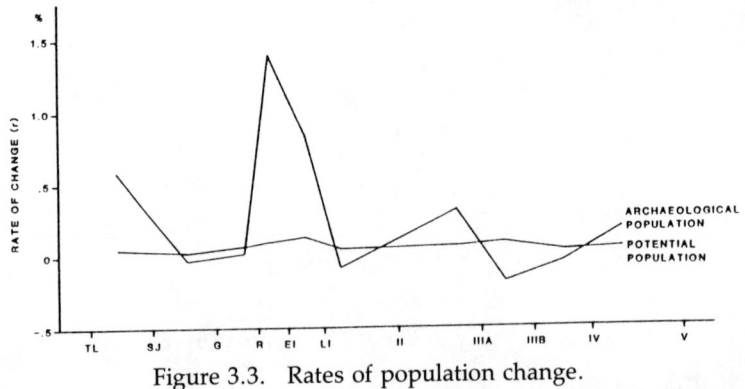

Figure 3.3. Rates of population change.

occurred later than those of its larger neighbor to the north. Ejutla was only very sparsely occupied until after the foundation of Monte Albán (during Early I), a period of rapid population growth in the Valley of Oaxaca. In contrast, Ejutla did not experience its first major

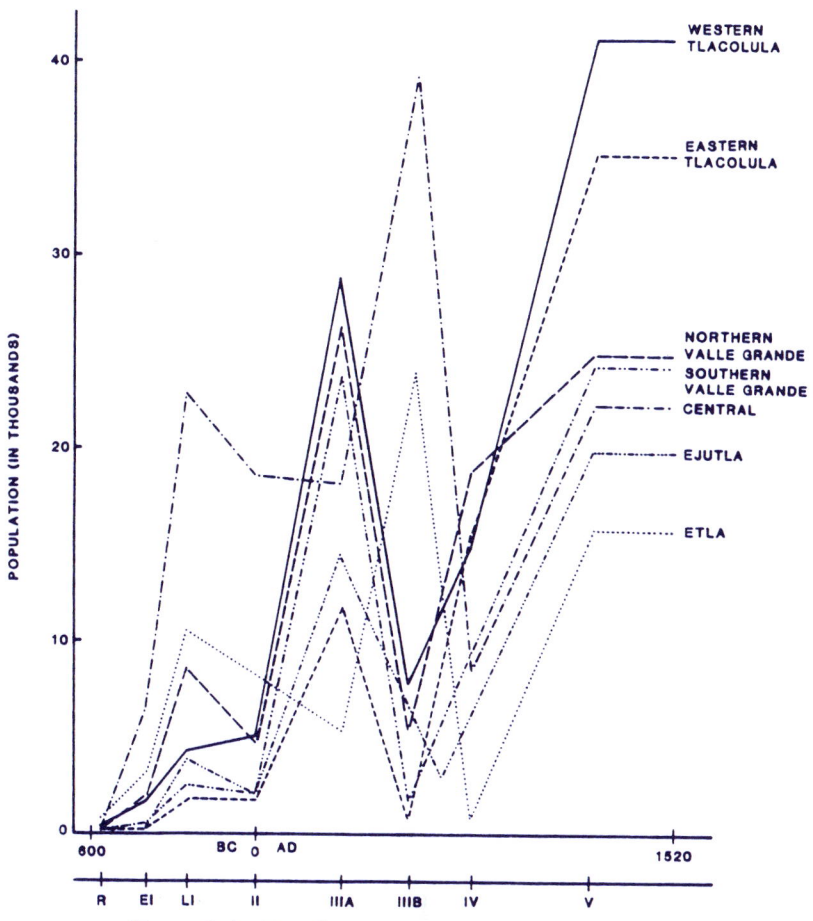

Figure 3.4. Population trends by valley subregion.

growth episode until the Early I–Late I transition, several hundred years later (Feinman 1985:64). Ejutla's less productive lands, relative to the Valley of Oaxaca as a whole, led us to expect this. However, Ejutla does have a greater proportion of good land than several of the Valley of Oaxaca's subregions (Table 3.1). If we factor in the different sizes of the subregions, Ejutla is more productive than eastern Tlacolula and ranks about the same as the Central area. Yet agricultural productivity does not appear to be the main factor affecting the pattern of population growth and distribution. In terms of the timing of growth episodes and the magnitude of population fluctuations from phase to phase, Ejutla exhibits the greatest number of similarities with the more peripheral parts of the Valley of Oaxaca, especially the

TABLE 3.1

Distribution of Good Land in Oaxaca (in ha)

Subregion	Class I	Class II	High Rainfall Class II	Total Class I and High Rainfall Class II
Etla	5117	88	16	5133
Central	1261	2652	678	1939
N. Valle Grande	3345	2600	882	4227
S. Valle Grande	2003	1180	1180	3183
W. Tlacolula	618	6118	918	1536
E. Tlacolula	396	1584	10	406
Ejutla	1527	3702	523	2050

TABLE 3.2

Wilcoxon Rank Sum Scores for Catchment Circles and Large Sites

Phase	Z Score	p-value
Tierras Largas	0.58	.2810
San José	1.84	.0329
Guadalupe	2.21	.0135
Rosario	2.89	.0019
M.A. Early I	3.20	.0007
M.A. Late I	3.52	.0002
M.A. II	2.88	.0020
M.A. IIIa	4.37	<.0001
M.A. IIIb	3.24	.0006
M.A. IV	5.27	<.0001
M.A. V	5.01	<.0001

more productive southern Valle Grande (Feinman and Nicholas, in press). Ejutla's spatial relationship to the Valley of Oaxaca core appears to be a more important factor than the productivity of its agricultural resources alone.

In general, eastern Tlacolula was characterized by the most drastic population fluctuations (Feinman et al. 1985). This may relate to the area's agricultural marginality. But one of the agriculturally richer portions of the valley, the southern Valle Grande, was also an area in which the demographic swings were rapid. These subregions have surprisingly comparable population histories, although they are markedly different agriculturally (Nicholas 1989:460–62). In part, their similar population patterns may be related to the fact that both areas were spatially peripheral, first to San José Mogote and then to Monte Albán, and so were only intensively occupied later in the valley's prehispanic sequence. As peripheries, along with the Ejutla Valley, these subregions seem to have been seriously affected by development strategies and shifts in the region's political economy in later Monte Albán times.

Interestingly, the most massive demographic shifts—both at the subregion (Fig. 3.4) and 4 km x 4 km grid-square level (Feinman et al. 1985)—took place *late* in the prehispanic era, both in the Valley of Oaxaca and the Ejutla Valley, when regional population was the highest (although not necessarily closer to potential productivity) and changes in the valley's civic-ceremonial organization were most marked. The occurrence of these more dramatic internal changes in the latter half of the prehispanic era, when the regional political economy was more complex, indicates a relationship between local-scale demographic instability and political/economic complexity, a pattern that also is seen for long temporal sequences in the domains of two other early states—ancient Mesopotamia (Adams 1981; Johnson 1973) and the Basin of Mexico (Sanders et al. 1979).

Settlement Location versus Land Quality

A second major issue we have addressed concerns the relationship between land quality and settlement location. We found that this question has neither one simple nor single answer. The specific answer depends upon the scale of the analysis, the time frame, and the particular questions asked. At the scale of the Southern Highlands, the answer would be: Yes, agricultural productivity is a very important variable in determining general settlement location. The Valley of Oaxaca has the largest expanse of flat land in the region, and both today as during most of the past, it has the highest population densities and the largest settlements.

However, this relationship is less clear as the scale of analysis is reduced to that of the Valley of Oaxaca system and its subregions. If we compare Ejutla to Oaxaca, we find that Ejutla is more marginal agriculturally and always had lower population densities and smaller settlements (Feinman 1985; Feinman and Nicholas 1988). Yet, land quality in the Valley of Oaxaca is quite variable, and its distribution by subregion is very uneven (Nicholas 1989:460-62). Ejutla has more good land than at least two of the valley's subregions (eastern and western Tlacolula), but for the most part it had lower population densities than either of them (Fig. 3.5). In general, through time, the highest prehispanic population densities were not found in the most productive parts of the valley. The discrepancy was particularly evident during the Postclassic period (Fig. 3.5, Table 3.1). When we compared the potential populations of each subregion with the estimated archaeological population for the same units, we found no strong positive correlation in any phase, and at some times the relationship was negative (Nicholas 1989:467-68).

At the local or 4 km x 4 km grid-square level, we found no significant correlation between actual prehispanic and potential population levels (Kowalewski 1982; Nicholas 1981). Even in the pre-Monte Albán phases, where we did find a settlement preference for better lands, the distribution of the population across the landscape did not match the distribution of the highest quality land (Fig. 3.6). However, based on preliminary analyses (Feinman 1985; Feinman and Nicholas, in press), there does appear to have been a clearer selection for good land in the placement of Ejutla settlements when compared to settlement location in Oaxaca. This was not completely unexpected, since Ejutla always appears to have been less politically developed than the Valley of Oaxaca. Yet, in Ejutla, scatter plots for each phase again show no strong consistent positive relationship between settlement size and potential population at the local scale (Fig. 3.7).

In sum, the role of potential agricultural productivity in settlement decisions was not constant and appears to have been of decreasing importance through time. In a more specific analysis of the location of the largest settlements in each phase relative to the distribution of the most productive tracts of land (Nicholas 1989:470-77), we found a clear decline in the relationship between the two variables through time (Table 3.2). The correlation was significantly positive only during the Tierras Largas phase. The weakest relationship was present when the valley system reached its highest levels of population and sociopolitical complexity in the Classic and Postclassic periods. While

SETTLEMENT AND LAND USE 89

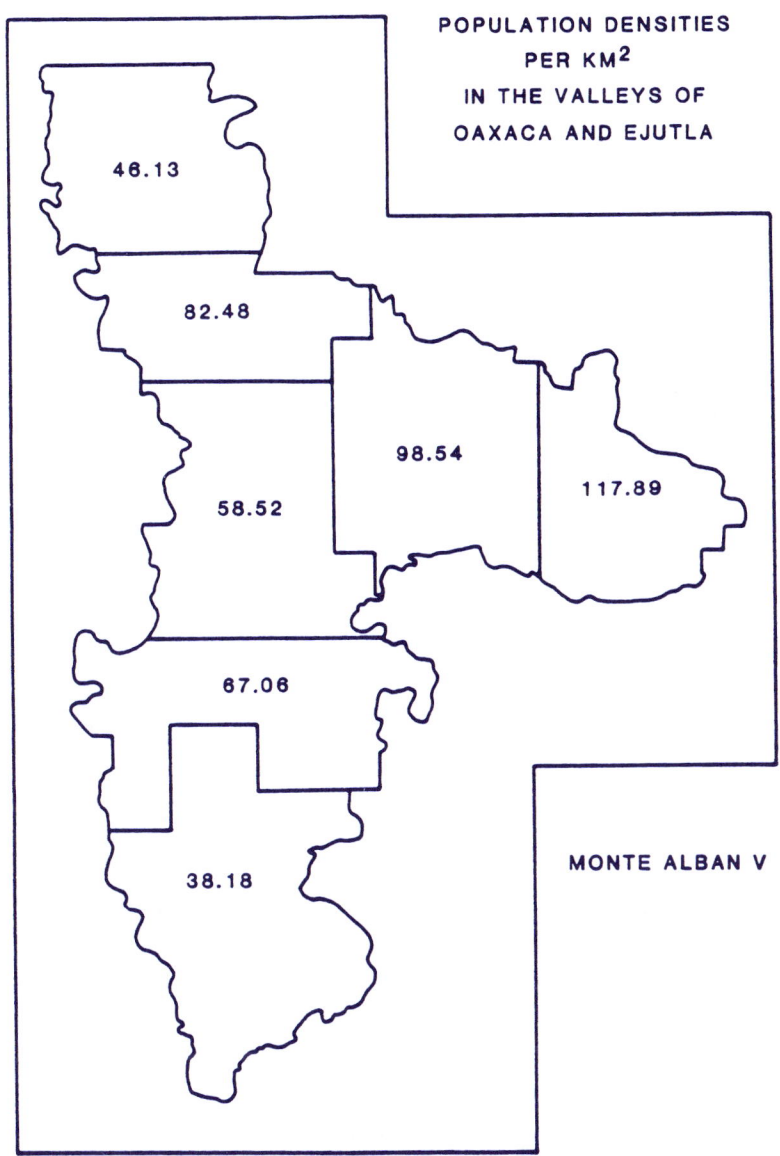

Figure 3.5. Population density in Period V.

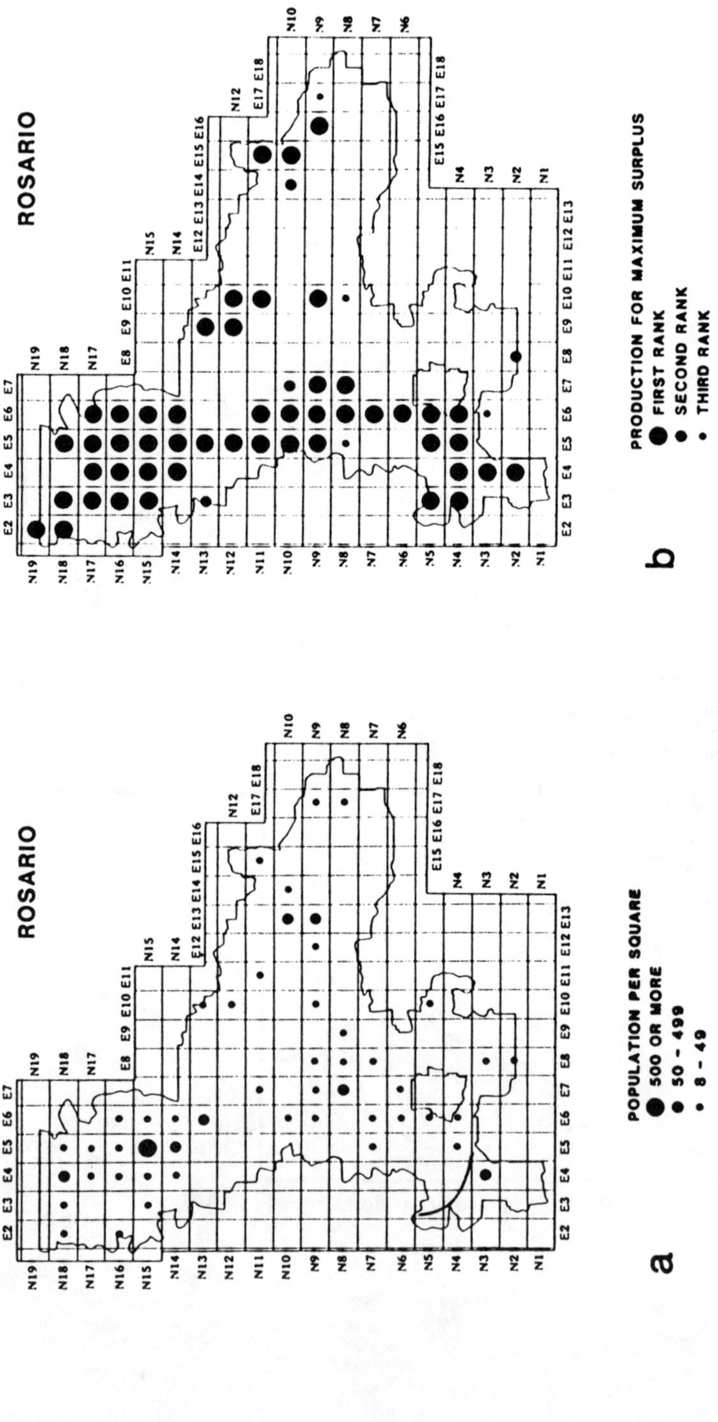

90 DEBATING OAXACA ARCHAEOLOGY

Figure 3.6. Distribution of Rosario phase population and good land.

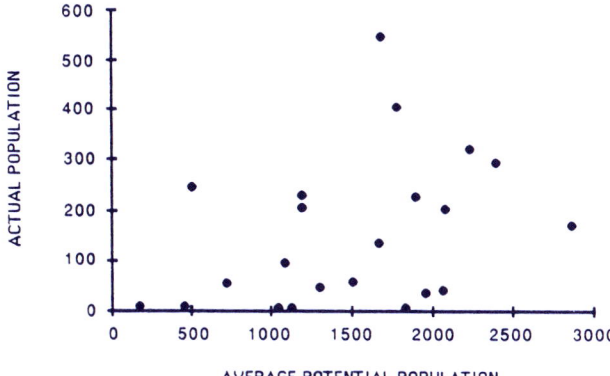

Figure 3.7. Scatterplot of actual and potential populations during Late Period I (Monte Albán Ic) in Ejutla.

some sites in the Valley of Oaxaca initially may have been located near good or satisfactory land, subsequent growth and changes in population distributions cannot be explained solely by environmental variables. This is especially clear in the case of the region's largest site, Monte Albán.

We have shown that consideration of good farmland was not the major factor in settlement decisions involving Monte Albán (Blanton et al. 1982; Kowalewski et al. 1989). To argue, as Sanders and Nichols (1988) do, that adequate amounts of good farmland can be found within 10 km of Monte Albán, and that this largely explains Monte Albán's location, is relatively meaningless. We do not argue that there is no good land near Monte Albán. Because of the patchy distribution of productive land and the narrowness of much of the valley floor (generally less than 20 km and in most places less than 10), most sites in the valley are within 10 km of parcels of good floodwater-irrigation land. This makes the utility of such a large catchment area (radius of 10 km) rather questionable for "explaining" the location of settlements. What is more important is that the 10 km catchment around Monte Albán is not one of the most productive in the valley. If land quality (potential productivity) *was* the most important variable, rather than the significance of central location as Blanton (1976; 1978:35-37) has argued, then there are other locations, in all three arms of the valley, that could have been selected. Similar 10 km catchments in either Etla or the Valle Grande were capable of producing 60 to 70 percent more food than the catchment area surrounding Monte Albán; in western Tlacolula, 22 percent more food could have been harvested.

It is not enough to assert that there is good land near the base of Monte Albán; this is evident and we know it from having worked there. To support their argument Sanders and Nichols must demonstrate that Monte Albán is located in one of the more productive parts of the valley. Sanders and Nichols (1988:39) endeavor to do this through reference to Kirkby's (1973:66) Figure 25, which shows the distribution of contemporary mean corn yields. Yet today, the land in the shadow of Monte Albán also is close to contemporary Oaxaca City, with its large population and major market places. Because of the proximity of a large number of consumers and the relatively low transportation costs that they face, modern farmers in this central area can invest heavily in technology to spur production. Hence, it is not surprising that Kirkby (1973:45, 51) noted an unusual reliance on mechanized pump irrigation in this central region today. As a consequence, Kirkby's Figure 25 shows the central region to be comparatively productive. But the relevant data are actually in Figure 18 (Kirkby 1973:48), which shows the distribution of the main agricultural water use methods. Mechanized pumps obviously were not available in prehispanic times. Reference to Kirkby's Figure 18 permits a consideration of farming and water use techniques implemented in the past, and an examination shows the central area to have been generally more marginal than several other subregions. If we divide the valley into 100 km^2 blocks, and calculate the potential prehispanic yields in each block, the 100 km^2 area that includes Monte Albán ranks in the *lower third* of 15 such blocks.

Sanders and Nichols (1988:43) also obfuscate the issue by stating that all major Oaxaca settlements located on steep, defensible hills (like Monte Albán) overlook large tracts of prime agricultural land. In doing so, they confuse valley floor land in general with the more restrictive category of prime agricultural land. While all hilltop sites in the Valley of Oaxaca overlook the alluvium (some at far greater distances than others), not all face large blocks of prime land. Furthermore, in Oaxaca, a hilltop site may peer down on choice farm land, but from experience we know that it may take more than an hour to walk down to that land and over two hours to get back up. What is relevant is the time involved in reaching land, and whether or not a community is likely to have had access to it.

Colonization

We also have examined the process of colonization in the valley (Nicholas et al. 1986) and found that, while satisfactory land was generally chosen over the least productive land, at the level of the grid squares there was no clear preference for situating settlements next to the best land available. Often, better lands were passed over as new settlements were established around existing centers and settlements. This pattern was especially evident during the San José phase, when settlements were clustered around San José Mogote in the Etla arm (Fig. 3.8). While some very productive land is located in this part of the valley, it was not all inhabited prior to the occupation of poorer-quality land. In addition, the largest tract of prime farmland, located in the Valle Grande, was only sparsely occupied when the Etla arm was inhabited much more densely. In the later Rosario phase, coincident with a dispersal of population away from Etla,

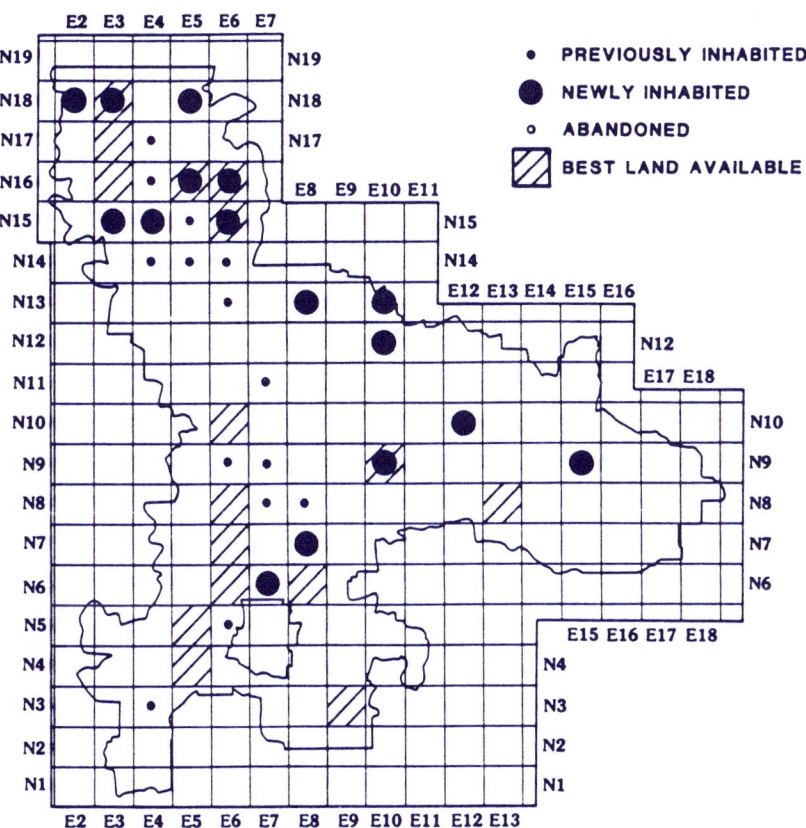

Figure 3.8. San José phase colonization map.

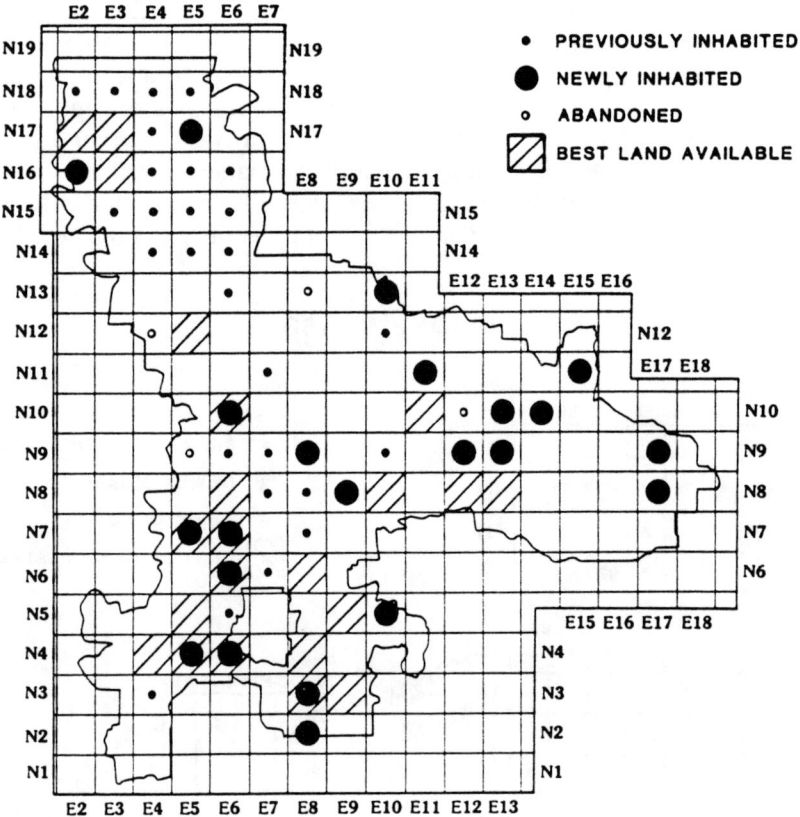

Figure 3.9. Rosario phase colonization map.

population concentrations occurred near several new secondary centers in the drier Tlacolula arm, but not in the more productive Valle Grande (Fig. 3.9). Some of the best land in the Valle Grande was not settled until Monte Albán I (Fig. 3.10), a thousand years after the first sedentary villages were established in the valley. Therefore, the spread of settlement seems as related to economic, political, and social factors as to environmental or purely demographic ones.

Throughout most of the sequence of sedentary villages in the Valley of Oaxaca, a hierarchy of settlements has been present. At least one settlement (beginning with San José Mogote during the pre–Monte Albán phases, and later Monte Albán) has dominated the landscape.

MONTE ALBAN LATE I

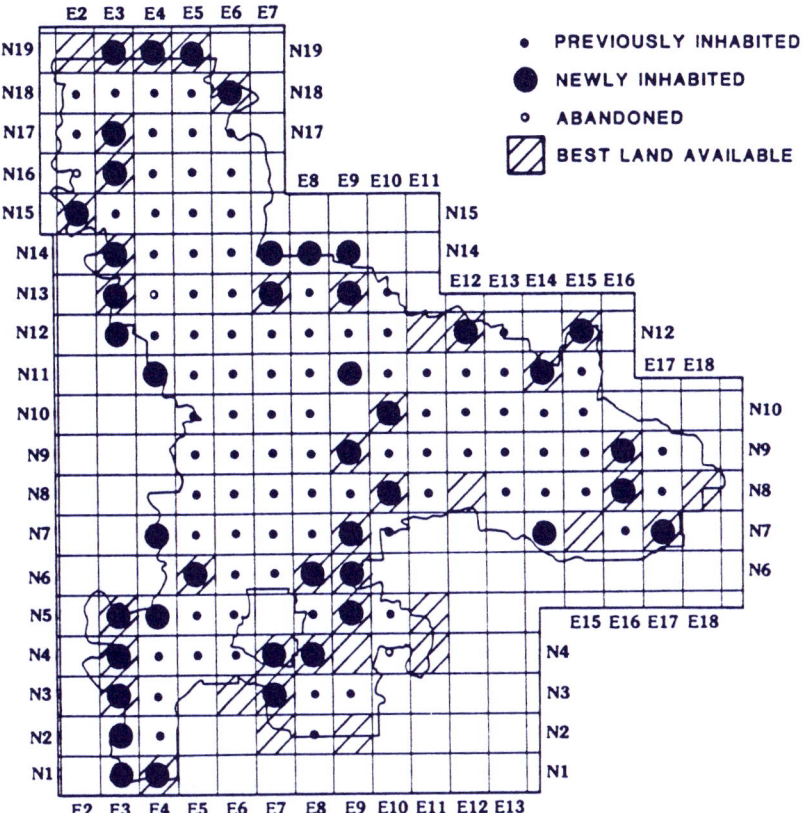

Figure 3.10. Late Period I (Monte Albán Ic) colonization map.

During much of the Oaxaca sequence, and particularly early on, new settlements were established in the most densely inhabited areas near existing large settlements. There is no evidence that population pressure pushed people to settle on progressively less desirable lands. In all but a few instances, such as at Monte Albán, where local populations exceeded the potential of the immediate area, actual populations in the Valleys of Oaxaca and Ejutla were always considerably below the absolute levels that could have been supported locally (Fig. 3.11). With little or no evidence of population pressure, it is difficult to defend the use of demographic variables alone to explain the process of colonization. Our analysis suggests that these larger towns

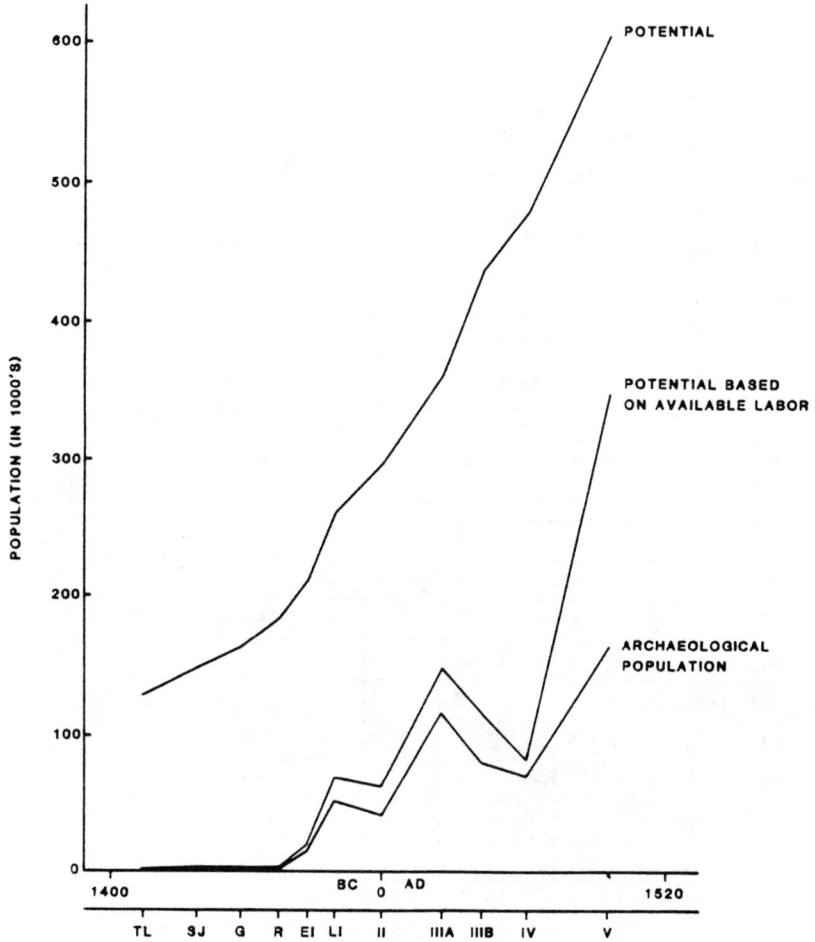

Figure 3.11. Potential population levels in the Valley of Oaxaca.

and cities had a continuing and important centripetal effect on the placement of other smaller settlements, either through coercion or by offering goods and services not available elsewhere (Nicholas et al. 1986).

Surplus

In a fourth series of analyses and simulations we addressed the issue of surplus production (Feinman and Nicholas 1987). In modeling surplus we cannot focus simply on absolute agricultural potential,

SETTLEMENT AND LAND USE 97

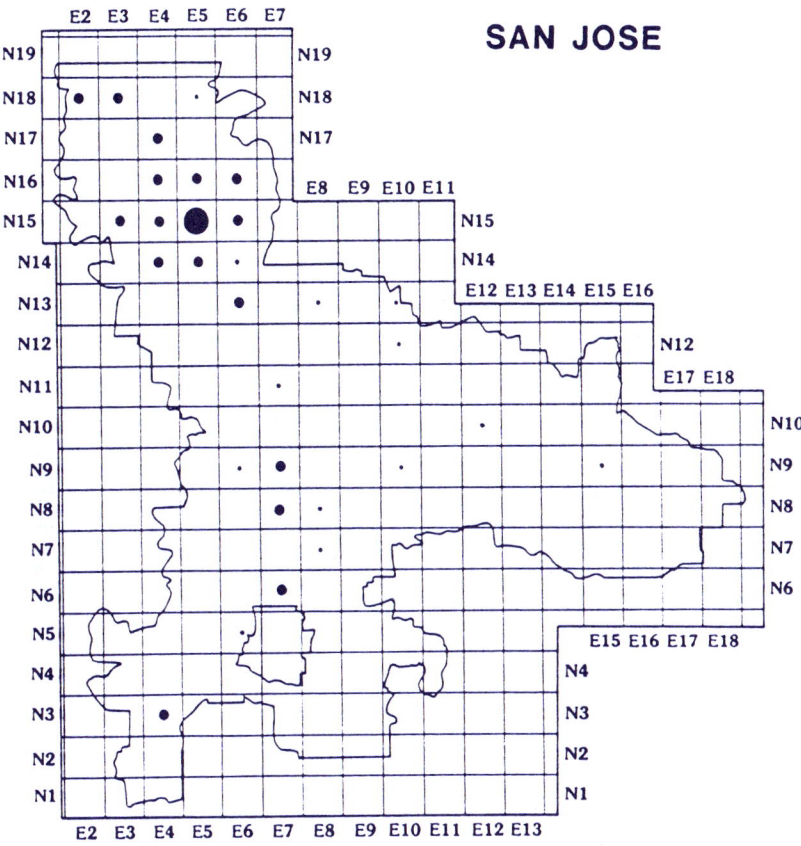

Figure 3.12. Distribution of surplus during the San José phase.

which in the Valley of Oaxaca has always greatly exceeded the estimated archaeological population (Fig. 3.11). Clearly, because of increasing maize yields, the amount of potential surplus that an individual Zapotec farmer could produce in an average year increased linearly through time. Yet the archaeological record does not indicate

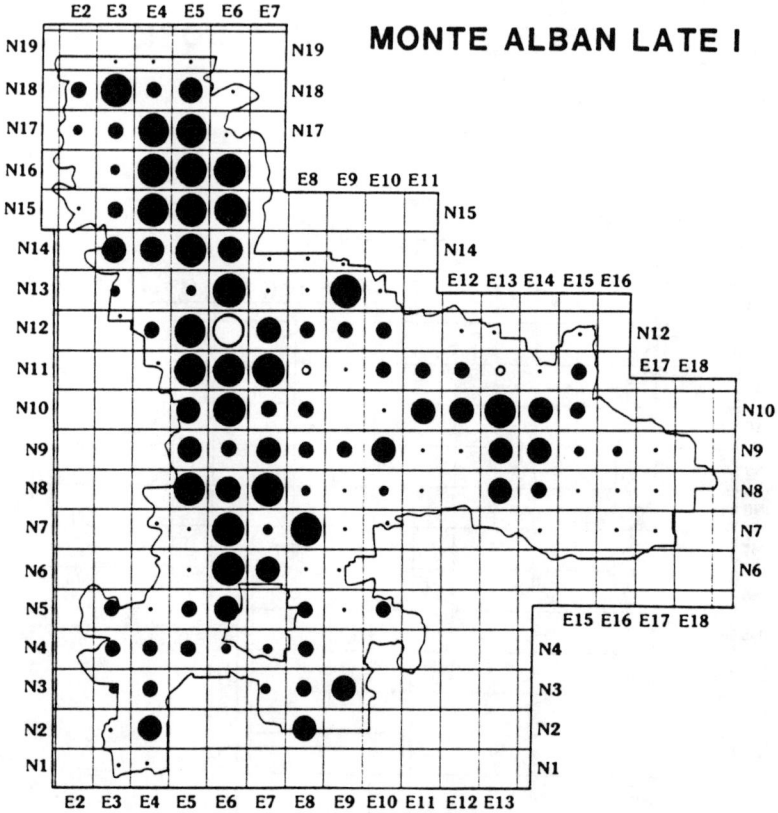

Figure 3.13. Distribution of surplus during Late Period I (Monte Albán Ic).

such a linear record of realized surplus (such as in monumental architecture, etc.). Obviously, surplus production occurs where there is available and conscriptable labor; hence surplus production cannot be predicted based only on an examination of environmental variables, such as land quality (Pearson 1957; Sahlins 1972; Wolf 1981).

SETTLEMENT AND LAND USE 99

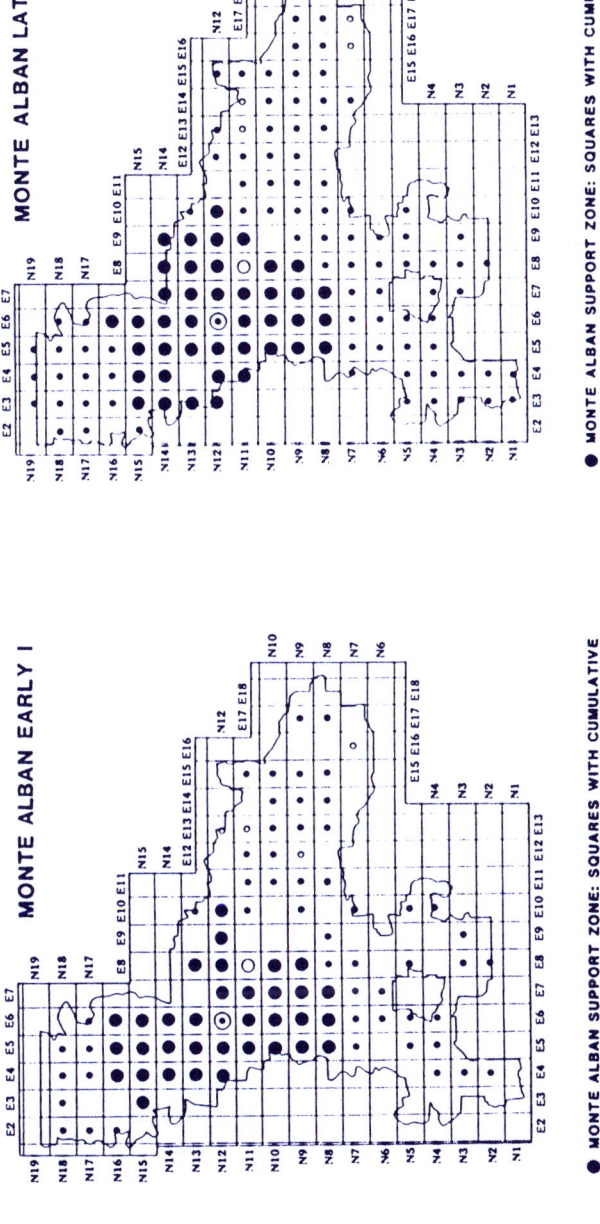

Figure 3.14. Monte Albán support zones in Early and Late I (Monte Albán Ia and Ic).

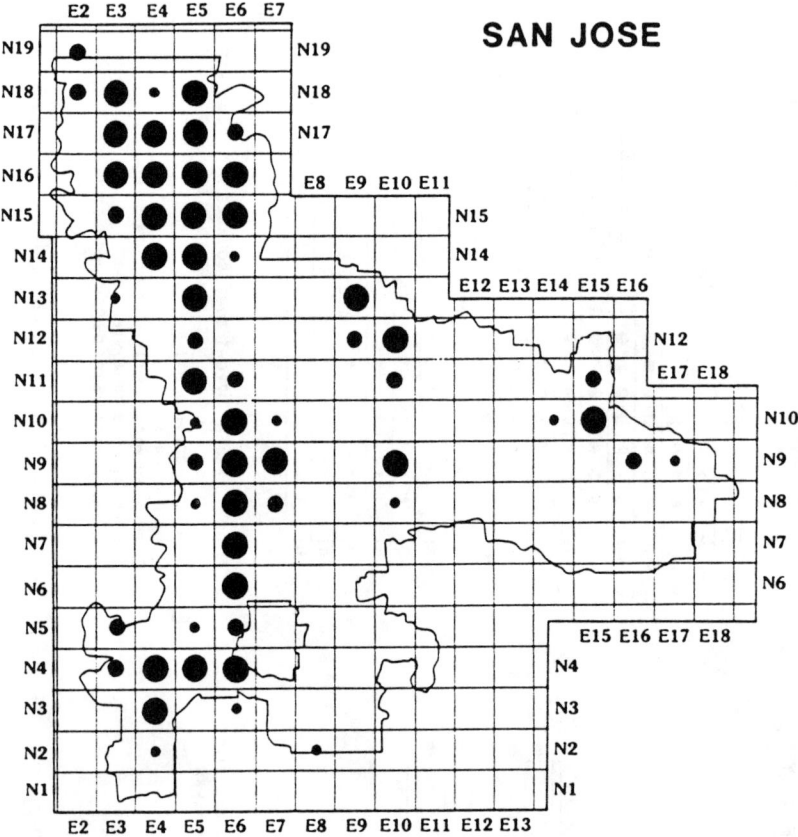

Figure 3.15. Distribution of population for maximum production during the San José phase.

To examine the valley's potential for surplus production, we calculated maximal production based on the size and distribution of the available labor (Kowalewski 1982; Nicholas 1989:478–80). Even these maximal production figues may be somewhat low because we conservatively assumed that the inhabitants of a particular site only farmed land in the grid square in which the site was located. The

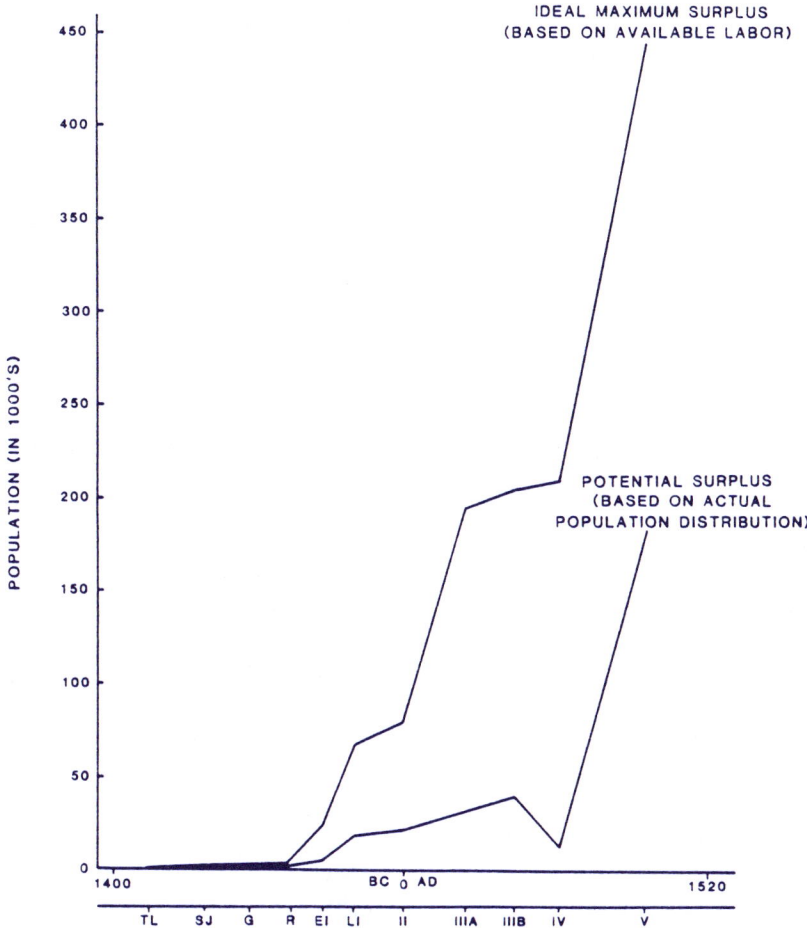

Figure 3.16. Ideal maximum surplus versus potential surplus.

impact of this restriction is greatest on larger sites, such as Monte Albán. Actual local imbalances may have been somewhat less than our figures imply.

During the pre-Monte Albán phases, the production of a surplus was limited because of the region's small population. Yet the greatest amounts of potential surplus could have been produced around the largest and most important centers, first around the site of San José Mogote (Fig. 3.12), and later around Monte Albán (Fig. 3.13). During the pre-Monte Albán phases, more surplus could have been produced within one day's round trip from San José Mogote, which is located near good alluvial land, than in the rest of the valley. Yet in the Rosario phase, fairly large surpluses also could have been produced near a series of smaller centers that were less well located relative to good farm land.

Beginning with Early I and the founding of Monte Albán, production increased considerably, even though a larger percentage of the population was engaged in non-farming activities. The focus for surplus production shifted from San José Mogote to Monte Albán, with more surplus produced within one day's round trip from Monte Albán than in the rest of the valley (Table 3.3). This shift became more pronounced in Monte Albán Late I, indicating the importance of distance from Monte Albán in the distribution of labor and hence potential surplus production. In Late I, population growth and potential surplus production increased most rapidly near Monte Albán, in spite of the quantity of poor Class III agricultural land in the area. Excluding Monte Albán's population, 65% of the growth in the valley occurred within 20 km of Monte Albán (Feinman and Nicholas 1987:41).

The importance of labor also is indicated by the rather static size of the support zone (the area within approximately 16 km, or one day's round trip, from Monte Albán) needed to provide food for the city's residents. In spite of the substantial growth at that center between Early I and Late I (Monte Albán grew from 5000 to around 16,000 people), the size of the necessary support zone remained essentially constant because of the increase in the availability of rural labor within that zone (Fig. 3.14). We see the growth of population in the rural support zone from Early I to Late I as integrally related to the increasing demand for agricultural production at the regional capital.

We also examined how potential surplus production deviated from what would be expected if the population had been located in a consistent fashion next to the best farm land available. To do this, we simulated "ideal" population distributions, in which the regional population was arranged to maximize agricultural resources, and then compared them to the actual population distributions (Feinman and Nicholas 1987). We found that the number of these "ideal" settlement patterns was initially very large (Fig. 3.15), and that they decreased through time as the population grew. But most importantly, they never closely matched the actual settlement pattern. Through time, with larger populations and the increasing productivity of maize, the potential to amass ever greater amounts of surplus existed, but in actuality, the amount and proportion of "unutilized" potential production probably increased (Fig. 3.16), as the regional

TABLE 3.3

Surplus Production by Distance from Major Centers[1]

Phase	<18 km		>18 km	
	Total Prod.	Surplus	Total Prod.	Surplus
Tierras Largas	314	88	132	31
San José	2297	564	430	89
Rosario	2247	1144	1234	502
M.A. Early I	10,859	5387	8580	4154
M.A. Late I	39,003	19,451	29,806	14,237

[1] San José Mogote in the pre-Monte Albán phases, and Monte Albán in Early I and Late I

TABLE 3.4

Maximum Potential Production in Dry Years with Valley Population Distributed on the Best Land

Phase	Archaeological Population	Maximum Potential in Dry Years
Tierras Largas	327	396
San José	1942	2825
Guadalupe	1788	3034
Rosario	1835	3560
M.A. Early I	14,652	33,670
M.A. Late I	50,920	60,940
M.A. II	41,319	62,462
M.A. IIIa	115,226	146,140
M.A. IIIb	78,930	133,116
M.A. IV	70,075	132,493
M.A. V	162,557	232,458

population was distributed in a way that was less in accord with available agrarian resources.

During this time we also noted the first instance of what we have called the "piedmont strategy" (Blanton et al. 1981; 1982). In Period I, when the expanding city of Monte Albán required agricultural surplus, much of the adjacent Class I land already was inhabited. Because of high transport costs and fewer opportunities for markets, rewards, and/or exchange, Class I lands far from Monte Albán remained sparsely settled, while nearby areas in the piedmont, which previously had been unoccupied, experienced large population increases. While farming in such hilly areas, dependent as it is on the vagaries of annual rainfall, may not yield much of a crop in dry years, production can be substantial in years with high precipitation. Because of the patchy nature of annual rainfall in Oaxaca, at least some piedmont farmers would most likely receive adequate rainfall and be able to produce an agricultural surplus. This surplus then could be used to provide food for Monte Albán, as well as those areas where crops were not as bountiful. In Monte Albán I, the piedmont strategy was employed principally in the central part of the valley, as it was in the Late Classic (Monte Albán IIIb). During the Early Classic (Monte Albán IIIa), when a more hierarchical political apparatus was in place, piedmont occupation was concentrated more to the south and east around secondary centers.

Boserup

While we are not able to address Boserup's thesis of population growth and agricultural intensification directly by examining changes in the frequency of cropping in the Valley of Oaxaca, we have collected data relevant to several facets of her model. As stated above, we found neither continuous population growth at the regional scale nor resource pressure in prehispanic Oaxaca. In the early phases when maize yields were lower, the regional population was low enough so that potential production was more than sufficient for the numbers of people inhabiting the valley. During later phases, when regional populations were higher, maize yields had increased substantially, so potential production still was more than adequate. The latter finding holds whether we examine potentials limited only by resources, or limited by both resources and available labor. Undoubtedly there were periodic local stresses due to the location of Monte Albán and other large settlements in less than ideal agricultural locations. Yet shortfalls in local production were engendered by the distribution of the population with respect to resources, not with respect to the inadequacy of the regional resource base. Valley-wide surpluses could have been produced in all phases, even in dry years, if the population had been optimally distributed with access to the most productive land (Table 3.4).

The "law of least effort" is a major underlying premise of Boserup's thesis. Yet, as should be evident from our discussion of settlement location, this law, at least in a strict interpretation, fails to explain prehispanic land use in the Valley of Oaxaca. In many phases, the valley population was not well-located relative to resources. As Flannery and his co-workers noted decades ago (Flannery et al. 1967), agrarian intensification and irrigation first occurred when populations were still low and population/resource balances were generally favorable. In a similar vein, Folke Dovring (1966:380–81) wrote in the *Journal of Economic History*:

> Mrs. Boserup's population theory is unfounded, to say the least. It disregards many facets of the problem. . . . If Mrs. Boserup had been less fettered by a single idea and instead had turned her attention to the paradoxes of historical experience, she might have noticed that the beginnings of modern agriculture in the Low Countries and in England were not associated with increase in farm population but with increased urban demand and intensified diffusion of ideas.

SUMMARY AND CONCLUSIONS

Overall, the Valley of Oaxaca's resources were more than sufficient for its prehispanic populations. Yet for the individual farmer, the unpredictable nature of rainfall patterns must have made farming a risky endeavor. For example, in Monte Albán I, with the establishment of the urban center, there was a greater reliance on riskier farm land. Yet this was not due simply to increasing numbers of people putting pressure on resources and forcing the less favorable land to be farmed. Pockets of prime farm land remained sparsely settled or unoccupied at the edges of the region and in Ejutla. To locate in areas of risk where good crops could be raised in some years, especially if these areas were located near a center, became a prominent strategy as intraregional exchange connections were intensified. While we most certainly recognize that land and water must be considered in examining these settlement decisions (and have structured our research accordingly), it appears that other social, political, and economic considerations altered purely environmental ones.

In this discussion of settlement and land use in prehispanic Oaxaca, we have presented the results of a series of analyses in which the

the focus was on the nature of the relationship between demographic and environmental variables on the one hand, and settlement location and distribution on the other. We have tried to take a balanced, integrative approach and examine the dialectic between the environment, population, and the region's political economy. Land and water are important variables, but they are not the only ones with predictive value. Likewise, we would not limit causal primacy to politics or ideology. Our approach is more multifaceted and systemic. We also have intentionally considered several different scales of analysis. Our regional investigations have emphasized the dynamic interplay among diverse factors that impinge upon human-environmental relations. In so doing, we hope to have followed the general directions laid out by Wolf, Palerm, and Flannery. In sum, we have become more convinced that Wolf was correct when he noted in the introduction to The Valley of Mexico volume:

> when interest turns to an analysis of the critical turning points in the spiral which connects population → technology → societal differentiation → controls, more complex models will be required. [1976:7]

Acknowledgments

We greatly appreciate the funding received from the National Science Foundation for the Valley of Oaxaca and Ejutla Valley Settlement Pattern Projects. Permission to implement the fieldwork and helpful support have been offered by the Instituto Nacional de Antropología e Historia and the Centro Regional de Oaxaca, particularly by Manuel Esparza, Ma. de la Luz Topete, and Joaquín García Bárcena. The assistance of the Department of Anthropology and the Latin American Studies program at the University of Wisconsin-Madison have aided us in completing this paper. We acknowledge the productive foundation for our investigations of human-land relations that was set forth by Stephen Kowalewski. Richard Blanton, Kent Flannery, Joyce Marcus, and Laura Finsten also provided many insightful comments and constructive suggestions over the years.

An earlier version of this work was presented in October, 1987, at the Fifth Annual Mesoamerica Conference in Philadelphia. We thank the organizers, Robert Sharer and Elin Danien, for inviting us to express our views in a productive and comfortable setting. Revisions were made while the senior author was a resident scholar at the School of American Research, and we thank Douglas W. Schwartz for the wonderful opportunity to spend a stimulating year in Santa Fe.

References Cited

Adams, John
1966   Review of The Conditions of Agricultural Growth (Boserup). Annals of the American Academy of Political and Social Science 367:224–25.

Adams, Robert McC.
1981   Heartland of Cities: Surveys of Ancient Settlement and Land Use on the Central Floodplain of the Euphrates. Chicago: University of Chicago Press.

Adams, Robert McC., and Hans J. Nissen
1976   The Uruk Countryside. Chicago: University of Chicago Press.

Armillas, Pedro
1948   A sequence of cultural development in Meso-America. In: A Reappraisal of Peruvian Archaeology, edited by Wendell C. Bennett, pp. 105–11. Memoirs of the Society for American Archaeology, 13(4). Menasha, Wisconsin.

Bernal, Ignacio
1965   Archaeological synthesis of Oaxaca. In: The Handbook of Middle American Indians, vol. 3, edited by Robert Wauchope and Gordon R. Willey, pp. 788–813. Austin: University of Texas Press.

Blanton, Richard E.
1976   The origins of Monte Albán. In: Cultural Change and Continuity, edited by Charles Cleland, pp. 223–32. New York, Academic Press.
1978   Monte Albán: Settlement Patterns at the Ancient Zapotec Capital. New York: Academic Press.

Blanton, Richard E., Jill Appel, Laura Finsten, Stephen A. Kowalewski, Gary Feinman, and Eva Fisch
1979   Regional evolution in the Valley of Oaxaca, Mexico. Journal of Field Archaeology, 6:369–90.

Blanton, Richard E., Stephen A. Kowalewski, Gary Feinman, and Jill Appel
1981   Ancient Mesoamerica: A Study of Change in Three Regions. Cambridge: Cambridge University Press.

Blanton, Richard E., Stephen A. Kowalewski, Gary Feinman, and Jill Appel
1982   Monte Albán's Hinterland, Part I: Prehispanic Settlement Patterns of the Central and Southern Parts of the Valley of Oaxaca, Mexico. Memoirs, 15. Museum of Anthropology, University of Michigan. Ann Arbor.

Blitz, Rudolph C.
1967   Review of The Conditions of Agricultural Growth (Boserup). Journal of Political Economy, 75:212–13.

Boserup, Ester
1965 The Conditions of Agricultural Growth: The Economics of Agrarian Change under Population Pressure. Chicago: Aldine.
1981 Population and Technological Change: A Study of Long-term Trends. Chicago: University of Chicago Press.

Bradley, Richard
1984 The Social Foundations of Prehistoric Britain: Themes and Variations in the Archaeology of Power. London: Longman.

Butzer, Karl W.
1976 Early Hydraulic Civilization in Egypt. Chicago: University of Chicago Press.

Byers, Douglas S.
1967 Climate and hydrology. In: The Prehistory of the Tehuacán Valley, vol. 1: Environment and Subsistence, edited by Douglas Byers, pp. 48–65. Austin: University of Texas Press.

Childe, V. Gordon
1950 The urban revolution. Town Planning Review, 21.

Choice
1966 Review of The Conditions of Agricultural Growth (Boserup). Choice, 3(5–6):434.

Cohen, Mark N.
1975 Population pressure and the origins of agriculture: An archaeological example from the coast of Peru. In: Population, Ecology, and Social Evolution, edited by Steve Polgar, pp. 79–122. The Hague: Mouton.
1977 The Food Crisis in Prehistory: Overpopulation and the Origins of Agriculture. New Haven: Yale University Press.

de Vries, Jan
1972 Labor/leisure trade-off. Peasant Studies Newsletter, 1:45–50.

Diebold, P. B.
1967 Review of The Conditions of Agricultural Growth (Boserup). Economic Development and Cultural Change, 16:151–54.

Dovring, Folke
1966 Review of The Conditions of Agricultural Growth (Boserup). Journal of Economic History, 26:380–81.

Drennan, Robert D.
1989 The mountains north of the valley. In: Monte Albán's Hinterland, Part II: The Prehispanic Settlement Patterns in Tlacolula, Etla, and Ocotlán, the Valley of Oaxaca, Mexico, by Stephen A. Kowalewski et al., pp 367–84. Memoirs, 23. Museum of Anthropology, University of Michigan. Ann Arbor.

Feinman, Gary M.
1985 Investigations in a near-periphery: Regional settlement pattern survey in the Ejutla Valley, Oaxaca, Mexico. Mexicon, 7:60–68.

Feinman, Gary M., Stephen A. Kowalewski, Laura Finsten, Richard E. Blanton, and Linda M. Nicholas
1985 Long-term demographic change: A perspective from the Valley of Oaxaca, Mexico. Journal of Field Archaeology, 12:333–62.

Feinman, Gary M., and Linda M. Nicholas
1987 Labor, surplus, and production: A regional analysis of Formative Oaxacan socio-economic change. In: Coasts, Plains and Deserts: Essays in Honor of Reynold J. Ruppe, edited by Sylvia Gaines, pp. 27–50. Anthropological Research Papers, 38. Arizona State University. Tempe.
1988 The prehispanic settlement history of the Ejutla Valley, Mexico: A preliminary perspective. Mexicon, 10:5–13.
in press Prehispanic interregional interaction in southern Mexico: The Valley of Oaxaca and the Ejutla Valley. In: Resource, Power and Interregional Interaction, edited by Edward Schortman and Patricia Urban. British Archaeological Reports.

Fisch, Eva
1982 The Early and Middle Formative periods. In: Monte Albán's Hinterland, Part I: Prehispanic Settlement Patterns of the Central and Southern Parts of the Valley of Oaxaca, Mexico, by Richard E. Blanton et al., pp. 27–36. Memoirs, 15. Museum of Anthropology, University of Michigan. Ann Arbor.

Flannery, Kent V.
1973 Introduction. In: The Use of Land and Water Resources in the Past and Present Valley of Oaxaca, Mexico, by Anne V. T. Kirkby. Memoirs, 5. Museum of Anthropology, University of Michigan. Ann Arbor.

Flannery, Kent V., Anne V. T. Kirkby, Michael J. Kirkby, and Aubrey W. Williams, Jr.
1967 Farming systems and political growth in ancient Oaxaca. Science, 158:445–54.

Flannery, Kent V., and James Schoenwetter
1970 Climate and man in formative Oaxaca. Archaeology, 23:144–52.

Flannery, Kent V., Marcus C. Winter, Susan Lees, James Schoenwetter, Suzanne Kitchen, and Jane Wheeler
1970 Preliminary Archaeological Investigations in the Valley of Oaxaca, Mexico, 1966–1969. Mimeographed preliminary report. Ann Arbor: University of Michigan.

Grigg, David
1979 Ester Boserup's theory of agrarian change: A critical review. Progress in Human Geography, 3:64–84.

International Labour Review
1965   Review of The Conditions of Agricultural Growth (Boserup). International Labour Review, 92:522–23.

Johnson, Gregory A.
1973   Local Exchange and Early State Development in Southwestern Iran. Anthropological Papers, 51. Museum of Anthropology, University of Michigan. Ann Arbor.

Jones, W. O.
1967   Review of The Conditions of Agricultural Growth (Boserup). American Economic Review, 57:679–80.

Kappel, Wayne
1977   Alternative Adaptive Strategies in Three Mexican Towns. Ph.D. dissertation. University of Arizona, Tucson.

Kirkby, Anne V. T.
1973   The Use of Land and Water Resources in the Past and Present Valley of Oaxaca, Mexico. Memoirs, 5. Museum of Anthropology, University of Michigan. Ann Arbor.

Kowalewski, Stephen A.
1980   Population-resource balances in Period I of Oaxaca. American Antiquity, 45:151–64.
1982   Population and agricultural potential: Early I–V. In: Monte Alban's Hinterland, Part I: Prehispanic Settlement Patterns of the Central and Southern Parts of the Valley of Oaxaca, Mexico, by Richard E. Blanton et al., pp. 149–89. Memoirs, 15. Museum of Anthropology, University of Michigan. Ann Arbor.

Kowalewski, Stephen A., Gary M. Feinman, Laura Finsten, Richard E. Blanton, and Linda M. Nicholas
1989   Monte Alban's Hinterland, Part II: The Prehispanic Settlement Patterns in Tlacolula, Etla, and Ocotlán, the Valley of Oaxaca, Mexico. Memoirs, 23. Museum of Anthropology, University of Michigan. Ann Arbor.

Meggers, Betty J.
1954   Environmental limitation on the development of culture. American Anthropologist, 56:801–24.

Nell, Edward J.
1972   The technology of intimidation. Peasant Studies Newsletter, 1:39–44.

Nicholas, Linda M.
1989   Land use in prehispanic Oaxaca. In: Monte Albán's Hinterland, Part II: The Prehispanic Settlement Patterns in Tlacolula, Etla, and Ocotlán, the Valley of Oaxaca, Mexico, by Stephen A. Kowalewski et al., pp. 449–505. Memoirs, 23. Museum of Anthropology, University of Michigan. Ann Arbor.

Nicholas, Linda M., Gary M. Feinman, Stephen A. Kowalewski, Richard E. Blanton, and Laura Finsten
1986   Prehispanic colonization of the Valley of Oaxaca, Mexico. Human Ecology, 14:131–62.

Nichols, Deborah L.
1989   Reply to Feinman and Nicholas: There is no frost in the Basin of Mexico? American Anthropologist, 91:1023–26.

Olmstead, Clarence W.
1970   Review The Conditions of Agricultural Growth (Boserup). Economic Geography, 46:208–9.

Palerm, Angel
1955   The agricultural bases of urban civilization in Mesoamerica. In: Irrigation Civilizations: A Comparative Study, by Julian Steward, R. Adams, Donald Collier, Angel Palerm, Karl Wittfogel, and Ralph Beals, pp. 28–42. Pan American Union Social Science Monograph, No. 1. Pan American Union. Washington, D.C.

Palerm, Angel, and Eric R. Wolf
1957   Ecological potential and cultural development in Mesoamerica. In: Studies in Human Ecology, pp. 1–37. Anthropological Society of Washington and Pan American Union Social Science Monograph, no. 3. Pan American Union. Washington, D.C.

Parsons, Jeffrey R.
1971   Prehistoric Settlement Patterns of the Texcoco Region, Mexico. Memoirs, 3. Museum of Anthropology, University of Michigan. Ann Arbor.

Pearson, Harry W.
1957   The economy has no surplus: Critique of a theory of development. In: Trade and Market in the Early Empires, edited by Karl Polanyi, C. Arensberg, and H. Pearson, pp. 320–41. Chicago: Henry Regnery Company.

Rubin, Julius
1972   Expulsion from the garden. Peasant Studies Newsletter, 1:35–39.

Sahlins, Marshall
1972   Stone Age Economics. New York: Aldine.

Sanders, William T.
1965   The Cultural Ecology of the Teotihuacán Valley. Ms. on file. Department of Anthropology, Pennsylvania State University.
1972   Population, agricultural history, and societal evolution in Mesoamerica. In: Population Growth: Anthropological Implications, edited by Brian Spooner, pp. 101–53. Cambridge, Mass.: MIT Press.
1976   The agricultural history of the Basin of Mexico. In: The Valley of Mexico, edited by E. Wolf, pp. 161–78. Albuquerque: University of New Mexico Press.

Sanders, William T., and Deborah L. Nichols
1988   Ecological theory and cultural evolution in the Valley of Oaxaca. Current Anthropology, 29:33-80.

Sanders, William T., Jeffrey R. Parsons, and Robert S. Santley
1979   The Basin of Mexico: Ecological Processes in the Evolution of a Civilization. New York: Academic Press.

Sanders, William T., and Barbara J. Price
1968   Mesoamerica: The Evolution of a Civilization. New York: Random House.

Schoenwetter, James
1974   Pollen records of Guilá Naquitz Cave. American Antiquity, 39:292-303.

Schultz, Theodore W.
1966   Review of The Conditions of Agricultural Growth (Boserup). Journal of Farm Economics, 48:486-87.

Sheffer, Charles
1971   Review of The Conditions of Agricultural Growth (Boserup). American Antiquity, 36:377-79.

Smith, Philip E.L., and T. Cuyler Young, Jr.
1972   The evolution of early agriculture and culture in Greater Mesopotamia: A trial model. In: Population Growth: Anthropological Implications, edited by Brian Spooner, pp. 1-59. Cambridge, Mass.: MIT Press.

Spooner, Brian (ed.)
1972   Population Growth: Anthropological Implications. Cambridge, Mass.: MIT Press.

Spooner, Brian, and Robert Netting
1972   Humanised economics. Peasant Studies Newsletter, 1:54-59.

Steward, Julian H.
1949   Cultural causality and law: A trial formulation of the development of early civilizations. American Anthropologist, 51:1-27.

Times Literary Supplement
1965   Review of The Conditions of Agricultural Growth (Boserup). September 30.

Tolstoy, Paul
1982-83 Advances in the Valley of Oaxaca. Quarterly Review of Archaeology, 3(3), 3(4), 4(1), 4(3), 4(4).
1988   Comment on Sanders and Nichols' Ecological Theory and Cultural Evolution in the Valley of Oaxaca. Current Anthropology, 29:66-67.

Williams, Barbara J.
1989   Contact period rural overpopulation in the Basin of Mexico: Carrying-capacity models tested with documentary data. American Antiquity, 54:715–32.

Wittfogel, Karl A.
1957   Oriental Despotism: A Comparative Study of Total Power. New Haven: Yale University Press.

Wolf, Eric R.
1959   Sons of the Shaking Earth. Chicago: University of Chicago Press.
1976   Introduction. In: The Valley of Mexico: Studies in Pre-hispanic Ecology and Society, edited by Eric R. Wolf, pp. 1–10. Albuquerque: University of New Mexico Press.
1981   The mills of inequality: A Marxian approach. In: Social Inequality: Comparative and Developmental Approaches, edited by D. Berreman, pp 41–57. New York: Academic Press.

Wolf, Eric R., and Angel Palerm
1955   Irrigation in the Old Acolhua Domain, Mexico. Southwestern Journal of Anthropology, 11:265–81.

4

IRRIGATED AGRICULTURE AT HIERVE EL AGUA, OAXACA, MEXICO

James A. Neely, Department of Anthropology, University of Texas

S. Christopher Caran, Department of Geological Sciences, University of Texas

Barbara M. Winsborough, Department of Zoology, University of Texas

---

This chapter deals with the operational characteristics and functions of a water control and terrace system which comprises the primary feature of a unique prehispanic archaeological site in the mountains just outside the southern extreme of the Valley of Oaxaca (Fig. 4.1). The uniqueness of Hierve el Agua is due to the well-documented long-lived use of the site, in addition to the well-preserved nature of the terraces and canals—the latter being a result of the deposition of travertine from the artesian spring waters that flowed through the system. It has been Neely's contention since 1966 (Neely 1967a, 1967b, 1970, 1972, in press, n.d.) that irrigation waters from the springs at Hierve el Agua supported a system of intensive terrace agriculture.

Upon learning that this volume of debates was being compiled, we decided to contribute a summary of certain parts of a nearly completed monograph (Neely, n.d.) reporting on four field seasons of field research at the site of Hierve el Agua. Specifically, this article debates the alternative hypothesis set forward by Hewitt, Winter, and Peterson (1987; also see Peterson, Winter, and Hewitt 1989; and Winter 1989) which states that the spring waters of Hierve el Agua were unsuitable for irrigation, and that the terraces were evaporative pans used to render comestible salts.

In support of their alternative hypothesis, Hewitt, Winter, and Peterson (1987) present evidence based on two chemical analyses of the spring waters, the site layout, ethnohistoric evidence, and an analogy to modern solar salt operations. This chapter will systematically reject all of these arguments by showing that: (1) the hydrochemical analyses presented by Hewitt, Winter, and Peterson (1987) are severely flawed because of the sampling procedures employed, and the analytical results they obtained from these analyses were misinterpreted; (2) the site layout argument suffers from a form/function tautology or assumption, rather than recognizing the form/topography/available resource relationships; (3) their ethnohistoric evidence is so inferential and "indirect" (Hewitt, Winter, and Peterson 1987:807) that it cannot specifically be applied to the Hierve el Agua site; and finally, (4) their analogies to modern solar salt operations overlook important characteristics and variations, which negate their analogy and argument in the very sites that they compare to Hierve el Agua.

Hewitt, Winter, and Peterson (1987:800) are correct in stating that an assumption was made in the past regarding the use of the primary non-architectural features at Hierve el Agua; no one has demonstrated that the spring-canal-terrace system functioned for growing crops. One of the purposes of this article is to rectify this failing by providing substantive data to show that irrigation waters from the resident springs at the site of Hierve el Agua supported a system of intensive terrace agriculture.

Our case for terraced irrigation agriculture at Hierve el Agua rests on several different lines of information that may be broken down into three broad categories of data: technological, diatom, and hydrochemical. Where applicable, these three categories of data will be addressed in each of the following subdivisions of this article. We will reserve the majority of the descriptive detail of Hierve el Agua, and our research there, for Neely's forthcoming monograph.

HISTORICAL BACKGROUND OF THE STUDY

Knowing of Neely's interest in prehispanic water control and agricultural technology and their effects upon cultural development, Kent Flannery notified him of Hierve el Agua, which Flannery had discovered during a search for dry caves in 1966. Having recently completed over a year's field research on water control and agricultural technology in the Tehuacán Valley (Woodbury and Neely 1972), Neely recognized the uniqueness and importance of Hierve el Agua.

IRRIGATION AT HIERVE EL AGUA 117

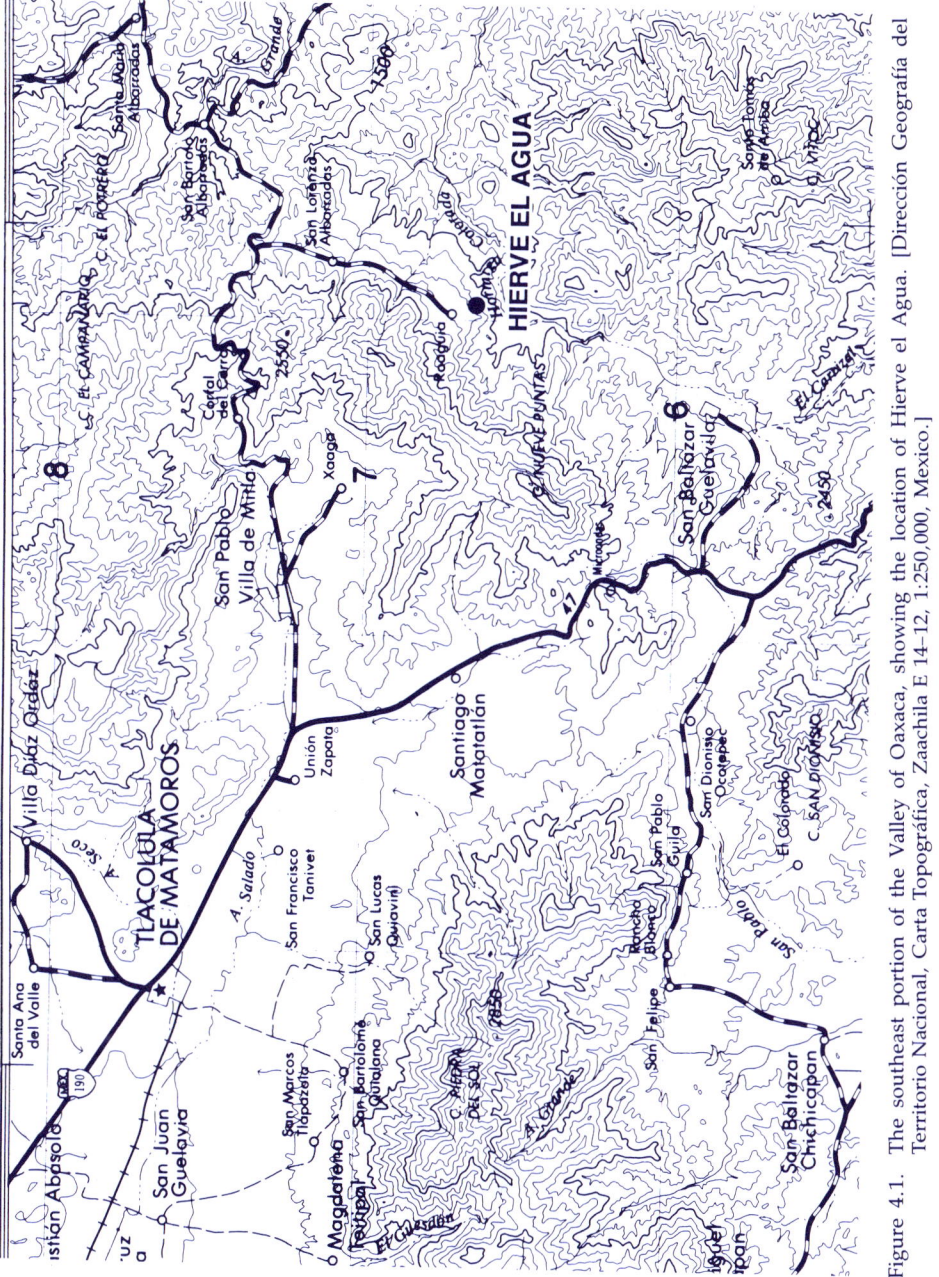

Figure 4.1. The southeast portion of the Valley of Oaxaca, showing the location of Hierve el Agua. [Dirección Geografía del Territorio Nacional, Carta Topográfica, Zaachila E 14-12, 1:250,000, Mexico.]

This site provided a very well preserved example of a terrace and canal system that was small enough to permit a detailed study of its use and function. Neely therefore joined Flannery's ongoing multidisciplinary project and began fieldwork at Hierve el Agua with permission from Mexico's Instituto Nacional de Antropología e Historia (INAH).

The original fieldwork was undertaken during the summers of 1966, 1970, and 1971. Following publication of the Hewitt, Winter, and Peterson (1987) article, Neely discussed their water analyses with several specialists. He also discussed the feasibility and value of undertaking additional studies and analyses. In August, 1988, with the kind assistance of the Oaxaca Regional Center for INAH, Caran, Winsborough, and Neely visited Hierve el Agua for five days. Our reconnaissance indicated that further studies and analyses were warranted, and we felt we could add needed data to the report in preparation. These impressions were further verified by the analyses of small samples of surface soils, travertine, and water collected during our short visit.

The results of our 1988 fieldwork led Neely to request a permit from INAH so that we could re-excavate several of his 1966 test pits to obtain additional well-stratified and dated soil samples. We also requested permission to take larger samples of soil, travertine, and water from the site. In April, 1989, Neely received the permit from INAH. Funded with a small grant from the University Research Institute of The University of Texas at Austin, Caran and Neely studied Hierve el Agua and its immediate environs for ten days in late April of 1989. Our work was facilitated by many staff members of INAH; Angel García Cook, Jefe del Dirección de Arqueología, Ernesto González Licón, Director de la Oficina Regional de Oaxaca, and Marcus C. Winter, staff archaeologist, were particularly helpful. Although the analyses and interpretations of some of the samples and data have not yet been completed, we feel the study has progressed to a point where we may present this summary of our findings to date.

GEOLOGIC AND HYDROLOGIC SETTING

The geology, hydrology, geomorphology, and soils of the region in which Hierve el Agua is located have been little studied, and are still incompletely known. The following overview of these subjects by Caran is based on his visits to the site, and from his research. These data are presented to set the scene of this study, to provide background data for sections of this paper, and to clarify certain statements and observations made by Hewitt, Winter, and Peterson (1987).

Hierve el Agua is located at the eastern end of the Sierra Madre del Sur of east-central Oaxaca (Fig. 4.1), overlooking the Hormiga Colorada River valley (López Ramos 1980: Fig. 2). Heavily faulted and folded Lower Cretaceous limestones and Miocene andesites are well exposed in the highlands north of this site (Barrera 1946: Plate 2; Morán Zenteno 1984: 63–64). Locally, older strata are buried beneath massive Pleistocene(?) and Holocene travertine deposits. Discharge from several small perennial springs continues to produce calcitic travertine at a rapid rate. Most springs at the site lie between approximately 1700 and 1740 m in elevation, but at least one spring was found at approximately 1470 m (Instituto Nacional de Estadística, Geografía e Informática 1988b). The waters from these springs are strongly effervescent, giving rise to the name Hierve el Agua, roughly "the place where water boils." This evocative image is somewhat misleading, in that the springs are essentially nonthermal. Spring water temperatures range from 22.7 to 25.5 degrees Celsius, well below the boiling point and only slightly higher than the mean surface-air temperature, which is 19 degrees Celsius (Instituto Nacional . . . 1984a, 1984b; Vivo Escoto 1964: Fig. 7).

Several lines of indirect evidence indicate that the springs at Hierve el Agua are artesian. The travertine forms ridges and mounds higher than the general land surface. The waters are heavily carbonated and slightly warmer than the mean air temperature, possibly as a result of deep circulation. The carbon dioxide effervescing from these springs probably derives from subterranean sources (see additional discussion below). Judging from the hydrochemistry of these waters, the aquifer is karstic limestone, which underlies the site and crops out nearby. Spring waters appear to issue along linear fracture zones that have propagated through older travertine deposits as well as bedrock. Although discharge rates were not measured, spring flow had diminished noticeably between August, 1988, during the rainy season, and April, 1989, at the end of the dry season. Solute content is distinctly seasonal, declining by approximately 10 percent during the rainy season. Thus, the hydrologic budget of Hierve el Agua includes a component of seasonal recharge, probably through cavernous limestones lying to the north. In contrast, properties of the artesian portion of the system may be essentially independent of the seasonal recharge.

Travertine-laden waters flowed upward along the fracture zones, and their deposits formed the plateau or tableland constituting the northern end of the site. They also formed the ridge or dike-like geological structure which runs generally north to south, to form the high western arm of the amphitheater-like formation (hence referred to as the amphitheater, though it is a geological formation) upon which the archaeological site was subsequently founded (Figs. 4.2 and 4.3). The central and eastern portions of the amphitheater were a result of travertine deposition from other springs effervescing a short distance to the east of the primary fracture zone. This deposition, from the east-west trending line of springs, some of which are now defunct, continued through the period of site use to the present day. Travertines deposited from the time of the origin of the springs, until after the site was abandoned some time in the prehispanic era, are seen as gray deposits. Modern and freshly deposited travertines range from yellowish-brown and yellowish-gray to pinkish-white and white in color.

At Hierve el Agua, the artesian springs formerly supplied water to an intricate system of artificial canals and terraces. With the abandonment of the site, roughly in the mid-1300s (see Site Chronology below), the canals were no longer maintained, and quickly filled with travertine precipitated directly from the diverted spring waters. Channelized flow through canals was replaced by unchannelized "sheet" flow and a system of rills following natural depressions. Both spring discharge and surface flow paths fluctuated through time because of the inactivation of some springs, the formation of new discharge points, and the continued differential accretion of travertine on slopes and along the poorly defined rills. These changes caused the flow to shift from one part of the site to another, blanketing many structures and activity areas with travertine.

Today, there is considerable environmental diversity at Hierve el Agua, reflecting the effects of prehistoric construction and use, weathering and uncontrolled travertine deposition following the abandonment of the site, and relatively minor alterations brought about by the modern residents of this area. Water use was essentially continual, although the method and intensity of use varied from prehistory to the present. Archaeological investigations have demonstrated the importance of this site for understanding regional patterns of prehistoric exploitation of natural resources. Unfortunately, little has been published concerning the area's geology, hydrology, geomorphology, or soils. Until the present investigations, no correlative studies of sediments and associated fossils (particularly diatoms) had been undertaken, even though information from studies of this kind would bear directly on questions concerning the local development of water and land resources. Careful sampling and analysis of the

IRRIGATION AT HIERVE EL AGUA 121

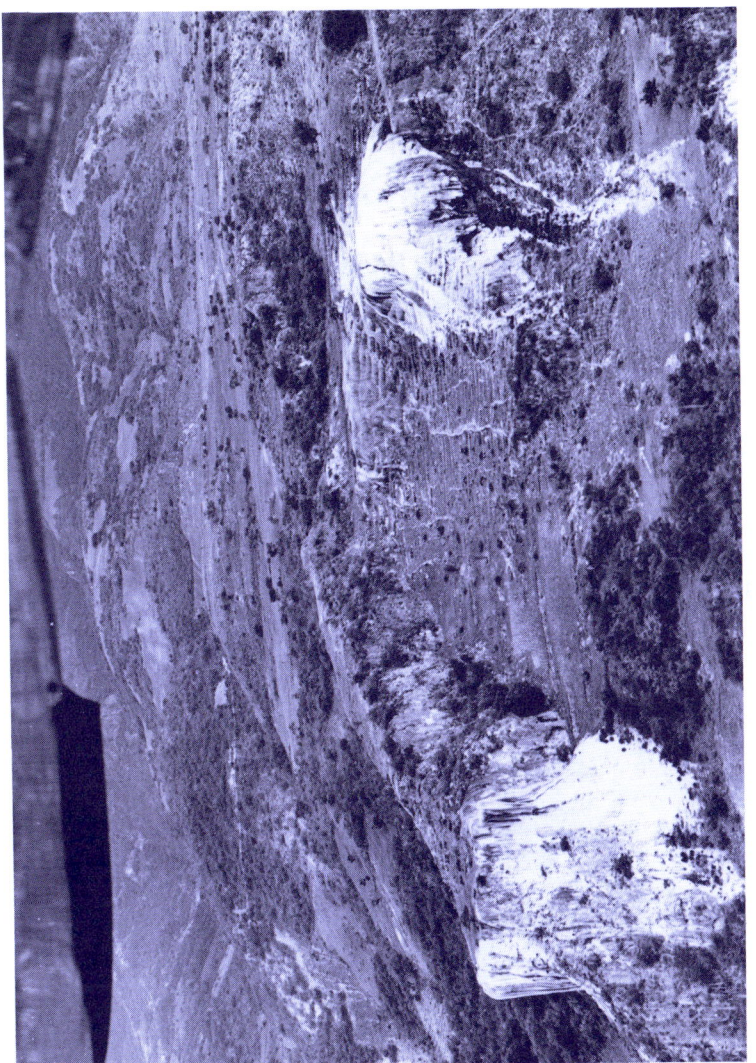

Figure 4.2. An oblique aerial photograph of Hierve el Agua, looking north-northwest. The scattered houses comprising the village of Roaguía may be seen center and right, between the site and the mountain in the background.

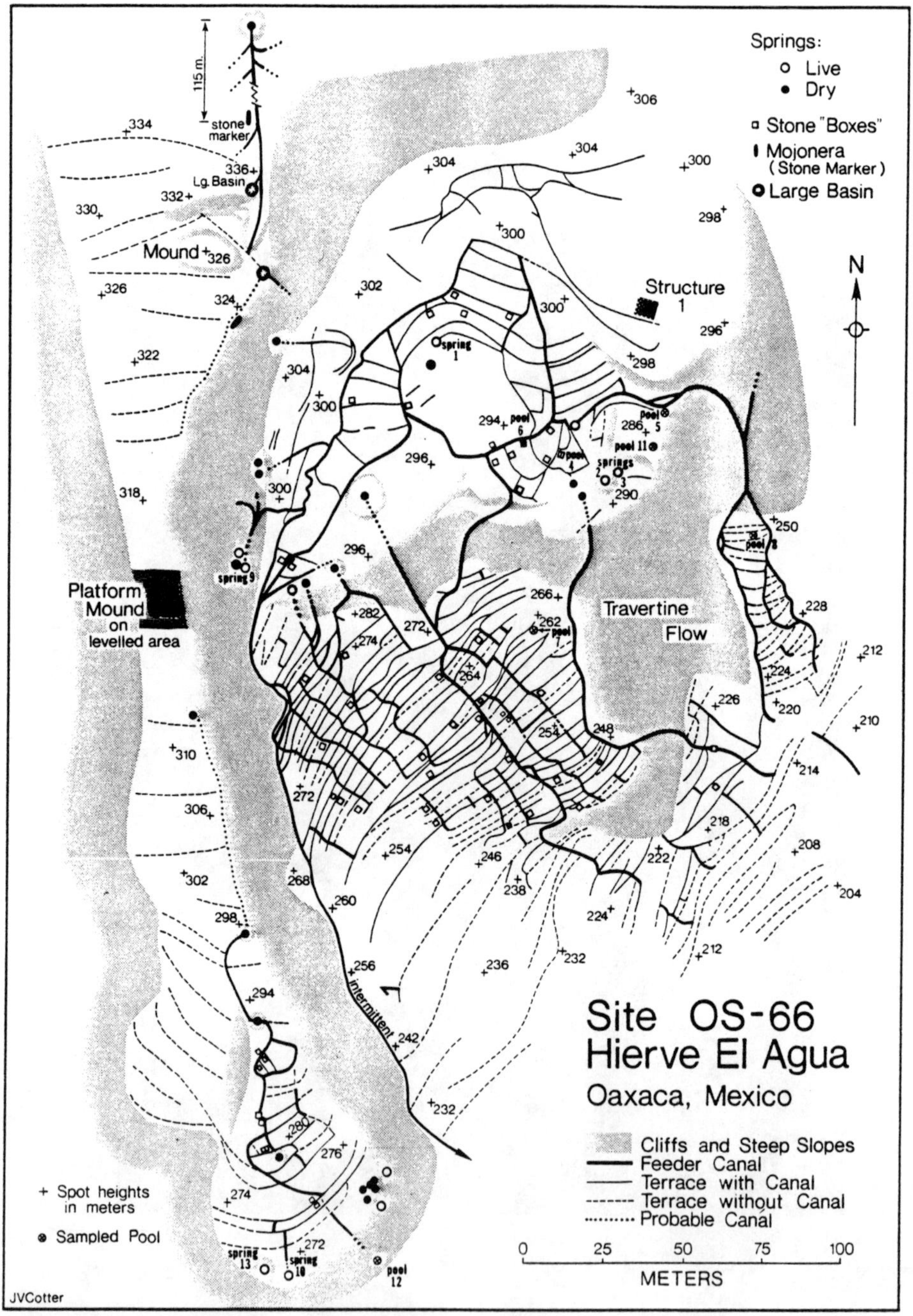

Figure 4.3. Plan view map of Hierve el Agua, showing the architectural features as well as the terrace and canal system in relation to spot elevations reflecting the site topography.

THE SURVEY AND TEST EXCAVATIONS AT HIERVE EL AGUA

The Survey

The survey of Hierve el Agua began in June of 1966. The central area of the site, illustrated in Figure 4.3, was traversed on foot, and the architecture, features, and artifacts visible on the surface were recorded. In 1970 the survey continued, with the reinvestigation of selected portions of the central area of the site for additional detailed information. When this work was completed, the coverage was extended to surrounding areas. The final phases of the survey took place during our 1988 and 1989 visits to the site, when Caran, Winsborough, and Neely traversed selected areas to the north and south of the central part of the site for data pertinent to their restudy.

The Excavations

In 1966, 41 one-by-one-meter test pits were excavated into the terraces throughout the site (Fig. 4.4). Two of these, Test Pits 40 and 41, were excavated into architectural terraces associated with the platform mound and other architecture located atop the high western arm of the site. All 41 of the test pits were carefully excavated in 10 cm arbitrary levels, by means of small hand picks and trowels. All soil matrix was screened through 5 mm mesh metal hardware cloth, and all sherds, chipped stone, bone, and other materials were collected and bagged separately for each 10 cm level. In the test pits exhibiting the most clearly defined stratigraphy, profile drawings were made and a pollen column was collected by James Schoenwetter of Arizona State University. The pits were backfilled at the end of the summer in 1966.

Initially, the test pits were excavated in likely locations throughout the site (e.g., terraces in various parts of the site that appeared to have relatively deep deposits of fill). As the work progressed, and Neely learned more about the site, he selected locations for additional test pits to answer specific questions that had arisen, or to provide additional information on poorly understood or untested portions of the site.

In excavating the original test pits we had seven goals. First, to find any stratified deposits that would place the site into a cultural and

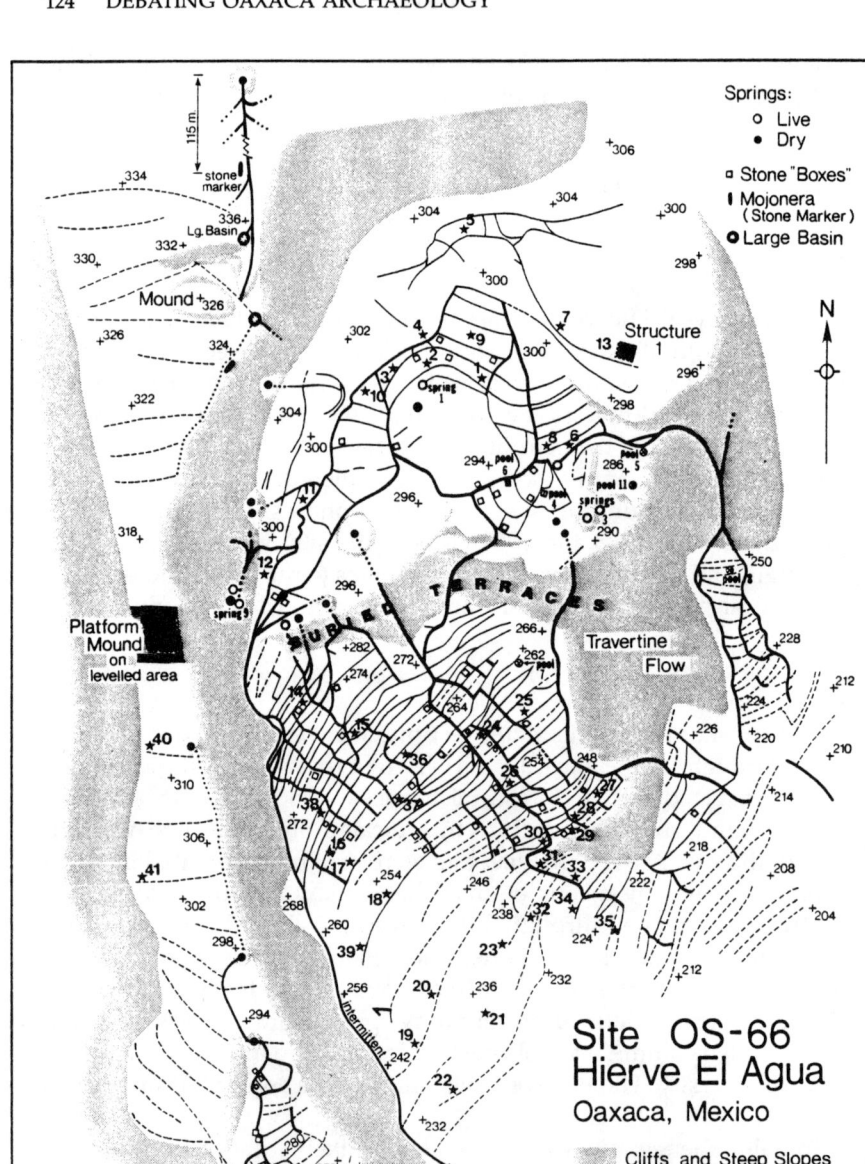

Figure 4.4. Plan view map of Hierve el Agua, showing the locations of the 41 one-by-one-meter test pits excavated in 1966.

chronological framework. Second, to find how the area grew or was modified through time. Third, to obtain data relevant to the technology employed in the construction, and subsequent modifications, of the terrace system. Fourth, to discover additional details pertaining to the construction and use of the canal system. Fifth, to determine as much as possible regarding the crops cultivated and the agricultural techniques employed. Sixth, to obtain at least some basic information regarding the architectural manifestations and occupations at the site. And seventh, to determine if the spring waters had been used for purposes other than domestic water supplies and agricultural irrigation.

Later, to collect new forms of data not covered in 1966, Neely reopened Test Pits 2, 16, 17, 21, 24, and 41 in April, 1989. During their re-excavation, these pits were enlarged to 1.5 by 1.5 meters to expose clean, clear fill profiles for study. The observations were recorded, photographs taken, and soil samples were collected. These pits were backfilled at the end of our brief re-study.

CHARACTERISTICS AND FEATURES OF THE SITE

Site Size

Hierve el Agua covers more than a square kilometer, but its exact dimensions vary according to the criteria used. The architectural part of the site is relatively small (i.e., approximately 17,015 m^2 or 1.7 ha) and, contrary to the observations of Hewitt, Winter, and Peterson (1987:806), is divided into several clearly visible, distinct units of construction (see Fig. 4.3 for some of these units).

The most obvious concentration of terraces and canals visible today lies within and just above the amphitheater (Figs. 4.2 and 4.3). This central concentration of terraces and canals has an area of approximately 59,220 m^2 or 5.92 ha (this area includes some 6,720 m^2 of non-architectural terraces and canals at the southern end of the high west arm of the site).

A thorough survey of the environs, however, indicates that remnants of terraces and associated canals extend for several hundred meters in all directions from the central amphitheater, making the total area of the site some 1,680,000 m^2 (168 ha or 1.68 km^2). As the terraces and canals in the locations surrounding the amphitheater have been broken up in modern times to permit contour plowing with ox teams, an intense survey was necessary to locate their remnants and trace their extent. We will discuss the modern destruction of these features in greater detail below.

Unfortunately, the amphitheater area was the only part of the site described by Hewitt, Winter, and Peterson (1987:801-2), and they have grossly understated its area, giving it as 22,500 m² in one citation and as "a little more than two hectares" in a second. Their article further suggests that they consider this amphitheater area—already underestimated—to be the total area characterized by the integrated system of terraces and canals.

Site Chronology

Sometime around 700–500 B.C., the inhabitants of the area began to construct the terraces and canals of Hierve el Agua. These constructions, as well as others to be discussed below, continued until the site was apparently abandoned, at about A.D. 1350.

The chronological placement of the construction and occupation at Hierve el Agua is based on a suite of eight radiocarbon dates, and on ceramic cross-dating, both the result of material from several of the 41 test pits excavated in 1966. Additional chronological information was obtained from two additional pits excavated in 1970 and by the 1989 re-excavation. All of the test squares yielded soils and sherds as well as other artifacts and, occasionally, a few examples of architectural construction.

Several of the test pits were nearly 2 m in depth, and provided a well-stratified series of sherds in proper chronological order from bottom to top in the fill. Most notable of these well-stratified tests were Pits 2, 16, 17, 38, 39, and 41 (Fig. 4.4). Each of these pits provides a long ceramic sequence that overlaps in at least two periods with neighboring pits, to present a total span of time some 1850 years in length, from Rosario or Early Monte Albán I to Monte Albán V (see Drennan 1983).

Our radiocarbon dates were also recovered from well-stratified deposits within some of the test pits. They are as follows:

UNIVERSITY OF MICHIGAN RADIOCARBON LABORATORY
(Crane and Griffin 1970:176)

M-2105	Test Pit 1, depth 75 cm	A.D. 940 ± 100
M-2106	Test Pit 40, depth 113 cm	A.D. 350 ± 130
M-2107	Test Pit 40, depth 175 cm	A.D. 140 ± 150
M-2108	Test Pit 40, depth 190 cm	310 B.C. ± 150
M-2109	Test Pit 41, depth 70 cm	420 B.C. ± 140

UNIVERSITY OF TEXAS RADIOCARBON LABORATORY
(Salvatore Velastro, Jr.—Personal Communication)

TX-5906	Test Pit 42, depth 20–30 cm	A.D. 500 ± 80
TX-5907	Test Pit 43, depth 54–66 cm	A.D. 450 ± 100
TX-6447	Test Pit 41, depth 110 cm	200 B.C. ± 140

Observations and Comments Regarding the Site Chronology

Obviously, we cannot agree with the suggestion made by Hewitt, Winter, and Peterson (1987:807) that use of the site spanned the period A.D. 500 to 1521, and may have lasted into the Colonial period. Their dating is based on the types of sherds they noted on the surface of the site, and on "indirect" reference made in the sixteenth-century Relación Geográfica of Tlacolula and Mitla (Hewitt, Winter, and Peterson 1987:814).

Neely's surface survey of the site recorded ceramics running from Monte Albán Ic (ca. 300 B.C.) to late in Monte Albán V (perhaps A.D. 1250–1521). These surface materials allowed him to assign general periods of use to various parts of the site.

However, more precise dates have been defined from well-stratified ceramic levels in the test pits. For example, although Neely had found a relatively large quantity of Monte Albán Ic ceramics, mixed in with later ceramic types, on the surface of the triangular-shaped area bounded by Test Pits 22, 16, and 35 (Fig. 4.4), it was not until he excavated his test pits in that part of the site that the intensity of the Monte Albán Ic use of Hierve el Agua became apparent. We cannot explain why Hewitt, Winter, and Peterson did not find ceramics dating earlier than Monte Albán IIIb on the surface of this portion of the site, since we found so many.

Furthermore, in this same part of the site, our chronology was extended back into Rosario (700–500 B.C.) or early Monte Albán Ia (500–300 B.C.) by the discovery of diagnostic ceramic types in the lowest levels of Test Pits 38 and 39 (Fig. 4.4).

Like Hewitt, Winter, and Peterson, Neely also found late Monte Albán V ceramics on the surface of the site; however, he did not find them in good, undisturbed stratigraphic contexts within any of his test pits. Thus, although general use of the site may have lasted until A.D. 1500, we hesitate to place the actual use of the terraces at Hierve el Agua any later than about A.D. 1350, midway through Monte Albán V.

Neither Neely's excavations, nor his intensive surface survey, produced any evidence for the site's having been used during the Colonial period. Hewitt, Winter, and Peterson (1987:807) point to comments about saltmaking in the *Relación de Tlacolula y Mitla* (Paso y Troncoso 1905:150) which they consider an "indirect" reference to Hierve el Agua. However, the actual *relación* says that the salt source "ai en este pueblo," that is, in Mitla. There is no proof that the document refers to Hierve el Agua, which is near San Lorenzo Albarradas, on the opposite side of Nueve Puntas mountain from Mitla.

Considering the usual difficulties in dating agricultural and water control features (Donkin 1973:17; Woodbury and Neely 1972:124, 135–39), the Hierve el Agua terraces and their associated canals can be considered relatively well dated. Furthermore, all available information suggests that the technology of terracing, terrace agriculture, and canal irrigation all occur earlier at Hierve el Agua than they do at other well-dated systems in Mexico, such as those in the Tehuacán Valley (Woodbury and Neely 1972:125, 135–39). And, in the light of the technological sophistication of the well-dated Purrón Dam Complex in the Tehuacán Valley (Woodbury and Neely 1972:82–99), a beginning date of ca. 500 B.C. for Hierve el Agua does not seem unreasonable.

NON-TERRACE ARCHITECTURE

The largest and most obvious single concentration of architecture occupies a large part (ca. 10,500 m^2, or a little over 1 ha) of the high western arm of the site (Fig. 4.4). Here we find a moderate-size platform mound, surmounted by remnants of a structure, and a series of architectural terraces. These terraces provided the level horizontal space needed for the construction of broad, open, lime plaster–floored plazas, individual masonry structures of varying sizes, and complexes of masonry structures flanking small patios or courtyards. Neely's intensive surface survey of this construction area, as well as the contents of Test Pits 40 and 41, indicate that this construction was quite complex and sophisticated, and was rebuilt or enlarged several times. Both radiocarbon dates and ceramics suggest that the buildings were continuously in use from Monte Albán Ic at least into Monte Albán IIIb.

Neely's surface survey recorded the presence of at least six other concentrations of non-terrace architecture, some of which were found within the area shown in Fig. 4.4. In addition, a number of areas of stone tool and sherd concentrations were recorded. Although these lacked visible evidence of architectural construction, it seems quite possible that they represent household structures or, at the very least, field houses.

Observations and Comments Regarding the Non-Terrace Architecture

The total area represented by non-terrace architecture (about 17,015 m^2 or 1.7 ha) and sherd/chipped stone concentrations (about 10,000 m^2 or 1.0 ha) amounts to approximately 27,015 m^2 or 2.7 ha. We suspect that this may be a rather conservative estimate for the area of non-terrace construction associated with the site, and our suspicion is based on two observations. First, there is additional household trash, including sherds, in the fill within the terraces (we will discuss the importance of this household trash to field use below). For example, the 50 to 60 cm level in Test Pit 2, a one-by-one-meter pit, produced 823 sherds. Such large amounts of household trash suggest that there was a relatively large and stable prehispanic population in fairly close proximity to the site. Second, although Neely's intensive survey did not extend that far, we have reason to suspect that the present village of Roaguía (Figs. 4.1 and 4.2) may be situated on the site of a prehispanic village. Considering the prehispanic and modern land-use patterns for the Valley of Oaxaca (Kirkby 1973), we doubt that the ancient farmers of Hierve el Agua would have wasted irrigable agricultural land by putting houses on it. The short walk from Roaguía (or anywhere in the general vicinity of the site) would be no problem, especially when we consider that some farmers from Roaguía and San Lorenzo Albarradas walk as far as 4 km (8 km per round trip) to tend some of their fields today (see our comments on Sr. Marcelino García in the section on terraces). Thus, Hewitt, Winter, and Peterson's (1987:806) comment that "there is no evidence of a large prehispanic community at Hierve el Agua," is open for debate.

In spite of Hewitt, Winter, and Peterson's (1987:806) suggestion of possible houses on the "broad" terraced fields in the southwestern portion of the amphitheater of the site, we found no evidence of habitations. Considering the nature of this specific location (discussed in detail in Terraces below) we are not surprised that Hewitt et al. did not find any evidences of house walls or floors. We doubt very much such structures would be present on irrigable land; rather, we would explain the concentration of sherds and chipped stone on the surface as household trash incorporated into terrace fill.

Artifact concentrations similar to some of those found at Hierve el Agua—and probably representing the one-time presence of perishable structures—were found in association with prehispanic terraced agricultural fields in the Tehuacán Valley of Puebla (Woodbury and Neely 1972:116, 120, 124, Figs. 45, 46). The present village of Roaguía, located less than 1 km north of Hierve el Agua (Figs. 4.1, 4.2), is largely composed of perishable single family structures. We would expect to find remnants of similar perishable structures adjacent to the irrigable lands at Hierve el Agua. Other indications of the presence of perishable architecture at or near the site took the form of grass-, reed-, and pole-impressed fragments of clay recovered from the stratified fill in several test pits. These presumably represent fragments of jacal or wattle-and-daub construction, present as part of the household garbage used as terrace fill.

THE TERRACES, CANALS, AND RELATED FEATURES AT HIERVE EL AGUA: THE TECHNOLOGY OF THE SYSTEM

The Terraces

The terraces comprise the major construction effort at Hierve el Agua, in terms of the quantity of construction materials used and the time and effort expended in their planning, construction, and maintenance. The terraces provide crucial information on the use and function of the site.

For the purposes of this study, we define a terrace as a raised embankment, bordered on its downslope side by a masonry wall constructed of dry-laid, unmodified, cobble and boulder-sized (cf. Wentworth 1922) pieces of travertine (Fig. 4.5). The pieces of travertine were evidently obtained by breaking them from exposed portions of the natural bedrock on the site. The top surface of the terraces are level, or nearly so, today. At Hierve el Agua, the terraces are divided into definably separate units (each of which we have considered as a separate terrace entity in our study) by canals that follow the direction of the land slope while they intersect and cross-cut the terraces as nearly perpendicular lines (Figs. 4.6, 4.7).

Terraces, of course, are not unique to the site of Hierve el Agua. Terraces are still extensively used in Oaxaca and throughout Mexico

Figure 4.5. Terrace walls located in the vicinity of Test Pit 24, looking north-northwest. The dry-laid construction of the unmodified travertine cobbles and boulders is evident in the central wall, while the wall just above it to the north has been covered with a travertine flow apron. The scale on the central wall is 15 cm in length.

today, as they were in prehispanic times (Donkin 1979, Woodbury and Neely 1972). What is unusual about the Hierve el Agua terraces is the number of terraces relative to the land area used; the steep slopes upon which most of these terraces were built; the extremely well-preserved nature of the terrace system; and the fact that almost every terrace has a small canal running the length of its masonry retaining wall. Obviously, the first two of these characteristics are related, for an efficient use of human energy requires the construction of a greater number of terraces per unit of land on steep slopes than is required on more level terrain. The preservation of the terraces and the importance of the terrace wall canals will be discussed below.

Figure 4.6. Overview of the central portion of Hierve el Agua, looking southwest up the canyon of the Hormiga Colorada River. Note the high western "arm" of the site with the travertine flow at its southern extreme.

A total of 416 terraces are illustrated on the site map (Fig. 4.3), with the majority of the terraces (338) concentrated in the 59,220 m² amphitheater area in the center of the map. Although the area represented by this map adequately represents the site center, as noted previously, we believe that the total area of the site was quite a bit larger. Remnants of travertine-coated terrace walls and canals were scattered over the terrain (including areas of agricultural fields still being dry-farmed today) for some distance in all directions. The number of terraces that may once have covered the site is roughly estimated at about 600.

Throughout the site, the surface area of the terraces is level, or slopes downward slightly from the rear of the terrace toward the terrace wall. Our test pits revealed the same general trend in the terrace fill layers. However, those which exhibited sloping strata had an angle of slope that decreased from bottom to top within the pit. The terrace walls themselves were seen to slope, frequently in two directions. The higher terrace walls—those supporting greater quantities of fill behind them—were constructed to slope inward, from bottom to top. This, in addition to an increase in the width of the wall

Figure 4.7. Overview of the central portion of Hierve el Agua, looking northeast toward the area of Springs 2 and 3. Note the travertine-covered terraces below and to the left (southwest) of the springs. The modern terraced fields, modified for contour plowing with ox teams, are shown in the lower right quadrant.

from top to bottom, provided the structural support required to maintain the mass and volume of the terrace fill. In nearly all cases, the upper edges of the terrace walls were found to slope longitudinally from one end of the terrace to the other. This gentle slope, averaging about 2.1% (1 degree, 11 minutes), was built into the small canal that formed the upper edge of most of the terraces, in order to permit an efficient flow of water along the top of the terrace wall. Many of the terraces shown in Figure 4.3 as not having these canals were also characterized by this slight longitudinal slope of the terrace's upper edge; this fact implies that canals once surmounted those terrace walls also.

The length of the terraces seems to have been affected, and perhaps limited, by three interrelated factors. First, the agriculturalists were faced with the need to efficiently distribute the available water from the flowing springs to all parts of the terrace system. The number, location, and productivity of the springs apparently had some effect on how the terraces were bordered or divided by the main "feeder" canals so as to conduct the water from the springs to the terrace-top canals. Second, it seems likely that the length of the terraces was kept relatively short to improve their structural stability on steeper slopes. The shorter terraces would reduce the mass and volume of the fill within a terrace, and thereby reduce the chance of a terrace wall collapse. With terraces broken up into shorter lengths, a wall collapse would be reduced to a relatively small-scale disaster. Third, the terraces may have been kept purposefully short because of the methods of agricultural technology being employed. We refer here to (1) the possibility of the terrace system being employed, at least in part, on seed beds for multi-cropping, (2) and the probability of hand-watering from the *pocitos*, which we will discuss in greater detail below.

The range of variation in the width, and to a great degree the depth, of the terraces was dictated by at least two factors: the natural topography of the original ground surface and a set of cultural factors, which includes the actual use of the terrace. The natural or original slope of the ground surface prior to terrace construction plays a large part in the resulting canal. In general, the steeper the slope of the original ground surface (i.e., the narrower the terraces (i.e., the closer the horizontal distance between terrace walls). Conversely, as the slope diminishes and the terrain is more level, the terraces are constructed as wider features, and the distance between the terrace walls increases. Cultural factors are also integrally involved in determining the width of terraces as they are constructed. While the specific use of a terraced field is important in determining its width, the most important of the cultural factors is the human energy factor. Briefly stated, there is a point of diminishing returns as far as the energy needed and the effort expended in the construction of terraces relative to the surface area each provides. Stated differently, there is an optimal ratio of terrace wall height and volume of fill relative to the degree of slope of the original ground surface on which the terrace is to be constructed.

As determined by a study of the soils exposed by Neely's test pits, the bulk of the fill within the terraces was brought in from elsewhere. The presence of ceramics and other artifacts suggests that household garbage/trash was used to augment or revitalize the terrace soils as a fertilizer and mulch, much in the same manner as Neely observed in the Tehuacán Valley in 1964; this practice has been documented elsewhere (Donkin 1979:2; Stewart and Donnelly 1943:42–43; Wilken 1969:231). Furthermore, a distinctive reddish-brown, iron-rich soil of unusually even texture and consistency, which Caran identified as some of the initial terrace fill at the bottom of several of the re-excavated test pits in 1989, appears to have its closest natural source just northeast of Roaguía, about 1.5 km away.

We may consider two other factors that probably affected the width of these terraces. The first is closely related to the optimum height of the terrace walls and the amount of effort it takes to construct them. This factor may be termed "lateral thrust." This is the additional effort necessary to build thicker, structurally stronger terrace walls to withstand the lateral thrust pressures exerted against the terrace walls as the amount of terrace fill increased in volume. The pressure is increased even further once the fill becomes moisture laden. The second factor involves the *pocitos* found in the small canals that run along the top edge of the terrace walls. We concur with Doolittle's (1989:842) interpretation of *pocito* use (see comments below), and believe that the use of these features may have had an effect on the width of the terraces. One would expect the width of the terrace not to exceed the reach of the agriculturalists as they drew water from the *pocitos* to apply small amounts of water to the plants growing on the terraced fields.

Observations and Comments Regarding the Terraces

The generalities of the "ideal" agricultural terraced field expressed by Peterson, Winter, and Hewitt (1989:848) are not realistic. An intensive study of prehispanic agricultural terracing in the Valley of Oaxaca (Neely 1967b, 1970) and the Tehuacán Valley (Woodbury and Neely 1972) indicates variability to be the rule rather than the exception. In almost every case, the location, size, and shape of the terraces and fields are dictated by the available natural resources—generally the soils and the topography. But in the case of Hierve el Agua we must include a third vital resource, the available water. Thus, we contend that the location, size, and shape of the terraced fields at Hierve el Agua were designed to take full advantage of the available terrain that could be serviced by the gravity flow of the perennially available spring waters.

We find Hewitt et al.'s comments on the size and shape of fields relative to their use very interesting in two ways. First, they are committing the same crime (i.e., correlating form with function) they have accused Doolittle (1989) of committing. We are not saying this merely to point out a case of the "pot calling the kettle black"; we are mentioning it to emphasize the inconsistency of their argument in relation to the high degree of variability in the size and shape of well-documented Mesoamerican agricultural terraces. We are certain they have seen large agricultural fields and small salt-rendering terraces or ponds, but we cannot overlook the variability resulting from natural as well as behavioral/cultural factors.

Second, Hewitt, Winter, and Peterson (1987:813) compare the terraces at Hierve el Agua with the solar evaporation salt works at Zapotitlán Salinas, located just west of the Tehuacán Valley in the southern part of the state of Puebla (Fig. 4.8). While there are some small salt pans present at Zapotitlán Salinas, we note that Hewitt et al. never mention the quite large terraces and pans used for solar evaporation which are also present (Fig. 4.9), and are apparently the most common terrace type in that area (Sisson 1973:80–102). Using the size, form, and function criteria that they have stated, Hewitt et al. would be forced to classify these large, solar, salt-rendering terraces at Zapotitlán Salinas (and elsewhere) as having been used for agricultural purposes. To be sure, one might argue that some of the large terraces at Zapotitlán supported a cellular conformation of many small (1.0 × 1.2 m) salt pans. Significantly, we found no evidence of salt pans or other partitioning modifications on the surface, or in the excavations, of the Hierve el Agua terraces.

Peterson, Winter, and Hewitt emphasize the southeasterly orientation of the site and terraces in relation to their contention that the site was used for solar salt rendering. They state that the site was so located to take advantage of " . . . the winter sunrises, which provided maximum exposure to the sun during the dry season and maximum evaporation on the terraces. This would have been beneficial in salt production but detrimental to irrigation agriculture" (Peterson, Winter, and Hewitt 1989:848). Our immediate response to this statement is that, due to the location of the springs and the topography, there is no other place where the particular segment of the site to which they are referring could have been situated. We also submit that, despite the southern exposure, the availability of the spring water for irrigation purposes outweighed the attractiveness of other locations which might not have had water perennially available. Southern exposure would also have been beneficial for crop growth, assuming an adequate supply of water.

Peterson, Winter, and Hewitt (1989:848) argue that salt production and crop irrigation employ different types of terraces. They then go on to describe the ideal type of terrace used for each. Unfortunately,

IRRIGATION AT HIERVE EL AGUA 137

Figure 4.8. The modern solar evaporation salt works at Zapotitlán Salinas, located about 2 airline kilometers west of the Tehuacán Valley just south of Mexico Highway 125.

Figure 4.9. Telephotograph of a portion of the solar evaporation salt works at Zapotitlán Salinas. Note the size and conformation of the salt pans.

no such ideal dichotomy occurs in Mexico. As we have noted, the range of variation in agricultural field morphology is amazing (see Donkin 1979), and we submit that a similar range of structural variation exists in salt-rendering loci (see Andrews 1983, Sisson 1973). There is, however, an even more compelling reason for rejecting Peterson, Winter, and Hewitt's (1989:848) functionally specific descriptions of terraces. This is the fact that certain of the characteristics they claim as being present at Hierve el Agua—thereby allegedly verifying the production of salt—either are not universally present at the site, are not present at all, or have not been documented as being part of the saltmaking process.

For example, consider the following five characteristics. (1) The terraces at Hierve el Agua are not flat. In fact, the apparent flatness of the terraces is an artifact of post-abandonment alluviation. Most of Neely's 39 test pits into the non-architectural terraces showed that the fill sloped downward from the back of the terrace to the front. (2) The Hierve el Agua terraces are not "impermeable pans." They are filled with relatively loosely compacted, household garbage-enriched, humic soils. In the few cases where a travertine cap or layer was found during the test excavations, they are interpreted by Caran as being post-abandonment accidents of canal overflow. (3) As noted elsewhere in this article, the presence of *pocitos* at Hierve el Agua in no way substantiates the presence of salt-processing activities. In fact, their ethnographically documented associations are *only* with agricultural fields. (4) There are no salt "hoppers" or small crystalline remnants in the terrace soils, nor are there piles of mineral waste scraped from the terraces (see Andrews 1983, Sisson 1973). Both these features are probably omnipresent at salt production sites, and would surely have been revealed during our test excavations even if they were not visible on the surface of the site. (5) The terraces at Hierve el Agua fall well within the broad range of variation in size, shape, and depth seen in well-documented prehispanic agricultural terraces elsewhere in Mexico (Donkin 1979; Woodbury and Neely 1972). This range of variation apparently overlaps that of solar salt-rendering pans; therefore, using size, shape, and depth as criteria for terrace function is at best tenuous.

While Figure 4.3 is an accurate rendering of the center of the site and its associated terraces as it appears today, there are two ways in which this site map does not precisely reflect the site as it was when it was in use in prehispanic times. First, although Hewitt, Winter, and Peterson (1987:803, 814) seem somewhat undecided as to their nature, there are definitely a large number of terraces that have been covered by travertine on the steep face of the central portion and eastern arm of the amphitheater just south of and below the sinuous, east-west trending line of springs (Fig. 4.3). Not only is the steplike conformation of these terraces clearly visible (Fig. 4.7), but a careful examination of the canals leading downward from the springs to the terraces below has revealed small canals leading from the well-defined, sometimes elevated, feeder canals to the terraces, where they blend into the travertine that has covered the terraces. The nature of these steplike features is further revealed in the lower half of the travertine apron extending down from Springs 2 and 3, as well as from their defunct counterparts just to the west. As one walks down the apron the thickness of the travertine deposit diminishes, and one may see the travertine-veiled outlines of the individual rocks that make up the terrace walls. In a few locations some pieces of the travertine coating have broken away as a sheet, revealing the actual terrace walls. The number of terraces that have been covered by travertine is not determinable; however, we would suggest a figure of about 60 as a conservative estimate.

The second way the map does not accurately reflect the prehispanic nature of the site is in the number and width of the terraces, as well as the absence of canals, in the southwestern quadrant of the amphitheater. Hewitt, Winter, and Peterson (1987:802, 806; see Fig. 4.2) also made note of these larger terraces. However, they did not realize that the fewer numbers and larger size of these terraces were the result of a recent modification of the prehispanic terrace system. In 1966 and 1970 these terraces, as well as those immediately south and east of Test Pits 10, 11, and 12 (Fig. 4.4), were under dry-land cultivation (i.e. without benefit of irrigation). The fields in the lower southwest quadrant of the site were actively being cultivated by means of contour plowing with an ox team. Our examination of these larger terraced fields, as well as interviews with several inhabitants of the hamlet of Roaguía and the town of San Lorenzo Albarradas, indicated that the fields had—only a few years prior to 1966—been generally similar in number, size, and shape to those located in other parts of the site. According to Sr. Marcelino García (a resident of San Lorenzo Albarradas, who was cultivating these fields with *ejido* permission in 1966), in order to facilitate contour plowing with an ox team for dry farming, he had purposely broken out most of the terrace walls and all of the connecting canal segments on this portion of the site. The fragments of these destroyed terrace walls and canals were stacked on roughly every fifth original terrace wall. This buried the original wall, with its travertine-encrusted canal on top, and produced a single relatively large, massive, high terrace wall. Our examination of the fields and terrace walls verified Sr. García's statements.

Following this destruction, the earth between the remaining terrace walls was then leveled, contour plowed, and planted in corn. To insure the stability of these augmented terrace walls, small maguey plants (*Agave* sp.) were planted at intervals along the top edge of the walls to tie together the loose rubble and soil with their root systems. By examining the extant terrace wall stubs to the east and west of these larger terraced areas, as well as the canal stubs to the north and south (off the site map), one may reconstruct the terrace and canal system that was originally present. It was a system that was apparently quite similar to the "narrow" terraces immediately to the north and east, and evidently was part of that same system.

In addition to not realizing how extensive these recent modifications were, Hewitt, Winter, and Peterson (1987:802) have mistakenly assumed that "the surface slopes more gradually" in this area of "broader" terraces. Referring to Figure 4.3, one may determine that the slope of this area, between spot elevation points 232 and 254, is approximately 35.2% (19 degrees, 24 min.). If one then calculates the slope between spot elevations 254 and 264 in an area some 50 m to the northeast which is characterized by "narrow" terraces, the result is about 31.3% (17 degrees, 22 min.). So in fact, the area of the "broad" terraces is nearly 4% (2 degrees, 17 min.) steeper than the area of the "narrow" terraces! This observation reinforces our statements regarding the adaptive construction and variability characterizing documented Mesoamerican agricultural technology in general, and that of Hierve el Agua specifically.

The practice of modifying the form and size of prehispanic terraces is not restricted to the area of the site discussed above. Our reconnaissance of the site revealed similar instances in nearly all of the modern agricultural fields surrounding the central, intensely terraced area of Hierve el Agua. This includes many of the identifiable non-architectural terraces located atop the high western arm of the site. The discovery of broken remnants of terraces and canals, as well as canals leading from now-defunct spring heads toward these fields, has resulted in our estimate of about 168 ha for the total area of the site.

Hewitt, Winter, and Peterson (1987:806) ask: "If the Hierve el Agua water control system was used for crop irrigation, why did the ancient inhabitants expend so much intensive labor on the small high terraces rather than channeling water directly down to the wide, more easily cultivated fields and terraces?" We have three immediate responses to this question.

First, the small terraces were most likely built to permit the irrigation of crops by hand on a plant-by-plant basis. This technique, known as pot irrigation or *riego a brazo*, is practiced in many parts of the Valley of Oaxaca today, especially in the flat alluvial zones characterized by a relatively shallow water table (Kirkby 1973:42). Archaeological excavations have indicated that this technique may also have been practiced in early prehispanic times in various parts of the Valley of Oaxaca (Flannery, Kirkby, Kirkby, and Williams 1967; Flannery 1970, Kirkby 1973:119; Orlandini 1967). Although other prehispanic and modern examples of *riego a brazo* have been found in a different environmental zone, and show different hydrological conditions than those found at Hierve el Agua, we believe the associated technology present at Hierve el Agua (i.e., terrace-top canals and *pocitos*) makes this analogy a valid one.

Second, the water was channeled to the more remote fields to the south and west of the center of the site, as well as to more remote fields on the north and east. And those remote fields were, until just a few years prior to 1966, very similar to those that Hewitt et al. call "small, high terraces."

Third, what does "more easily cultivated" mean in prehispanic terms? Hewitt, Winter, and Peterson's perspective is one of modern farmers doing contour plowing with ox teams. When one considers the prehispanic tilling techniques that were probably employed (see Donkin 1979:3–16), it makes little difference whether the fields and terraces were small (narrow) or large (wide).

To the best of our knowledge Hewitt, Winter, and Peterson did not carry out any test excavations at Hierve el Agua. We are therefore puzzled by their comment: "If terraces at Hierve el Agua show successive layering of carbonate laminations and soil containing sherds, one possibility is that soil was brought in to raise the levels of the pans" (Peterson, Winter, and Hewitt 1989:848). Possibly it represents misinterpretation of a letter from Neely to Hewitt (Neely 1969) or of verbal descriptions of test pits passed on to Winter during August, 1988, or April, 1989. The truth is that there was *no* layering of carbonate laminations and soils containing sherds in Neely's excavations. In fact, there was little evidence of any carbonate deposition whatsoever in the terrace fill, and certainly no evidence for interbedded carbonate laminations and soils. As noted above, a few terraces exhibited a natural travertine cap resulting from post-abandonment canal overflow.

In one other case, Peterson, Winter, and Hewitt (1989:848) have misunderstood an article by Neely. They write that "Neely (1967:15) describes broken-up travertine below the terraces he excavated"; this they interpret to mean that he discovered " . . . an earlier travertine buildup which would have been disadvantageous, if not impossible, for agriculture." This is not what Neely said or meant. What he found were occasional chunks of old fossilized canals which had been added to the terrace fill or used as stones in the terrace walls.

Based on this misunderstanding, Peterson, Winter, and Hewitt (1989:848) suggest that "there may have been years or even decades when the system was not used." This, of course, is a possibility; however, two lines of evidence suggest there were no long periods of disuse. First, in the 39 test pits excavated into terraces throughout the site, the only evidence of a travertine crust appeared as a single layer varying from 5 to 20 cm in thickness, the upper surface of which began about 10 to 25 cm below the present ground surface. In a few cases Caran believes this layer may illustrate temporary terrace disuse, with subsequent terrace rejuvenation for additional short-term use. However, in most cases, Caran has interpreted this layer as a post-abandonment event, occurring when a canal broke and uncontrolled water flowed over the terrace surface. Probably, such disasters were quickly discovered and corrected so that a travertine layer usually did not have time to form. A second line of evidence for long-term use comes from the cross-sections of several canals at the site. The layers of travertine that are plainly visible in these cross-sections (Fig. 4.10) indicate that little trauma or long-term cessation of travertine deposition occurred.

We suspect that Hewitt, Winter, and Peterson's (1987:807-808) quandary regarding the absence of "flowstone aprons" in certain locations at Hierve el Agua may be answered by more closely studying the prehispanic terraces and canals. It would be surprising if the ancient inhabitants of Hierve el Agua did not take advantage of this flowstone, which breaks away from its underpinnings in laminar sheets with relative ease, for construction material to build their terraces and the walls on top of which some of the feeder canals have been constructed (see Canals). Also, in at least one instance, we suspect that some of the flowstone material that was present along the base of the eastern face of the high western arm of the amphitheater was removed to facilitate the construction of a large feeder canal, parts of which are intermittently visible in that location today.

THE CANALS

We conservatively calculate that there are about 6375 m of canals still visible and *in situ* at Hierve el Agua. This figure, however, may represent only about half the linear distance of canals once present. The disappearance of many canals can be attributed to recent farmers

Figure 4.10. A canal and *pocito* that have been cross-sectioned to show the original size of the *pocito* and the layering of the traverine filling it. The two rectangular, black-colored inclusions at the center and lower part are cross-sectioned sherds that fell into the *pocito* prior to the last use of the system. The scale is in centimeters.

having modified the ancient terraced areas to permit contour plowing with ox teams. An additional number of canals have been lost through being buried, along with their associated terraces, by the travertine apron that has formed over the cliff face just below the east-west line of springs (Fig. 4.7). A few canals have been displaced by erosional processes (and occasionally by mischievous visitors to the site).

The Hierve el Agua canals can be visualized as a single large system, composed of several interrelated subsystems. Each subsystem originates at a separate spring head, conveying water downslope by means of the relatively large primary canals we have termed "feeder" canals. As the water reaches the area of the terraces, it is diverted laterally into smaller "terrace-wall" canals. Any water that remains in the small canals at the end of the terrace is diverted back into another feeder canal, or into a small "side canal" paralleling the feeder canal, to flow downslope to the next terrace to be irrigated.

Originally, these canals appear to have been made either by the excavation of a small channel in the earth or by forming a small channel in a linear mound of clay or lime mud. The latter technique was employed to construct (1) the terrace-wall canals, (2) those feeder canals where the presence of bedrock would not permit easy excavation, or (3) canals in areas where there was a need to elevate the stream of water by means of a stone wall, in order to achieve the most efficient angle of grade. As soon as the spring waters started flowing through these channels, the bottom and sides of the canals came to be coated with travertine deposits precipitated from the water. The outer surfaces of the canals also received a similar coating, apparently due to water infiltrating into the walls and splashing over the edges of the channels. This precipitate literally cemented or "fossilized" the canals in place, and it largely accounts for the well-preserved nature of the canal system as well as the associated terraces.

Observations and Comments Regarding the Canals

Peterson, Winter, and Hewitt (1989:849) claim that the narrow canals at Hierve el Agua do not resemble the wider irrigation canals in use in the Valley of Oaxaca today. They use this as an argument against the Hierve el Agua canals having been used for irrigation agriculture. Yet paradoxically, in the same paragraph, they go on to state: "One would not expect large canals and rapid flow of a large volume of water at Hierve el Agua simply because the springs and the natural flow are small." Why should one expect large canals if only a small water supply was available?

Two additional considerations are relevant to the size of the canals. First, as in the case of the *pocitos* (see below), the readily visible remnant of the canals one sees today is roughly half the size of the canal when first built. Cross-sections of the canals (Fig. 4.10) show that gradual travertine deposition inside them over the centuries has narrowed them to their present size. Second, it is likely that the irrigation technology used at Hierve el Agua was different from many of the larger canal systems currently functioning in the Valley of Oaxaca. The Hierve el Agua system, with its associated *pocitos*, was a hand-watering system rather than a flood-watering system; its analogies are to be found in the Zaachila piedmont system described by

Kirkby (1973:117). Smaller canals are more amenable to such a system, just as they are when a relatively small water supply is available.

Once again, we must emphasize the variability of irrigation systems in Mexico. While Peterson, Winter, and Hewitt (1989:849) note that most modern Valley of Oaxaca canals are "generally 30 centimeters or more in width," we can certainly attest to having seen smaller ones. Furthermore, Wilken (1987) notes similar variability in the sizes of canals associated with "scoop irrigation" systems in Guatemala which we believe form an ethnographic analog to the Hierve el Agua system. Wilken (1987:182) states: "The canals or zanjas bordering each tablón vary in size from the large, meter-wide drains of Almolonga and La Ciénaga to the tiny canals of Zunil, which are only a few centimeters wide and deep." Of the Guatemalan examples described by Wilken, the scoop irrigation system at Zunil seems to be the closest analog to the Hierve el Agua system in nearly every respect.

Peterson, Winter, and Hewitt's (1989:849) generalization that "salt production focuses on concentrating water while irrigation agriculture spreads it out" is simply not applicable to the case of Hierve el Agua. Because of the special irrigation technology utilized, and the fact that water was a scarce resource in this area, Hierve el Agua irrigation concentrated water flow and use. The presence of small feeder canals, and even smaller terrace-wall canals, attests to this emphasis on water concentration.

There is no reason why all irrigation systems have to have the same size and layout. Nevertheless, by comparing the area of the Hierve el Agua terrace-and-canal system to that which Neely and his students found on the Xoxocotlán piedmont near Monte Albán (Neely 1972; O'Brien, Mason, Lewarch, and Neely 1982), Hewitt et al. attempt to show that Hierve el Agua is too small to have been used for irrigation agriculture. But as we have already noted, they have grossly underestimated the total area of Hierve el Agua. Therefore, even if we disregard the discussions of site variability presented above, their argument of site size relative to function is not really applicable.

POCITOS

Pocitos are small, generally circular, shallow depressions that have been excavated or modeled at fairly regular intervals into the clay or lime mud used to form the channel of the terrace canals. They form integral parts of the terrace-wall canal channels; as it passes down the canal, the water flows in a straight-line through the *pocitos*, which are centrally positioned and are deeper than the bottom of the channel (Fig. 4.11). Although *pocitos* are found elsewhere (e.g., in the channels of some of the smaller feeder canals, and excavated into the soil adjacent to the feeder canals) in relatively small numbers (about 10 percent of the total number of *pocitos* present), their context is inevitably the canal and terrace system.

These features have been given an appropriate name by the inhabitants of the region. The name *pocito* (little well) is derived from the fact that the small, circular depressions hold water, like small wells or cisterns, after a rainfall; the name is also appropriate to the probable

Figure 4.11. A terrace wall located in the vicinity of Test Pit 24. Note how a small canal has been constructed atop the terrace wall, and that *pocitos* have been excavated at regular intervals into the canal. This small canal flows southwestward into the main feeder canal seen in the background. The scale is 15 cm in length.

function of the feature. Using Flannery's and Kirkby's observations of *riego a brazo* as a general analogy, in 1966 Neely suggested to Kirkby that the *pocitos* might be places from which to dip water to apply to crops planted on the terraces (Kirkby 1973:117-19). Kirkby's (1973:117) subsequent observations in the Zaachila Valley of Oaxaca, as well as those by Wilken (1987:178-93) in Guatemala, have supported Neely's reconstruction and have provided additional details as to the procedures involved and the crops grown.

The *pocitos* at Hierve el Agua have been preserved by minerals precipitated from the spring waters. As in the case of the canals, which have narrowed through travertine deposition, a similar process has reduced the size of the *pocitos* until all that remains is a depression approximately half the depth and diameter of the original (Fig. 4.10).

Observations and Comments Regarding the Pocitos

Hewitt, Winter, and Peterson seem uncertain as to whether the *pocitos* at Hierve el Agua are natural or artificial constructions (see Hewitt, Winter, and Peterson 1987:806 [Fig. 10 caption], and Peterson, Winter, and Hewitt 1989:848). We have no doubt that these were deliberately constructed as part of the canal and terrace system to provide locations where water could be dipped up and directly applied to individual plants for irrigation purposes. Our conclusions are based on three sources of archaeological and ethnographic field observation, those of Kirkby (1973:117-19), Neely (1966, 1970, 1971), and Wilken (1987:178-93). Doolittle's (1989:841-42) discussion concerning the origin and function of *pocitos* is also derived from these sources, something Hewitt, Winter, and Peterson were apparently unaware of. Significantly, our survey of the available literature on prehispanic and modern salt production in Mexico and Central America (e.g., Andrews 1983; Apenes 1944; Charlton 1969, 1971; Drennan 1976; Lozano García 1946; MacNeish, Peterson, and Neely 1972; Noguera 1975; Parsons 1971; Sisson 1973; Zárate 1917) reveals no mention of *pocitos* or *pocito*-like features associated with salt production. As a result, we concur with Doolittle's (1989) critique, since the documented association of *pocitos* with irrigation agriculture activities seems more convincing than Peterson, Winter, and Hewitt's (1989:848) undocumented claim that these features "could have been used in salt production."

STONE BASINS AND BOXES

Because we are not yet certain of the function of the stone basins and boxes at Hierve el Agua, we prefer to use simple descriptive terms rather than the functionally loaded term *registros* (inspection boxes) adapted by Hewitt, Winter, and Peterson (1987:805-6).

The majority of these features were constructed by setting relatively thin slabs of travertine (which were more than likely trimmed to the desired shape and thickness) into the earth to form a single box or a pair of boxes. These features were usually partially buried in the fill of a terrace, so that soil formed the bottom of the box while its upper end remained open. Most boxes were situated at the base of the next terrace wall upslope, and a small canal carried water to each box from the upslope terrace-top canal or from an adjacent feeder canal. When two boxes were present, one was set in front of the other in such a manner that the upper edge of the lower box was even with, or just below, the bottom edge of the upper box. In almost all cases where the latter arrangement occurred, it was possible to see a drain hole in the center of the lower edge of the front side of the upper box. This would allow water from the upper box to flow into the lower box. Although Hewitt, Winter, and Peterson (1987:807) do not make note of it, this arrangement can be seen in Figure 9 of their article.

While we are still researching the stone basins and boxes, and our minds are open, we strongly suspect that their functions go beyond merely providing a tank or collecting basin from which one could use a vessel to dip out water, as Hewitt, Winter, and Peterson (1987:806) suggest. We agree with Doolittle's (1989:843-45) criticisms of Hewitt, Winter, and Peterson's analysis of these features; we see only the grossest similarity between the stone boxes from Hierve el Agua and the water collection basin at Fábrica San José (Drennan 1976:257), and hence must reject their idea that the stone boxes were used for salt production. As in the case of the *pocitos*, our survey of the literature on prehispanic and modern salt production in Mexico has not revealed any mention of *registros* or *registro*-like features associated with this activity.

This does not mean that we are convinced by Doolittle's (1989:844-45) interpretation of the stone boxes as representing Colonial period hispanic technology in the form of "drop structures" or "stilling basins" to slow the flow of water from the canals onto the terraces. Our doubts are based not only on our view of the way the system operated (that is, by hand-dipping of water from the *pocitos* rather than direct flow of water onto the terraces) but also the evidence that the site went out of use around A.D. 1350.

Of course, the travertine-laden waters that flowed into the boxes left a coating on all surfaces. We suspect that in most cases the stone boxes were carefully maintained so as not to allow the deposits to build up. This is suggested by the fact that the drain holes between the boxes were not closed by travertine, even though the joints between the side-wall slabs were crusted shut. In a few cases, however, the deposition was evidently not controlled, and those boxes turned into elliptical basin-like features when seen in plan-view. With a careful examination of these basins, however, one can discern the original slabs used for the walls and determine the original shape and size of the box.

ADDITIONAL COMMENTS REGARDING TERRACES, CANALS, AND RELATED FEATURES

Hewitt, Winter, and Peterson (1987:813) describe Hierve el Agua as "a descending series of small level terraces designed to maximize water evaporation and mineral precipitation." We believe that this characterization and interpretation of the system is incorrect. In fact, we submit that, except possibly for the terraced basin-like areas near the springs, the system was specifically designed to *minimize* water evaporation and mineral precipitation, most especially in the terraced fields! This minimization was accomplished in several ways.

First, the canals are small. This was because of the need to distribute small amounts of water over a relatively large area. Small canals accomplish this task by exposing minimal surface area to the atmosphere, which reduces water loss through evaporation.

Second, the canals were frequently constructed with *saltos*, or waterfall-like drops, in their courses. This was done partially out of necessity to drop the water over steep slopes, such as that below Springs 2 and 3. In addition, however, the major feeder canal just below Springs 2 and 3 has several artificially elevated drop-offs in its route downslope. These artificially elevated drop-offs are also seen on a smaller scale in the northwest quadrant of the amphitheater. One possible explanation for these drop-offs (in addition to their obvious role in transporting water downslope) is that they purposefully increased the agitation of the waters so as to drive out additional CO_2 gas and increase the deposition of minerals and salts in the canals and on the splash areas at the base of the drop-offs. This was done in order to reduce the deposition of minerals in the terraced fields.

Third, the system of small terrace canals with *pocitos* would permit small amounts of water to be delivered by hand-held scoops directly to the base of the plant stems at the point where they entered the soil. The fact that this could be done with minimal quantities of water, and only when the plants demanded additional moisture, would greatly minimize evaporation and mineral precipitation. Furthermore, since the water was probably placed at the base of the plant, this would have prevented mineral deposition on the plant leaves—which is the prime way plants are adversely affected by mineral precipitation (see discussion below). Yet another benefit may be seen in this plant-by-plant watering process: only a small part of the terrace soils would be affected at any one planting. The subsequent crop could have been planted in the spaces between the spots where the plants of the previous crop were placed. The upper layers of the deep, organic-refuse-enriched soils of the terraces could have been easily turned between crops. And because the network of canals was designed so that the flow to each terrace could be controlled, specific fields could be allowed to lie fallow while the surrounding fields were cultivated. The discovery of maize pollen in the fill of Neely's Test Pits 16, 17, and 23, plus cucurbit pollen in Test Pit 23, suggests that several different crops may have been grown on the same terrace. This has been shown to prolong soil life for agricultural pursuits (Donkin 1979:2).

Maize pollen usually does not travel more than 10 or 15 m, so the large amounts at Hierve el Agua (up to 17 grains in one sample from Test Pit 23) suggest maize was grown right on the terraces. To be sure, some pollen could have been introduced with household trash (although pollen does not always survive such transportation); this cannot be the case with the 130–140 cm level in Test Pit 23, however, since it was found in reddish-brown soil with no evidence of sherds or other household trash.

Fourth, even if larger amounts of water did happen to enter the terraced fields through the breaking of a canal wall, or due to run-off mixed with spring waters in the rainy season, this eventuality had been foreseen by the designers of the Hierve el Agua system. The terraces had enough fill soil, perhaps purposely maintained as a relatively loose matrix by the inclusion of more sandy/loamy soils and sherds, to permit the water to flow down past the root system of the plants rather quickly. This would allow the moisture to be utilized by the plant, but reduce evaporation and mineral precipitation on the roots. Once the water reached the lower soils it could pass from the terraces, either through the interstices of the dry-laid stone terrace walls, through the porous travertine rocks themselves, or, if the water reached the bedrock floor of the terrace, through a series of drainage or "weep holes" maintained at intervals along the base of the terrace walls. We fortuitously found these weep holes while making small test excavations to see how deeply the bottom of the terrace walls were buried and to determine the heights of the walls. Obviously, this whole arrangement was designed to reduce evaporation and mineral precipitation in the terraced fields; it is not a feature appropriate for salt rendering.

SALT PROCESSING AT HIERVE EL AUGA

Ironically, it was Neely in 1967 who first raised the possibility of saltmaking at Hierve el Agua when he mentioned that "algunas [de las areas funcionalmente distintas] están cerca de los manantiales y se componen de grandes depresiones someras y ciertas formas que podrían ser sistemas para extraer sales comestibles por métodos primitivos mediante procesos de evaporación"* (Neely 1967a:15). Despite this suggestion of saltmaking, which preceded that of Hewitt, Winter, and Peterson (1987) by twenty years, Neely now wishes to revise his opinion. After a detailed consideration of the terraced field and canal technology, as well as the diatom and hydrochemical analyses to be given below, it is now clear to us that comestible salts could not have been produced in those basinlike areas close to the springs. If any comestible salts at all were produced at Hierve el Agua (and we consider this only a remote possibility), they would have been available in quite small quantities several hundred meters south and downslope from the springs and the greater portion of the terrace and canal system (see Hydrochemistry below).

Inspired by the fact that saltmaking took place at Lambityeco forty years ago, Peterson, Winter, and Hewitt (1989:848) comment that "it would be interesting to know when salt was last produced at Hierve el Agua." If such production ever took place at Hierve el Agua, we doubt that it was that recently. Neely interviewed several inhabitants of Roaguía and San Lorenzo Albarradas over the years from 1966 to 1989, and none acknowledged the use of Hierve el Agua for any pursuits other than dry farming, watering their animals, and mineral bathing (for example, on picnics and Sunday family outings).

Hewitt, Winter, and Peterson (1987:814) propose that future research include experimentations with salt production. This is probably not necessary, since the same end can almost certainly be achieved through hydrochemical modeling with the SOLMNEQ computer program (see Hydrochemistry). This program can accurately

---

*"some [of the functionally distinct areas] are near the springs and consist of impressive depressions and other features which could be systems for extracting edible salts by primitive methods involving evaporation."

determine when, or at what point, in the rendering process comestible salts will be produced (if at all), as well as estimate the productivity of such production. Caran is currently in the process of implementing this computerized modeling program. The results of these efforts will be published in Neely's forthcoming monograph on Hierve el Agua.

Much as Neely suggested twenty years ago (Neely 1967a:15; 1967b; letter to Hewitt, June 11, 1969), Peterson, Winter, and Hewitt (1989:849) believe that holding ponds were constructed in close proximity to the spring heads to "function as an initial evaporation stage" for salt production. For various reasons, we no longer hold this belief. We now believe that these basins near the spring heads may well have functioned as degassing areas where CO_2 was allowed to escape, in order to accelerate solute deposition before the spring waters were channeled to the fields for irrigation. In our view, the basins functioned to improve the water for irrigation, while increasing the life of the system and reducing the amount and frequency of maintenance of the system by decreasing the amount of precipitate in the water. Thus, these basin-like features were analogous to the soil retention dam (TR-15) of the Purrón Dam Complex which Neely discovered in the southern part of the Tehuacán Valley (Woodbury and Neely 1972:82–99).

It is also conceivable that some basinlike features may have served the site occupants as bathing areas, as Flannery has suggested (letter to Hewitt, January 15, 1969); following a suggestion by William T. Sanders, Flannery compares them to the baths of Nezahualcoyotl near Texcoco. Hewitt (1968), himself, has also suggested the possibility of mineral baths at the site.

Other evidence for saltmaking proposed by Hewitt, Winter, and Peterson will, we believe, not stand up to close scrutiny. Worked sherds recovered from Neely's test excavations, believed by Winter (personal communication, April, 1989) to be "salt pan scraping tools," could just as well have served for pottery manufacture and other scraping tasks. The fact is that Neely found no salt pans to scrape.

Peterson, Winter, and Hewitt (1989) even contradict themselves on the possibility of evaporation surfaces. In one paragraph they predict a "successive layering of carbonate laminations and soil containing sherds" at the site (p. 848), while in a subsequent paragraph they state that " . . . [salt] collection terraces . . . need not have had a carbonate floor or show alternating layers of travertine and soil" (p. 849). The fact is that none of Neely's test pits—which were widely distributed throughout the terrace system, both near the springs and far downslope—showed the presence of alternating layers of carbonates and soils. And if no carbonate floors were present, what would prevent the water from soaking down into the relatively deep terrace fill soils? A careful geological examination of these soils did not reveal any salt crystals or "hoppers," which are omnipresent in such situations. Also, the hydrochemical analysis of Hierve el Agua spring waters (see below) showed little, if any, comestible salt present in solution that could be rendered. Current hydrochemical modeling by computer, as well as analyses of the soil samples taken from stratified layers of fill from some of the test pits, should provide additional statements concerning the feasibility of salt production at Hierve el Agua.

Hewitt, Winter, and Peterson persist in comparing the terraces and canals at Hierve el Agua with the modern salt processing system at Zapotitlán Salinas near Tehuacán. We strongly disagree with their statement regarding the similarity of the two sites. As noted in Terraces above, it is only in the most general sense that the two sites are visually similar (i.e., both consist of terraces built on a piedmont hillslope). Furthermore, although our minds are open, we know of no examples of salt processing systems similar to that of Zapotitlán Salinas which date to prehispanic times. Those at Venta Salada in the Tehuacán Valley (MacNeish, Peterson, and Neely 1972:463–68, 492–94), which are well dated to the Postclassic period, do not show terrace construction similar to that found at the Zapotitlán salt works (MacNeish, Peterson, and Neely 1972; Neely 1964; Sisson 1973) or Hierve el Agua.

Finally, a word should be said about the mineral water at Hierve el Agua: it tastes awful. As Michael Kirkby once said when asked if he thought the springs had been used for comestible salt, he replied, "That's the last thing I'd want on my *huevos rancheros*."

PRELIMINARY RESULTS OF THE DIATOM STUDY

One way to answer some of the questions about Hierve el Agua is through a study of the diatom paleoecology of the site. In this section, we give some preliminary results of an ongoing study by Winsborough.

Diatoms are single-celled algae (microfloral organisms) encased within a silica cell wall. Many diatom species have specific autecological preferences and tolerances determining where they will grow, and they are often sensitive to physical and chemical conditions in their environment. Salinity, pH, substrate type, light, current, flow seasonality, and available nutrients are some of the most common parameters affecting the composition of a diatom community.

Taking advantage of these responsive characteristics of diatoms, Winsborough designed a study to characterize the modern and fossil diatom assemblages of the site; assess their similarity; and determine, by the diatom signature, the nature of several distinct microhabitats associated with the aquatic and moist areas of the site at the time of prehispanic use. Diatoms were collected from modern habitats at Hierve el Agua, including the same contexts from which samples were taken for water chemistry analysis (see Hydrochemistry). Diatoms were also extracted from discrete travertine layers in canals, *pocitos*, stone boxes, terrace walls, and soils from well-stratified test pits, in order to obtain information on the diatoms living when the site was in use. The following results of Winsborough's study are based on her analysis of 11,211 specimens—9000 modern diatoms, and 2211 diatoms from old deposits.

To date, a total of 54 species of diatoms have been identified. Table 4.1 lists the relative abundance of those species which occur with a relative abundance of at least 0.5% in either the modern or ancient samples. From this list it can be seen that *Achnanthes gibberula, Denticula elegans, Hantzschia amphioxys, Navicula heufleri,* and *Navicula mutica* are common in both sets of data. Five other species were common only in the modern collections, and present in very low numbers in the old travertines. These are *Amphora coffeaeformis, Cymbella norvegica, Diploneis oblongella, Nitzschia tropica,* and *Rhopalodia gibberula.* An entirely different set of six species were common only in the old travertine material, and rare to absent in modern habitats. These are *Amphora perpusilla, Fragilaria lapponica, Gomphonema intricatum* var. *vibrio, Navicula salinarum, Nitzschia dissipata,* and *Nitzschia filiformis.*

Because no canals or terraces today are being used as they were in the past, it is not possible to examine modern counterparts to some of the ancient habitats. One of the most similar modern habitats, in terms of the diatoms present, was a sample of sediment taken from the bottom of a *pocito* with rainwater standing in it.

Four of the diatom species found in samples of old material prefer a sand or gravel substrate (*A. perpusilla, N. salinarum, N. dissipata,* and *N. filiformis*). *N. mutica* accounted for 39.8% of the diatoms in the old material, and *H. amphioxys* another 13.4%. Together they account for over half the diatoms extracted from old materials. The presence of these two species is probably not a matter of differential preservation, since small, thinly silicified species such as *A. gibberula* were well preserved and accounted for 14% of the assemblage. Only two of the species found at Hierve el Agua are known to tolerate hypersaline

TABLE 4.1

Percentages of the Relative Abundance of the Most Common Diatoms at Hierve el Agua with a Relative Abundance of at least 0.5%.

Species	Modern Sites	Old Materials
Achnanthes gibberula	46.1	14.1
Amphora coffeaeformis	11.8	---
Amphora perpusilla	--	3.1
Cymbella norvegica	11.6	---
Denticula elegans	11.6	1.8
Diploneis oblongella	0.8	---
Fragilaria lapponica	---	1.8
Gomphonema intricatum	---	8.8
Hantzschia amphioxys	0.5	13.4
Navicula heufleri	8.7	2.4
Navicula mutica	2.4	39.8
Navicula salinarum	---	1.6
Nitzschia dissipata	---	1.5
Nitzschia filiformis	---	1.6
Nitzschia tropica	4.9	---
Rhopalodia gibberula	0.9	---

environments: *Amphora coffeaeformis* and *Rhopalodia gibberula*. However, as both these species have broad environmental tolerances (from fresh to hypersaline waters), their occurrence in no way indicates the presence of hypersaline conditions. Furthermore, they were found only in our modern samples, where water chemistry analyses have shown the maximum measured total dissolved solids (TDS) to be 6645 mg/l (i.e., moderately saline).

Winsborough believes that the presence of these two species does not imply any change in the saline content of the water or the general environment of the site through time, nor do they indicate the presence of hypersaline microenvironments.

The preliminary results of this study suggest that the overall diatom assemblage at Hierve el Agua may be characterized as a benthic community which prefers neutral to alkaline pH conditions, well-aerated spring or stream habitats and subaerial conditions, such as splash zones and wet areas. Many of the species are adapted to conditions of periodic desiccation and are characteristic of warm bicarbonate-rich water which is fresh to moderately saline (0–10,000 mg/l TDS). The modern samples show that habitat variability may be responsible for determining the proportion of different species in a sample, but that the same general set of species is found over the entire site. The old material is more diverse, and includes soil forms, species which prefer a solid carbonate substrate, and species which are epiphytic on other plants, such as mosses and filamentous cyanobacteria. Because some of the species in the old material did not occur in the modern collections, it is possible that there was a wider variety of habitats at some time in the past, which may have included rather permanent bodies of relatively fresh standing water. It also seems quite probable that the waters were more eutrophic, with the additional nutrients present encouraging an increased number and greater variety of diatom species. Overall, there is no difference in the autecology of the modern and ancient diatom samples from Hierve el Agua, in terms of salt preferences and tolerances. This implies that the present environment at Hierve el Agua is a reasonable approximation of the past environment, as represented by the old/ancient travertine samples examined to date. Details regarding the modern hydrological environment at the site are presented in the following section.

Preliminary Results of the Hydrochemistry and Water-Resource Development Study

Neely asked Caran, who is a research scientist associate of the University of Texas at Austin (Department of Geological Sciences and

Texas Archaeological Research Laboratory) and president of a private geological consulting firm, to undertake the hydrochemical studies at Hierve el Agua because of Caran's interest and expertise in geomorphology, Cenozoic stratigraphy, and hydrology/hydrochemistry. As with Winsborough's investigations, Caran's work is in progress. However, his inquiries have progressed sufficiently to allow him to offer some preliminary observations on the hydrochemistry and water-resource development of this site. These observations are crucial indicators of water use at Hierve el Agua in the context of its intricate canal and terrace system.

The objectives of these hydrochemical studies are (1) to evaluate previously published hydrochemical data in terms of their analytical credibility; (2) to provide new data from 13 carefully collected, stabilized, curated, and analyzed water samples from Hierve el Agua; and (3) to assess potential uses for these waters based on their present hydrochemistry.

EVALUATION OF PREVIOUS WATER ANALYSES

Three analyses of spring water from Hierve el Agua have previously been published. Hewitt, Winter, and Peterson (1987: Table 1) presented two analyses, one of which was a 1968 study by the Laboratorio Central de Agrología, Secretaría de Recursos Hidráulicos, Mexico. The other study was on a sample collected in 1984 by Hewitt (and/or colleagues) and analyzed at the Mineral Studies Laboratory of the Bureau of Economic Geology, University of Texas at Austin. An additional data set, comprising one sample collected in 1986, was published by the Instituto Nacional de Estadística, Geografía e Informática (1988b). The laboratory that performed this analysis was not specified.

Based on two of these samples, Hewitt, Winter, and Peterson (1987) have argued that spring waters at Hierve el Agua are suitable for salt rendering but unsuitable for irrigation. The two analyses (samples 222-68 and 84-793) on which they based their conclusions are here reproduced in Table 4.2. Unfortunately, potential use for Hierve el Agua water cannot be accurately judged from these data. The analyses are fraught with numerous, conspicuous errors, making them unusable. Description of the analytical methods was incomplete, and there was no mention of techniques employed in sampling, sample preparation, or curation. Sample 222-68 was analyzed three days after collection, which is well within the recommended period for storing water samples to be analyzed for major ions. But sample

TABLE 4.2

PREVIOUSLY PUBLISHED ANALYSES OF WATER AT HIERVE EL AGUA

	Sample 222-68 (mg/l)	Sample 84-793 (mg/l)	Sample 31 (mg/l)
Undissociated			
B	10.00	nd	nd
Cation			
Ba	nd	0.30	nd
Ca	nd	245.00	8.00
Mg	nd	43.00	44.40
Ca+Mg	438.00	nd	nd
K	nd	211.00	193.00
Na	1,688.00	1,610.00	1,575.50
Sr	nd	4.50	nd
Anion			
CO_3	971.10	nd	138.00
HCO_3	nd	1,700.00	353.80
Cl	2,238.70	2,280.00	2,378.50
SO_4	42.20	60.00	26.40
TDS	5,388.00	6,153.80	4,729.00
pH	6.65	6.90	9.00

NOTES: nd = no data

Sample 222-68 collected in Spring 1 area, 02-26-68; analyzed 02-29-68 at the Laboratorio Central de Agrologia, Secretaria de Recursos Hidraulicos, Mexico. Data originally reported in parts per million, ppm (= mg/l at TDS<7,000). Total dissolved solids (TDS) is the sum of ion concentrations (erroneously reported as 5,378 ppm).
SOURCE: Hewitt, Winter, and Peterson (1987: Table 1).

Sample 84-793 collected in Spring 1 area, 06-23-84; analyzed 10-11-84 at the Mineral Studies Laboratory, Bureau of Economic Geology, The University of Texas at Austin.
SOURCE: Hewitt, Winter, and Peterson (1987: Table 1).

Sample 31 collected in Spring 1 area (?), 10-07-86. In addition to the constituents reported above, the laboratory also reported 11.8 mg/l nitrate (NO_3), which was entered into the calculated TDS.
SOURCE: Instituto Nacional de Estadistica, Geografia, e Informatica (1988b).

84-793 had been stored for three and a half months before analysis, far longer than the maximum permissible storage of samples for anion determination.

Neither sample appears to have been collected and stored in accordance with standard hydrochemical procedures. These procedures include (1) simultaneous collection of duplicate samples for separate analyses of cations and anions (at least 500-milliliter samples for cations, 1-liter samples for anions); (2) filtration of the samples to remove particles (suspended solids) larger than 0.45 microns; (3) treatment of the cation sample with nitric acid to stabilize the concentration of cations by preventing formation of mineral precipitates; and (4) storage of the anion sample on ice prior to analysis in order to stabilize the concentration of individual anions. Some of these procedures may have exceeded the prevailing laboratory standards at the time of the analyses, especially the 1968 sample. However, methods of sampling and treatment that do not comply with these practices may affect analytical results adversely.

SAMPLE 222-68

This sample was collected in February, 1968, during the dry season. The precise sampling location was not specified, but was presumably one of the large perennial springs in the northern part of the Hierve el Agua site area, perhaps at the Spring 1 locality (Fig. 4.12) of the present study. There are several obvious errors in the analytical results as published. The total dissolved solids (TDS) concentration was incorrectly reported to be 5378 mg/l. The sum of the ionic concentrations is actually 5388 mg/l. Electrical conductivity (specific electrical conductance or SEC) was reported in the wrong unit of measurement, micro-Ohms, rather than the proper unit, micromhos, which is the reciprocal of micro-Ohms. It is unclear whether pH was measured in the field at the time of sampling, or in the laboratory at the time of sample analysis. Water temperature at the sampling point was not recorded, and presumably was not measured. Ionic concentrations were noted for sodium (Na), carbonate (CO_3), chloride (Cl), sulfate (SO_4), boron (B), and TDS. However, only the sum of calcium (Ca) and magnesium (Mg) concentrations was provided; their individual ionic strengths were not differentiated. Many of the reported ionic concentrations were similar to those for ions in the second sample, 84-793. But there were striking inconsistencies as well, for which no explanation was offered.

These problems did little to inspire confidence. However, the analysis was rejected for other, more compelling reasons. In most natural waters, potassium, calcium, and magnesium are among the principal cations, yet none of these concentrations were reported for sample 222-68. Hewitt, Winter, and Peterson (1987:809-10) recognized this shortcoming in their data, but failed to note several others. Most importantly, bicarbonate, an obvious major constituent of carbonated waters, had been omitted from the data set. Instead, the data included an anomalous figure for carbonate concentration at the reported pH of 6.65. Below a pH of 8.3, ionic carbonate is essentially absent (Hem 1970:156, Fig. 19). Therefore, almost all of the reported "carbonate" must have been bicarbonate, although bicarbonate would still be grossly underrepresented in this analysis, even relative to that for the other sample reported by Hewitt, Winter, and Peterson (1987), number 84-973 (Table 4.2; see additional discussion below). For sample 222-68, the pH was given as 6.65, which is higher than that of any of the spring water pH measurements obtained in the field during the present study. The comparatively high value indicates that the pH of sample 222-68 probably was measured in the laboratory after partial destabilization of the sample, rather than in the field. This also suggests that the ionic composition of the sample had not been stabilized in the field, casting further doubt on the credibility of this analysis.

One additional point must be discussed. Boron concentration was reported for sample 222-68. Initially, this value, 10.0 mg/l, appeared anomalously high in relation to most other nonthermal ground waters (White et al. 1963: Tables 24, 25). Excessive boron in irrigation water is toxic to many plants, including all major cultivated varieties. Boron concentrations greater than 1.25 mg/l are considered unsuitable for sensitive cultivars, but most plants with even high tolerance for boron generally cannot flourish in waters containing more than 3.75 mg/l (Scofield 1936, as cited by Richards 1954: Table 14; Hem 1970: Tables 27 and 28).

Hewitt, Winter, and Peterson (1987) recognized this fact. Initially, it was their most compelling argument against prehistoric use of Hierve el Agua spring waters for irrigation. However, they were silent on the issue of possible contamination of the sample through collection or storage in glass vessels. For many years, it has been widely recognized that many types of laboratory glassware are composed of borosilicate glass, which contains trace amounts of boron that can leak into samples (see American Petroleum Institute 1968). Unless both the collector and the laboratory which processed sample 222-68 were known to have rigorously avoided glass, boron contamination was a very real possibility that should have been critically evaluated.

As it happens, the present study confirmed the high concentration of boron in waters at Hierve el Agua (Tables 4.3 and 4.4). In fact, boron concentrations are even higher than that noted by Hewitt, Winter, and Peterson (1987). Maximum observed boron concentration was 22.56 mg/l. Careful field and laboratory techniques ensured that this and other new values were not the result of contamination. This might have been irrefutable evidence that irrigation with these waters was not possible. However, a review of literature concerning the effects of boron on crops disclosed two decisive mitigating factors: (1) boron absorption and toxic effects are inhibited by high concentrations of calcium carbonate in the soil and in aqueous solution (Kabata-Pendias and Pendias 1984:133, Muhr 1940:222, 224); and (2) boron is readily adsorbed on soil organic matter, retarding uptake by plants (Yermiyaho, Keren, and Chen 1988). As will be discussed below, spring waters at Hierve el Agua are supersaturated with respect to calcium carbonate, counteracting any possible toxicity of boron. In addition, as we have already mentioned, the prehistoric inhabitants of Hierve el Agua applied household garbage and comminuted organic matter to terraces at the site. Organic matter would have imparted many benefits, including the adsorption of boron, thereby limiting the exposure of crop plants to toxic concentrations of this element. Certain other agricultural practices also may have helped to lessen the effective boron toxicity.

SAMPLE 84-793

Sample 84-793 was collected in June, 1984, during the rainy season (Hewitt, Winter, and Peterson 1987:808-810), apparently from Spring 1. Analytical techniques were reported and results of this analysis are shown in Table 4.2. Neither pH nor water temperature was measured in the field, and the sample was not filtered. Within 24 hours of collection, a mineral precipitate formed in the sample bottle. The precipitate was later determined to consist primarily of calcium carbonate, presumably as calcite. Formation of a precipitate indicates that no steps had been taken to stabilize this sample. Unfortunately, the lag between collection and analysis of the sample was three and a half months, allowing ample time for changes in ionic concentration relative to chemistry of the spring waters. Despite this problem, some of the results appear reasonable, although calcium and bicarbonate concentrations are anomalously low, sulfate is moderately high, and chloride and pH are surprisingly high in relation to the body of field and analytical data now available.

Ground water that is highly charged with carbon dioxide (CO_2), such as that at Hierve el Agua, can have pH values well below neutral (pH 7) because dissolution of CO_2 in water creates carbonic acid. However, the pH of these waters becomes highly unstable when the water reaches the surface, as when springs discharge. Equilibrium CO_2 saturation of water at depth is far greater than CO_2 saturation at the surface, where ambient pressure is considerably lower. As ground water reaches the spring port, there is a marked decrease in confining pressure, and CO_2 is liberated as a gaseous phase. This produces the effervescence that characterizes these springs. Degassing causes pH to increase, which reduces the water's capacity to retain some ions in solution. Relatively insoluble minerals, particularly calcite ($CaCO_3$), readily form precipitates as the pH rises abruptly. Deposits of calcite formed in this manner are called travertine. The mineral that precipitated in the 84-793 sample bottle prior to analysis was almost certainly calcite. Precipitation selectively depleted the sample's solute load, particularly the Ca and HCO_3 concentrations, thereby compromising results of the analysis. In addition, the high levels of chloride and sulfate indicate possible evaporative concentration of residual ions in the sample, probably as a result of prolonged sample storage. Because of improper curation prior to analysis, the sample cannot be considered representative of the spring waters from which it was collected.

ANALYSES PUBLISHED BY THE INSTITUTO NACIONAL DE ESTADISTICA, GEOGRAFIA E INFORMATICA

A regional ground water hydrologic map published by the Instituto Nacional de Estadística, Geografía e Informática (1988b) denotes a spring at Hierve el Agua that was sampled (sample 31) in October, 1986, at the beginning of the dry season. The map indicates that water from this spring was used for recreation. Indeed, three small bathing and swimming pools were constructed over part of the prehistoric canal and terrace system by area residents in December, 1975. Water is diverted into these pools from Spring 1, the largest and most centrally located of the springs now active at Hierve el Agua (Fig. 4.12). Spring 3 and a diffuse area of seepage also discharge into the lowest and largest of the three pools. It is not clear which spring was the source of water sampled by the INEGI, and although it was likely

TABLE 4.3

MAJOR-ION HYDROCHEMISTRY OF THE SPRING WATERS AT HIERVE EL AGUA

Site No. (Sample No.)	Date (Time)	Undis-sociated B	Cations					Anions			Calculated TDS	Metered pH	Temp. W (Temp. A)	Effervescence
			Ca	Mg	K	Na	Sr	HCO$_3$	Cl	SO$_4$				
1 (5463c)	8-16-88 (10:50 am)	9.12	647.1	32.52	149.1	1,370	4.17	2,260	2,017	27	6,516.01	6.2	25.1 (27.7)	Steady, moderate, medium bubbles
1 (8900862)	4-26-89 (11:50 am)	22.07	770.5	45.25	201.1	1,606	nd	2,464	1,500	36	6,644.92	6.4	25.0 (25.5)	Variable, moderate to strong, medium bubbles with large bubbles every ≈2 sec
2 (5466c)	8-17-88 (9:45 am)	nd	293.8	32.36	124.9	1,420	nd	1,100	1,810	<5	<4,786.06	6.3-6.4	23.2 (26.5)	Variable, weak to strong, tiny to large bubbles
2 (8900863)	4-26-89 (12:20 pm)	22.56	754.6	45.87	207.5	1,586	nd	2,424	1,560	30	6,630.53	6.3-6.4	23.5 (nd)	Variable, weak with tiny bubbles for ≈20 seconds, strong with medium and large bubbles for 1 min, 20 sec
3 (5467c)	8-18-88 (9:50 am)	nd	681.87	22.57	121.3	1,412	nd	2,300	1,983	32	6,552.74	6.2	23.3 (23.0)	Steady, strong, medium bubbles
3 (8900864)	4-26-89 (12:30 pm)	21.31	752.6	44.05	208.6	1,550	nd	2,370	1,540	27	6,513.56	6.1-6.2	23.0 (nd)	Steady, strong, medium bubbles
9 (5470c)	8-17-88 (2:15 pm)	nd	167.3	31.25	113.6	1,157	nd	1,330	1,461	28	4,288.15	6.5	25.1 (31.1)	Sporadic, very weak, small bubbles
10 (5471c)	8-17-88 (3:00 pm)	nd	598.4	32.55	138.9	1,375	nd	2,240	1,879	27	6,290.85	6.3	23.1 (23.0)	Steady, moderate, small bubbles
13 (5472c)	8-18-88 (3:30 pm)	nd	641.3	21.40	125.3	1,497	nd	1,420	2,115	33	5,853.00	6.2	22.7 (28.8)	Steady, moderate, small bubbles

NOTES

nd = no data
Site No.: see Figures 3 and 8.
Sample No.: number assigned at Environmental Laboratory, Lower Colorado River Authority, Austin, Texas.
Date (Time): date and time of sample collection and stabilization, as well as measurement of pH and air and water temperatures.
Undissociated B: boron, primarily undissociated
Cations: Ca, calcium; Mg, magnesium; K, potassium; Na, sodium; Sr, strontium; all values in milligrams per liter (mg/l).
Anions: HCO_3, bicarbonate; Cl, chloride; SO_4, sulfate; all values in mg/l.
Calculated TDS: total dissolved solids in mg/l; sum of the concentrations of all ions (and B).
Metered pH: pH ,in standard units, measured at the spring port with a Cole-Parmer portable pH meter.
Temp. W (Temp. A): temperature of water (W) and air (A), in degrees Celsius (dC), measured at spring port with a submersible thermometer and an air thermometer, respectively
Effervescence: intensity of carbon dioxide effervescence (discharge of bubbles), using the following criteria: steady = little change in effervescence over 5 minutes (min); variable = clearly definable change over 5 min; sporadic = great change over 5 min; weak = isolated bubbles in water column; moderate = bubble streams in water column; strong = bubble streams deform water surface; bubble size = tiny, <2mm; small, 2-5mm; medium, 5-10 mm; large, >10mm.
All cation samples were filtered to remove particles≥0.45 microns and treated in the field with sufficient 1:1 nitric acid to reduce pH to <2. In the laboratory, undissociated boron and cations were analyzed according to EPA and ASTM standard procedures by ICP analysis within 30 days of sample collection.
All anion samples were filtered to remove particles 20.45 microns and were placed on ice within one minute of collection. Samples were kept on ice until delivered to the laboratory. In the laboratory, anions were analyzed according to EPA and ASTM standard procedures by Technicon Autoanalyzer (AAII) analysis as follows: bicarbonate within 14 days of sample collection; chloride and sulfate within 28 days of sample collection.

TABLE 4.4

MAJOR-ION HYDROCHEMISTRY OF THE WATERS IN POOLS LOCATED ALONG THE FLOW PATHS AT HIERVE EL AGUA

Site No. (Sample No.)	Date (Time)	Undissociated B	Cations					Anions			Calculated TDS	Metered pH	Temp. W (Temp. A)	Comments
			Ca	Mg	K	Na	Sr	HCO$_3$	Cl	SO$_4$				
6 (5468c)	8-16-88 (12:45 pm)	17.4	139.9	19.75	128.7	1,440	nd	840	2,121	42	4,748.75	7.7	27.6 (29.2)	Pool 6 is ≈51m below Spring 1 along channel
7 (5469c)	8-17-88 (10:30 am)	22.7	126.0	15.35	130.8	1,575	nd	600	2,293	52	4,814.85	8.7	29.2 (30.0)	Pool 7 is ≈65m below Pool 6 along a channeled flow path
8 (5464c)	8-17-88 (12:01 pm)	16.34	53.63	30.70	143.3	1,404	2.08	770	2,086	39	4,545.05	8.3	24.4 (31.6)	Pool 8 is ≈60m below lower swimming pool (Pool 11)
11 (5465c)	8-18-88 (9:55 am)	14.65	543.1	26.25	150.5	1,362	3.64	1,900	1,966	32	5,998.14	6.6-6.7	23.3 (28.6)	Lower swimming pool (Pool 11); recieves both spring and surface-water discharge.

NOTES
See Table 3.

IRRIGATION AT HIERVE EL AGUA 167

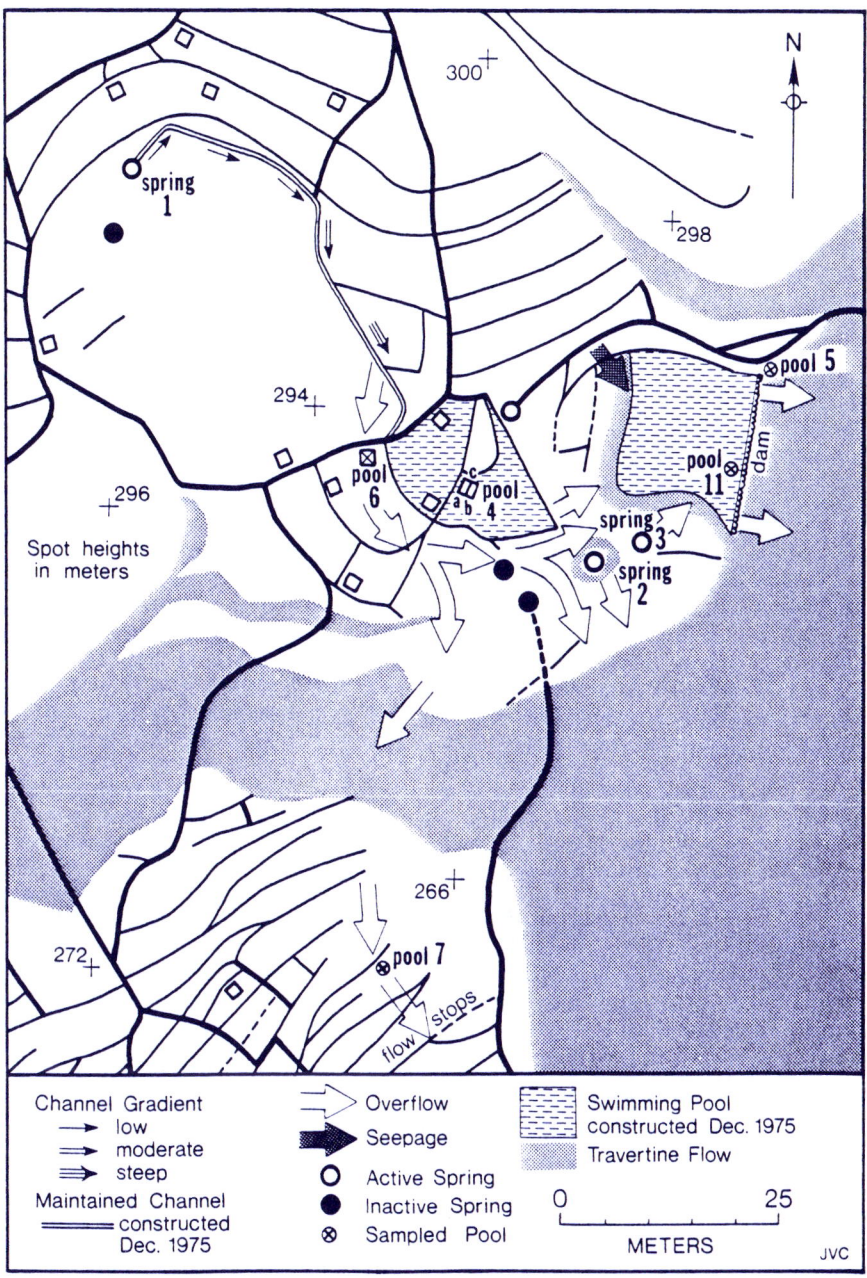

Figure 4.12. The upper central portion of Hierve el Agua, showing the sampling locations (see Tables 4.3, 4.4, 4.5, and Fig. 4.13) as well as the spring water flow paths.

Spring 1 or 3, samples may have been collected from pools below these springs. No information regarding sampling and analytical procedures was provided. Most of the analytical data for sample 31 are consistent with findings of the present study except that calcium and bicarbonate are very low, and chloride and pH are very high (Table 4.2). Clearly, this sample was thoroughly degassed by the time it was analyzed. As a consequence, pH became extremely elevated, while calcium and bicarbonate were severely depleted. Whether degassing and depletion occurred in the sample bottle during prolonged storage, or were the result of surface drainage and possible impoundment of spring discharge, is uncertain. Sample 11 of the present study was collected at the lowest swimming pool, but the hydrochemistry of this sample differs significantly from that of sample 31 of the INEGI study. Therefore, sample 31, like the samples discussed by Hewitt, Winter, and Peterson (1987), appears to have been stored improperly and at the time of the analysis was no longer representative of spring waters at Hierve el Agua.

Review

Three previously published analyses of spring waters from Hierve el Agua were evaluated. None of these data sets was found to be free of conspicuous defects and none accurately reflects the hydrochemistry of these unusual springs. The failing of these data is not the result of poor analytical practice. Laboratories involved in these studies appear to have performed the analyses competently, although some of the data were reported incorrectly or incompletely. Chief among the causes for rejecting these analytical results is the manner in which samples were collected and curated. In all three cases, the samples had destabilized prior to analysis because of inadequate preparation. Therefore, reliability of the results was impaired before the analytical process even began. Relying on two of these analyses, Hewitt, Winter, and Peterson (1987) attempted to address the suitability of local spring discharge for prehistoric irrigation as originally postulated by Neely (1967, 1970). Hewitt, Winter, and Peterson (1987) concluded that these waters were unsuitable because of their solute load. Instead, these authors suggested that the terraces and canals at this site were used for salt rendering. However, the quality and number of water analyses then available must be considered inadequate, and do not justify the far-reaching conclusions of Hewitt, Winter, and Peterson (1987) regarding the type and intensity of water use. Clearly, a program of controlled sampling, field observation, and laboratory analysis was needed to provide a sufficient hydrochemical data base. Only in this way could potential uses for spring waters at Hierve el Agua be assessed.

The Hydrochemistry of the Spring Waters

Ten new cation and anion pairs of water samples were collected in August, 1988, during the rainy season, and were submitted for analysis at the Environmental Laboratory of the Lower Colorado River Authority (LCRA), Austin, Texas. Three additional sample pairs were collected and submitted to the same laboratory in April, 1989, at the end of the dry season. Sampling localities are illustrated in Figure 4.12. For each sample pair, pH, water temperature, and air temperature were measured in the field. Techniques for sample collection, stabilization, storage, and analysis met or exceeded current standards set by the United States Environmental Protection Agency (EPA) and the American Society for Testing of Materials (ASTM) (see notes accompanying Table 4.3). The results of these analyses, as reported by the laboratory, are presented in Tables 4.3 and 4.4, along with sampling dates, field observations, and identification of the analytical methods.

Nine samples of spring water were analyzed during the present study (Table 4.3). Discharge from some of the springs drains a few tens of meters into pools in various parts of the site, where four additional water samples were collected (Table 4.4). Of the nine samples taken directly from springs, six were collected in August, 1988. Three of these springs, numbers 1, 2, and 3, were resampled in April, 1989. The dry season extends from November through April and the rainy season from May through October (García-Quintero 1951; Instituto Nacional . . . 1984a, b). Conditions at the times of sampling were typical of the seasonal rainfall pattern. Therefore, Springs 1, 2, and 3 were sampled both at the peak of the rainy season in August and at the end of the dry season in April.

Table 4.5 provides a direct comparison of three sets of seasonal hydrochemical data. In addition to wet and dry season figures for Springs 1, 2, and 3, results of analyses of wet season samples from Springs 9, 10, and 13 are included. Internal consistency within each of the three data sets is indicated by the percentage deviation of the numerical difference between the highest and lowest concentration of each ion (numerical range) from mean concentrations of the respective ions among the three analyses in that data set. Consistency among data sets is indicated by comparing both the mean concentrations of each ion and the percentages of deviation. Wet-season hydrochemistry of waters from Springs 1, 2, and 3 closely matches the chemistry of samples from Springs 9, 10, and 13, which were collected at the same time, but differs significantly from results of the repeat sampling of Springs 1, 2, and 3 during the dry season. This pattern provides a clear indication of strong seasonality in the hydrochemistry of Hierve el Agua spring waters.

Spring waters at Hierve el Agua are unusual: they are naturally carbonated and strongly effervescent, giving rise to the site's name. Geological evidence (mineral and fossil) indicates that water chemistry and relative flow rates in the prehistoric past did not differ significantly from conditions at present (see discussion by Winsborough). Perennial discharge, coupled with the site's unique hydrochemistry, undoubtedly posed special opportunities and problems for resource development. All of the springs are moderately saline, with TDS values ranging from 4288 to 6645 mg/l (see Hem 1970:219). Boron concentrations are very high, as much as 22.56 mg/l seasonally, but maximum sulfate concentration is only 36 mg/l. Sodium is the principal cation, composing 56% of total cations (in mg/l) during the dry season and 66–68% during the wet season. Calcium is the next most abundant cation, representing 35% of cations in the dry season, 24–26% during the wet season. Bicarbonate has the highest percentage of total anion concentration during the dry season, 61%, compared to the second most abundant anion, chloride, with 39%. In wet months, bicarbonate and chloride are codominant, with bicarbonate representing 47–49% of total anions and chloride representing 50–52%. Presumably, spring waters were most frequently used for irrigation during the dry season. Therefore, the dry season hydrochemistry of these springs may most closely approximate the initial composition of waters used for irrigation.

In December, 1975, area residents constructed three small pools for swimming and bathing at the site (Fig. 4.12). A narrow channel was cut into the travertine deposits to convey water to these pools from Spring 1, currently the most active of the springs. Some of the water overflows from the channel and spreads downslope across travertine-covered terraces. The channel is maintained regularly between Spring 1 and the swimming pools, and is similar in many ways to the canals constructed and used by prehistoric inhabitants of this area. This channel is thus a functioning analog of the ancient water-distribution system.

Because none of the relict canals carry spring water at present, the existence of the modern channel presents a unique opportunity to model hydrochemical behavior of the prehistoric irrigation network. Vigorous carbon dioxide effervescence at Spring 1 and other springs indicates that water chemistries are highly unstable because the amount of carbon dioxide in solution is the principal control on solute load. Therefore, water chemistry should change rapidly with distance from the point of discharge. By sampling the water at points along the modern channel, and along the unchanneled portion of the flow path farther downslope, we were able to approximate changing conditions along canals used for prehistoric irrigation. Of course, the analogy is imperfect, but it offers a reasonable basis for comparison. Clearly, construction of the modern channel was, for our purposes, a fortuitous turn of events.

Table 4.4 is a compilation of analyses of waters collected at four locations along various flow paths downslope from springs at Hierve el Agua. Of these, data concerning Pools 6 and 7 are the most useful, because these sampling points lie along a direct, continuous flow path and receive water from only one source, Spring 1. Therefore, differences in the chemistries of water samples from Spring 1, Pool 6, and Pool 7 may emulate changes that would have occurred through the canal distribution network. Pool 6 is a stone box, part of the ancient irrigation system, whereas Pool 7 is a small natural depression at a break in the travertine-covered slope (Fig. 4.12). Pools 6 and 7 are not the larger, artificial, swimming and bathing pools, although they, too, were sampled (results of these analyses are shown in Table 4.4 but, because of space limitations, are not otherwise treated in the present discussion).

Figure 4.13 illustrates variations in hydrochemistry along the flow path from Spring 1 to Pools 6 and 7 successively. Water reaches these intermittent pools via overflow from the modern channel. Samples were collected along this hydrologic gradient in August 1988, during the rainy season. As noted above, dry-season hydrochemistry may approach that of prehistoric irrigation waters more closely than does the composition of waters collected during the rainy season. Therefore, absolute numerical values shown in Figure 4.13 may be less significant than the nature of the trends. Perhaps the most striking trend is that of changes in the pH. Waters emerging from Spring 1 are slightly acidic, with a pH of 6.2. Approximately 51 m downslope from Spring 1 along the channel, water enters the stone box at Pool 6, where the pH is 7.7. A 1.5 unit increase in pH over so short a distance is remarkable. The pH scale is logarithmic, such that each pH unit represents a tenfold difference with respect to the next higher and lower units. A rise in pH indicates a reduction in hydrogen-ion activity and, in this case, a shift from acidic conditions to basic. This change has dramatic effects on solutes, particularly bicarbonate and calcium.

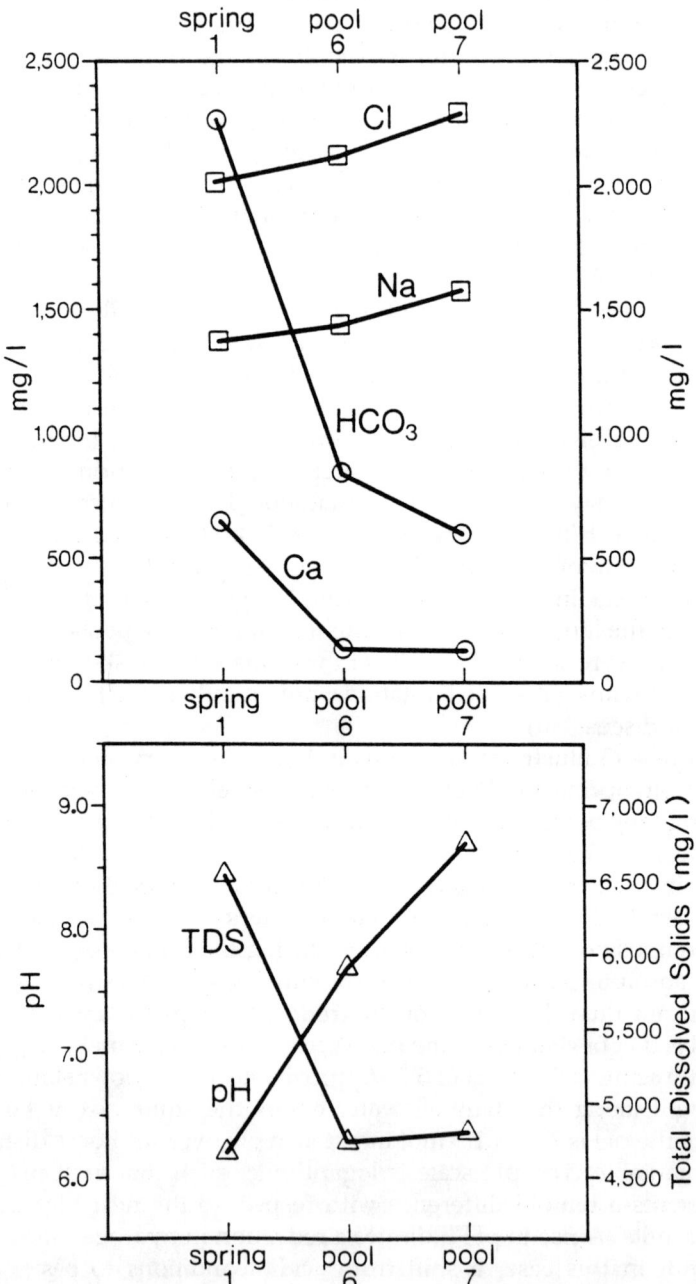

Figure 4.13. Changes in hydrochemistry along a direct flow path at Hierve el Agua.

Most of the springs at Hierve el Agua effervesce spontaneously and vigorously. They are naturally carbonated, a very unusual condition, particularly in nonthermal waters, requiring a rare combination of hydrologic and hydrochemical factors in an appropriate geologic setting. Deep underground, where hydrostatic pressures are substantially greater than atmospheric pressure, carbon dioxide is more easily held in solution. The carbonated ground waters of Hierve el Agua attain very high concentrations of dissolved CO_2, forming carbonic acid (H_2CO_3). Waters rich in carbonic acid (in solution) are extremely aggressive in terms of their capacity to dissolve limestone, which is primarily composed of calcium carbonate. This is the case at Hierve el Agua, where Lower Cretaceous limestones comprise the aquifer. Calcium is a major cation in local spring waters, and bicarbonate concentrations are anomalously high. When these waters emerge as springs into the relatively low-pressure surface environment, they are in fact supersaturated with calcite, the major precipitate of calcium and bicarbonate (which converts to carbonate during precipitation). Theoretical sources of carbon dioxide at depth include magma bodies. However, there is no indication of neovolcanism in this area and observed water temperatures are too low to suggest it. An alternate explanation is that the CO_2 derives from decomposing organic matter in the recharge area. This process can produce up to 100 times the partial pressure of CO_2 in the atmosphere, but is effective only under aerobic conditions existing above the water table (Wood 1985: Fig. 2). Therefore, aerobic decomposition of organic matter probably cannot solely account for the very high dissolved CO_2 content of ground water at Hierve el Agua. Instead, the most likely explanation is suggested by yet another anomaly in the spring water data, the very low concentration of sulfate (Tables 4.3, 4.5).

Sulfate is a major anion in many ground water systems of karst terranes. But under certain conditions, sulfate may be removed from a system by chemical reduction, forming sulfide. When this occurs, the reaction usually is mediated and accelerated by sulfate-reducing bacteria. Sulfate is reduced deep within the aquifer, in the anaerobic environment well below the water table. However, in addition to anaerobic conditions and sulfate, the bacteria require some form of organic matter as a nutrient. Crude oil and/or natural gas commonly serve this purpose. The reaction consumes organic matter and sulfate and produces bicarbonate, water, and sulfide (generally as hydrogen sulfide). Sulfide often reacts with metals and precipitates near the site of the reaction. Bicarbonate remains in solution and may become a major anion. But bicarbonate concentration is very dependent on pH and pressure. An increase in pH will cause the bicarbonate to react

TABLE 4.5

SEASONAL VARIATION OF THE SPRING-WATER
HYDROCHEMISTRY AT HIERVE EL AGUA

Ion	Wet season (Aug., 1988): Springs 9,10, and 13				Wet season (Aug., 1988): Springs 1, 2, and 3				Dry season (April, 1989): Springs 1,2 and 3			
	Analytical range (mg/l)	Numerical range (mg/l)	Arithmetic mean (mg/l)	Range/mean x 100%	Analytical range (mg/l)	Numerical range (mg/l)	Arithmetic mean (mg/l)	Range/mean x 100%	Analytical range (mg/l)	Numerical range (mg/l)	Arithmetic mean (mg/l)	Range/mean x 100%
Undissociated B	nd	nd	nd	nd	9.12 (1 analysis)	0.0	9.12	0.0	21.31-22.56	1.25	21.98	5.7
Cations												
Ca	167.3-641.3	474.0	469.0	101.1	293.8-681.87	388.07	540.92	71.7	752.6-770.5	17.9	974.9	1.8
Mg	21.40-32.55	11.15	28.4	39.3	22.57-32.52	9.95	29.15	34.1	44.05-45.87	1.02	45.06	2.3
K	113.6-138.9	25.3	125.9	20.1	121.3-149.1	27.8	131.8	21.1	201.1-208.6	7.5	205.73	3.6
Na	1,157-1,497	340.0	1,343	25.3	1,370-1,420	50	1,400.7	3.6	1,550-1,606	56.0	1,580.7	3.5
Sr	nd	nd	nd	nd	4.17 (1 analysis)	0.0	4.17	0.0	nd	nd	nd	nd
Anions												
HCO$_3$	1,330-2,240	810	1,663.3	48.7	1,100-2,300	1,200	1,886.7	63.6	2,370-2,464	94	2,419.3	3.9
Cl	1,461-2,115	654	1,818.3	36.0	1,810-2,017	207	1,936.7	10.7	1,500-1,560	60	1,533.3	3.9
SO$_4$	27-33	6	29.3	20.5	<5-32	>27	<21.3	>126.8	27-36	9	31	29.0
TDS	4,288.15-6,290.85	2,002.7	5,477.3	36.6	<4,786.06-6,552.74	>1,766.68	<5,951.6	>29.7	6,513.56-6,644.92	131.36	6,596.35	2.0
pH	6.2-6.5	0.3	6.3	4.8	6.2-6.4	0.2	6.25	3.2	6.1-6.4	0.3	6.3	4.8
Temp. W (dC)	22.7-25.1	2.4	23.6	10.2	23.2-25.1	1.9	23.9	7.9	23.0-25.5	2.5	24.5	10.2
Temp. A (dC)	23.0-31.1	8.1	27.6	29.3	23.0-27.7	4.7	25.7	18.3	25.5 (1 measurement)	0.0	25.5	0.0

NOTES
See Table 3.

with calcium in solution to form $CaCO_3$. A decrease in ambient pressure causes degassing of CO_2.

In the upper panel of Figure 4.13, HCO_3 and Ca concentrations drop abruptly between Spring 1 and Pool 6, in association with the increase in pH. Bicarbonate, for example, undergoes a 63% decrease, compared to a 78.4% decrease in calcium. Calcium leaves the solution as calcite, a mineral precipitate of calcium carbonate, which forms travertine. This process causes bicarbonate to convert to carbonate, which immediately leaves solution in the precipitate. Precipitation is an important process affecting water quality. The lower panel of Figure 4.13 shows that TDS actually declines, by 26%, between Spring 1 and Pool 7 in spite of a small amount of evaporative concentration. This decrease in TDS occurs because of the loss of substantial quantities of Ca and HCO_3.

In addition to the formation of carbonate minerals, much of the loss of bicarbonate results from release of carbon dioxide from solution, which simply effervesces and is lost to the atmosphere. The flow path is steep and rough and flow becomes turbulent, which produces significant pressure variations. Even small pressure reductions cause additional degassing and consequent loss of bicarbonate. However, the initial concentration of bicarbonate was so much greater than that of calcium that there is more than enough bicarbonate to combine with calcium ions, causing them to leave solution, even though the percentage decrease in calcium concentration is greater than that for bicarbonate. It is the degassing of these waters, as evolved carbon dioxide, that is most responsible for the increase in pH. For this reason, pH continues to rise steeply between Pools 6 and 7, some 55 m apart, while Ca and HCO_3 concentrations begin to level off. Additional precipitation of calcium carbonate would largely depend on further concentration of the ions in solution as water evaporates.

That some evaporation has occurred is indicated by the steady increase in sodium and chloride concentrations along this flow path. Concentrations of these ions in solution is far less pH dependent, and they are virtually unaffected by downslope transport of the spring water except as influenced by evaporation. These ions would precipitate primarily as sodium chloride (NaCl), the mineral halite, which is the principal component of table salt. However, no precipitation occurred, nor would any be expected. Sodium chloride is highly soluble in water at normal atmospheric temperatures and pressures, and its ions do not easily leave solution. A number of minerals would precipitate before halite, and concentrations of other major ions would have to be substantially lower than those seen at Pool 7 before the first crystal of halite would form. Even some of the Na and Cl ions may enter other precipitates first. This fact has important implications for potential water use at Hierve el Agua.

Potential Water Use: A Summary

From about 500 B.C. to A.D. 1350, perennial ground water resources at Hierve el Agua were developed intensively. A complex battery of canals conveyed water from artesian springs to hundreds of small terraces perhaps as much as half a kilometer downslope. Based on archaeological criteria, two competing hypotheses for water use at Hierve el Agua have been advanced previously. The hydrochemical analyses described above shed new light on these two hypotheses. Observations to date have eliminated some possibilities and suggested probable scenarios for resource management. It is clear that prehistoric occupants of Hierve el Agua were able to manipulate water chemistry in a surprisingly sophisticated manner.

SALT PRODUCTION

Hewitt, Winter, and Peterson (1987) argued that spring waters at Hierve el Agua were best suited for salt production, and that canals and other structures there were very similar to those at known salt-rendering sites in the Tehuacán Valley. It is intriguing to consider the possibility of local salt production, in that it would imply highly complex resource management by these peoples. Partial evaporation and mineral precipitation would be induced in the first pan to remove undesirable salts, then the supernatant fluid would be diverted into subsequent pans until the concentrated fluid primarily contained solutes of comestible salts, from which salt could be produced in purified form. For this purpose, the steep slopes at Hierve el Agua would be ideal, because gravity feed offers the only practical means of moving fluids from one pan to another. But under close scrutiny, this hypothesis must be firmly rejected. Only two points need be discussed here: (1) the accuracy of water analyses presented by Hewitt, Winter, and Peterson (1987), as well as the calculations by which they treated their data; and (2) the physical requirements for a system capable of producing appreciable quantities of comestible salt.

Credibility of the two chemical analyses published by Hewitt, Winter, and Peterson (1987) was evaluated in detail earlier in this article. The data were found to have numerous conspicuous errors, and neither analysis was deemed useful—although sample 84-793 did provide a general indication of the spring water chemistry, if we ignore depletion of Ca and HCO_3 and its effects. Because the data were faulty, all calculations based on them are likewise erroneous. Yet even if the data had been accurate, some of the methods used to assess them were inappropriate, or based on false premises.

In the worst of these compounded errors, the authors calculated potential salt yield from the analysis of sample 84-793, then developed an entire production scenario based on the expected yields (Hewitt, Winter, and Peterson 1987:808-13). They had assumed that evaporation of spring water would produce the same precipitates and the same proportional yields of specific salts that would result from complete evaporation of sea water. This assumption is false. Initial ionic strengths in the spring water are very different from those in sea water, and would produce different kinds and quantities of precipitates. Predicting the formation of precipitates from waters as complex as those at Hierve el Agua requires thermodynamic modeling and is not a trivial exercise.

Salt production from sea water is a common practice the world over (Fiedelman and Diamond 1969). But compared to the composition of sea water and many saline ground waters, concentrations of the ions of comestible salts in the spring waters of Hierve el Agua are relatively low. For example, in August, 1988, there were 1370 mg/l of sodium in solution at Spring 1 (Table 4.3). Evaporative concentration had raised sodium levels to 1575 mg/l, only a 15% increase, by the time the flow had reached Pool 7 (Table 4.4). In contrast, sodium concentration in sea water averages 10,500 mg/l, almost seven times that of Pool 7 (Hem 1970: Table 2). And even sea water is not saturated with respect to halite. Approximately 95% of sea water must be evaporated before halite will precipitate (Fiedelman and Diamond 1969: Fig. 1).

It is obvious that considerably greater evaporative concentration would have been necessary to produce salt from spring waters at Hierve el Agua, which are grossly undersaturated with respect to the chlorides of sodium, potassium, and magnesium, the chief comestible salts. This means that water would have to be shifted from pan to pan in order to remove impurities and adequately concentrate the desired brines. Hewitt, Winter, and Peterson (1987) alluded to this practice, but presented no evidence from this site to support it. They stated that spring waters would have been held in ponds in the upper part of the site to allow initial precipitation of calcium carbonate as a consequence of CO_2 degassing. Then, water would have been diverted to a pan, or series of pans, for additional evaporative concentration and removal of undesirable minerals. Finally, comestible salts would precipitate, leaving only a concentrated liquid residue or bittern to be discarded.

The most obvious criticism of this scenario is that few of the structures required to accomplish salt rendering are found at the site today except for the canals, which actually served other functions. Only two relatively small features that may be construed as holding ponds have been found near the springs, other than the swimming pools constructed in 1975. It is possible that larger holding ponds may have been dismantled or were buried beneath travertine, but there is in fact no evidence that they ever existed. Canals are present and do, in fact, lead to terraces, which Hewitt, Winter, and Peterson (1987) would call pans. However, none of the canals actually extend onto the terraces themselves, as they would have to if water were being added periodically. Likewise, there are no drains or other exit points through which concentrated fluids could have been diverted. Terraces consist of soil placed upslope from vertical retaining walls to create generally level benches on what was previously a steep bedrock (Pleistocene? travertine) slope. These soils are highly permeable, and do not allow water to stand. In addition, Neely found that weep holes had been deliberately placed in the terrace walls to further enhance drainage. For the purpose of salt rendering, drainage through the terraces would have been counterproductive. These terraces, therefore, bear absolutely no similarity to evaporative pans other than by their relative flatness and rectilinear shape.

There are no layered mineral accumulations on the terraces or in the soil profiles except occasionally for travertine, which has precipitated spontaneously at this site for many thousands of years and continues to form today, long after abandonment of the site. Salt rendering produces a large volume of waste minerals. One might imagine the enormous quantity of waste left on the "pans," or scraped into piles that would have built up over the some 1850 years that the site was occupied. Yet no trace of this material is found at the site today. Perhaps it was deliberately removed, but to where and what purpose? Was it leached away by rainfall? Some salts are highly soluble and might have dissolved in this manner. But dissolution would not have been instantaneous, and the less soluble minerals such as calcite, which forms travertine, would retain cavities or growth patterns in the diagnostic shapes of more soluble minerals. Such structures are common elsewhere, but have not been discovered at Hierve el Agua despite efforts to find them.

Irrigation

Hewitt, Winter, and Peterson (1987:809) concluded that spring waters at Hierve el Agua were unsuitable for irrigation "due to high salinity, sodium, residual sodium carbonate, and boron." They based their assumption on salt tolerances and water quality recommendations published by the Salinity Laboratory of the U.S. Department of Agriculture (Richards 1954). Although these recommendations provide a basis for comparison, Hewitt, Winter, and Peterson (1987) overstated their significance in the present context. The USDA recommendations were promulgated to address large-scale irrigation programs on high-yield commercial farms, where the volume of water is very large, and fields may be irrigated for many months every year. Typically, water is sprayed onto crops from above, thereby enhancing evaporation and coating the leaves. In many areas where such irrigation is practiced, precipitation may be sparse or unreliable throughout the year, not just during a specific growing season. Under these conditions, soil salinization is common and water quality may be a critical factor affecting irrigation potential.

Irrigation practices at Hierve el Agua would have been very different from those described above. Rainfall is sufficient during half the year, when perhaps only an occasional watering would have been necessary. During the dry season, water was most likely removed by hand from *pocitos* along the canals, and perhaps from stone boxes at more widely spaced intervals. Water was then poured onto the ground around individual plants. This simple practice would greatly reduce splash losses and avoid mineral buildup on leaves. Leaf damage ("salt burn") is one of the principal hazards associated with use of saline waters for irrigation (Maas 1986:19). Damage of this kind probably was prevented because water applications were small and restricted to the area immediately surrounding each plant. One may speculate that if prehistoric inhabitants of the site wished to further restrict evaporative concentration of solutes in the irrigation waters, they might have watered at night when evaporation rates are relatively low.

Hand watering in the manner described above is the most likely method of irrigation practiced at Hierve el Agua. Certainly, the level of technology required to construct and maintain the intricate network of canals and terraced fields was extremely sophisticated. But the actual process of irrigation was performed on a relatively modest scale. For example, there is no evidence to indicate that the terraces were ever deliberately flooded. Preservation of canals and related structures at Hierve el Agua is excellent. Canals surround the terraces, within reach of the farmers, yet there are no canal segments or sluice-like structures leading onto the terraces themselves. In modern large-scale irrigation, it is most efficient to apply large volumes of water a few times each growing season. Irrigation equipment must be brought to the fields and assembled, wells must be pumped, water is sprayed onto fields or run into furrows, and the equipment is disassembled, hauled away, and stored until the next use. At Hierve el Agua, the irrigation system was always in place and water, from continuously discharging springs, was always available. There would have been no reason to apply large volumes of water to fields at any one time.

Recent re-excavation of test pits originally described by Neely (1967a, 1970) has shown that terrace soils were highly permeable, allowing excellent drainage. All of this soil had been hauled to the terraces by the prehistoric farmers themselves, so it is likely that fill materials were selected specifically for their drainage properties. Furthermore, Neely found that terrace walls were equipped with weep holes to ensure thorough drainage. The combination of limited, localized water applications and good drainage would prevent saturation of the soil with mineralized water, effectively retarding salt buildup. Rains during the wet season might easily flush away small, seasonal mineral accumulations. Despite the steep slope, stepped terraces would capture most of the runoff, further enhancing flushing. Indeed, we found no evidence of mineralization at any of the re-excavated terraces except at two locations. At one locality, a highly indurated calcic deposit had formed when part of the upslope canal broke, allowing uncontrolled leakage of water onto the terrace. At the other location, low-density travertine capped the terrace. In both cases, the respective upslope canals had then been repaired and additional fill material had been placed on the terraces. Presumably, irrigation-assisted agriculture then continued normally.

Even those elaborate precautions for which there is physical evidence may not have been sufficient to prevent local mineralization over 1850 years of irrigation at Hierve el Agua. Periodically, remedial measures may have been required. Neely discovered that, occasionally, household garbage had been added to the terraced fields. Any organic matter included in the garbage would gradually decompose, yielding nutrients and carbon dioxide. The CO_2 would enter solution in the residual soil water, where it would tend to reduce pH and inhibit precipitation of carbonate minerals, particularly calcite. Neely also found that the height of some terrace walls had been raised once or twice during their period of use, and that new fill material had been added. In this way, the unsaturated thickness of terrace soils could be increased, allowing continued cultivation. Where walls were raised, the grade of the terrace canals had to be adjusted to the new wall height. Grade changes of this type necessitated complex modification of junctures where terrace canals (oriented approximately parallel to topographic contours) diverted part of the flow from the main supply canals (oriented perpendicular to topographic contours). The level of effort indicated by such careful maintenance attests to the importance of irrigation to year-round crop success.

Prehistoric farmers at Hierve el Agua may have differed from modern commercial crop managers in one particularly important respect: their expectations. Crop yields from the ancient terraced fields may have been low compared to current production standards. Yet, in the past, such yields may have been considered high by a population whose alternative was exclusive reliance on wet-season production. Certainly, crop yields were sufficient to justify construction and maintenance of an extensive and intricate canal system for augmenting dry-season agriculture.

In modern agricultural practice, saline waters do not necessarily have to kill crop plants to be considered problematic. Any reduction in productivity would be avoided. Over a wide range of salinities, crop yield decreases in inverse proportion to salinity, although even salt-sensitive plants maintain some production (Maas and Hoffman 1977). Sea water has been used experimentally for certain types of agriculture (Epstein and Norlyn 1977). The normal dissolved solids load in sea water is 35,000 parts per million, more than five times the maximum observed solute load (much of it calcium and bicarbonate) at Hierve el Agua.

The total dissolved solids concentrations of samples taken from springs and pools at Hierve el Agua does not exceed 6645 mg/l, a moderate salinity. Principal cations are sodium and calcium, principal anions are bicarbonate and chloride. For agriculture, concentrations of some of these major ions are higher than desirable. Yet waters of similar composition and TDS are routinely used for irrigation in the Pecos River Valley and adjacent areas of New Mexico and Texas (Hood, Mower, and Grogin 1960; Lee 1986; Moore and Hefner 1976) and in many other parts of the world as well (Grillot 1956; Hayward 1956).

In terms of the USDA recommendations, boron and sodium concentrations at Hierve el Agua are especially high. As noted above, boron absorption may be inhibited when there is ample calcium carbonate in solution, and most of the toxic effects of sodium result from accumulation in the soil column (Maas 1986:22). Therefore, high concentrations of boron and sodium in solution would not necessarily prevent use of these waters for irrigation. Such waters might be used seasonally, if applied in appropriate quantities on well-drained soils. In addition, ancient farming practices at Hierve el Agua appear to have been deliberately intended to retard mineralization and ensure good soil drainage. These measures included use of soil amendments and adoption of specialized methods for constructing and maintaining terraces and terrace walls. Figure 4.13 shows that the irrigation system itself was responsible for improving water quality to a degree, at least along short flow paths, because TDS values would have declined as gradual degassing caused calcite to precipitate in the canals. Although spring flow at Hierve el Agua was not ideal for irrigation, it represented an available perennial water resource in an area where tillage agriculture generally is restricted to the rainy season. Clearly, irrigation was the primary water use at Hierve el Agua.

Ongoing and Proposed Studies

Work to date has served to characterize the general hydrochemical environment of Hierve el Agua, and to explain apparent water quality anomalies that might have affected water use in the past. This effort will be extended in the near term to include hydrochemical modeling, whereby the relative solubilities of potential precipitates can be calculated under a variety of conditions. In this way, we may accurately predict the evolving composition of spring waters as they are conveyed along selected flow paths. Only then can we definitively state whether comestible salts might have been produced anywhere at this site, even in small quantities or incidental to irrigation. Other tasks will include integration of the results of the hydrochemical investigation with findings concerning travertine petrology and diatom micropaleontology. Additional coordinated studies will address the mineralogy of precipitates in various parts of the canal system, to determine whether there was deliberate segregation of waters of varying composition. Soil samples collected in April, 1989, will be analyzed in an effort to: (1) identify the source of fill materials in the terraces; (2) detect any trace of precipitates related to salt production; and (3) learn whether soils in one fill layer had become mineralized before another layer was added.

Future investigations may involve resampling of springs and the waters at various points along flow paths, in order detect short-term fluctuations of water chemistry. Such changes could mask fundamental hydrochemical properties that may have affected water use in the past. Detailed analyses of major ions, selected trace constituents, and perhaps certain isotopes would help to identify the source of spring waters and to better explain aspects of their unusual hydrochemistry. Possible long-term changes in water chemistry could be detected through serial analysis of the extremely thick deposits of laminated travertine, which cover the site and extend hundreds of meters farther up- and downslope. The analysis would focus on travertine mineralogy, ionic and isotopic geochemistry, and fossil diatoms.

Diatoms are especially sensitive indicators of paleo–water chemistry and can therefore provide indirect, surrogate hydrochemical data when the environmental tolerances of represented taxa are known. An added advantage of diatom studies is that diatoms are siliceous, and are therefore easily separated from the calcareous travertine. Most other major microfossils of this environment are themselves calcareous, and are separated from travertine only with great difficulty. In conjunction with the archaeological investigation, ongoing and proposed analyses of water chemistry, soils, travertine deposits, and fossils at Hierve el Agua will provide the basis for a detailed reconstruction of resource development. At present, the importance of this site in prehistory can be assessed only tentatively. However, results of this investigation should provide a model for studies of resource utilization throughout the region.

CONCLUSIONS

This chapter has addressed Hewitt, Winter, and Peterson's contention that Hierve el Agua was used for saltmaking rather than irrigation agriculture. We feel we have refuted their arguments through four different lines of evidence, as follows.

(1) A search of the literature shows that there are many places throughout the world where waters higher in salt content than Hierve el Agua's are successfully used for crop irrigation. (2) The diatoms from both modern and ancient contexts at the site do not suggest that the terraces would have been a highly saline environment. (3) A restudy of Hewitt, Winter and Peterson's (1987) water analyses, augmented by additional hydrochemical analyses undertaken on properly collected, recorded, and curated water samples, has in fact shown that their water analyses, and the interpretations based thereon, are not correct. Our computerized hydrochemical modeling and terrace soil analyses, currently in progress, are expected to further refute their salt production hypothesis. (4) Studies of site morphology, and the technology of the terrace and canal system at Hierve el Agua, provide an additional body of data that

counters the salt production hypothesis while bolstering evidence for irrigation agriculture as the prime function of the site.

Our conclusion is that Hierve el Agua represents a unique and adaptively designed system of terraces, canals, and related features to efficiently utilize perennial spring waters, which are a scarce and limited natural resource in this region, for irrigation agriculture conducted by means of an equally efficient and adaptively designed, but labor intensive, system of hand watering.

Additional details concerning the site, its architecture, artifact assemblages, agricultural techniques, and plants grown, as well as its impact on the greater Valley of Oaxaca will be presented in Neely's forthcoming monograph.

References Cited

American Petroleum Institute
1968   API Recommended Practice for Analysis of Oil-Field Waters, 2nd ed. American Petroleum Institute, Report 45. Dallas.

Andrews, Anthony P.
1983   Maya Salt Production and Trade. Tucson: The University of Arizona Press.

Apenes, Ola
1944   The primitive salt production of Lake Texcoco. Ethnos, 9(1):25–40.

Barrera, Tomás
1946   Guia Geología de Oaxaca. México, D.F.: Universidad Nacional Autónoma de México.

Charlton, Thomas H.
1969   Texcoco fabric-marked pottery, tlateles, and salt making. American Antiquity, 34(1):73–76.
1971   Texcoco fabric-marked pottery and saltmaking: A further note. American Antiquity, 36(2):217–18.

Crane, H. R., and J. B. Griffin
1970   University of Michigan radiocarbon dates XIII. Radiocarbon, 12(1):161–80. American Journal of Science. New Haven: Yale University.

Donkin, R. A.
1979   Agricultural Terracing in the Aboriginal New World. Viking Fund Publications in Anthropology, 56. Tucson: The University of Arizona Press.

Doolittle, William E.
1989   *Pocitos* and *registros*: Comments on water control features at Hierve el Agua, Oaxaca. American Antiquity, 54 (4):841–47.

Drennan, Robert D.
1976   Fábrica San José and Middle Formative society in the Valley of Oaxaca. Memoirs, 8. Museum of Anthropology, University of Michigan. Ann Arbor.
1983   Radiocarbon dates from the Oaxaca region. In: The Cloud People: Divergent Evolution of the Zapotec and Mixtec Civilizations, edited by Kent V. Flannery and Joyce Marcus, pp. 363–70. New York: Academic Press.

Epstein, E., and J. D. Norlyn
1977   Seawater-based crop production: A feasibility study. Science, 197:247–51.

Fiedelman, H. W., and H. W. Diamond
1969   Salt, solar. In: The Encyclopedia of Marine Resources, edited by F. E. Firth, pp. 594–97. New York: Van Nostrand Reinhold Company.

Flannery, Kent V.
1969   Correspondence addressed to Dr. William P. Hewitt, Utah Geological Survey, University of Utah, Salt Lake City, Utah. Dated January 15.

Flannery, Kent V. (ed.)
1970   Preliminary Archaeological Investigations in the Valley of Oaxaca, Mexico, 1966–1969. A report to The National Science Foundation and the Instituto Nacional de Antropología e Historia. Museum of Anthropology, University of Michigan. Ann Arbor.

Flannery, Kent V., M. J. Kirkby, A. V. T. Kirkby, and Aubrey W. Williams, Jr.
1967   Farming systems and political growth in ancient Oaxaca. Science, 158:445–54.

García-Quintero, Andres
1951   Hydrology of Mexico. American Society of Civil Engineers Transactions, 116:1197–17.

Grillot, Georges
1956   The biological and agricultural problems presented by plants tolerant of saline or brackish water and the employment of such water for irrigation. In: Utilization of Saline Water. Paris: UNESCO.

Hayward, H. E.
1956   Plant growth under saline conditions. In: Utilization of Saline Water. Paris: UNESCO.

Hem, J. D.
1970   Study and Interpretation of the Chemical Characteristics of Natural

Waters, 2nd ed. United States Department of the Interior, Geological Survey Water-Supply Paper 1473. Washington, D.C.

Hewitt, William P.
1968   Letter to the Editor of Science. October 11.

Hewitt, William P., Marcus C. Winter, and David A. Peterson
1987   Salt production at Hierve el Agua, Oaxaca. American Antiquity, 52(4):799–816.

Hood, J. W., R. W. Mower, and M. J. Grogin
1960   The Occurrence of Saline Ground Water Near Roswell, Chaves County, New Mexico. New Mexico State Engineer, Technical Report 17. Santa Fe, New Mexico.

Instituto Nacional de Estadística, Geografía e Informática
1984a Zaachila–Carta de Efectos Climáticos Regionales Mayo-Octubre. (Map.) Mexico, D.F.
1984b Zaachila–Carta de Efectos Climáticos Regionales Noviembre-Abril. (Map.) Mexico, D.F.
1988a San Pedro Quiatoni, Oaxaca. (Map.) Mexico, D.F.
1988b Zaachila–Carta Hidrológica de Aguas Subterráneas. (Map.) Mexico, D.F.

Kabata-Pendias, Alina, and Henryk Pendias
1984   Trace Elements in Soils and Plants. Boca Raton, Fla.: CRC Press, Inc.

Kirkby, Anne V. T.
1973   The Use of Land and Water Resources in the Past and Present Valley of Oaxaca, Mexico. Memoirs, 5. Museum of Anthropology, University of Michigan. Ann Arbor.

Lee, J. N.
1986   Shallow Ground-Water Conditions, Tom Green County, Texas. United States Department of the Interior, Geological Survey Water-Resources Investigations, Report 86–4177. Washington, D.C.

Lozano García, Raul
1946   Estudio Tecnológico de la Industria de la Sal en México. Instituto de Geología, Universidad Nacional Autónoma de México. México, D.F.

López Ramos, E.
1980   Geología de México, 2nd ed. Vols. 2 and 3. Published privately. México, D.F.

Maas, E. V.
1986   Salt tolerance of plants. Applied Agricultural Research, 1(1):12–26.

Maas, E. V., and G. J. Hoffman
1977   Crop salt tolerance-evaluation of existing data. In: Managing Saline Water for Irrigation, Texas Tech University, International Salinity Conference Proceedings, pp. 187–198. Lubbock.

MacNeish, Richard S., Frederick A. Peterson, and James A. Neely
1972   The archaeological reconnaissance. In: Excavations and Reconnaissance. The Prehistory of the Tehuacán Valley, vol. 5, edited by Richard S. MacNeish, pp. 341–495. Austin: The University of Texas Press for the R. S. Peabody Foundation.

Moore, J., and J. V. Hefner
1976   Irrigation with saline water in the Pecos Valley of West Texas. In: Managing Saline Water for Irrigation, Texas Tech University, International Salinity Conference Proceedings, pp. 339–44. Lubbock.

Morán Zenteno, D. J.
1984   Geología de la República Mexicana, 2nd ed. México, D.F.: Instituto Nacional de Estadística, Geografía e Informática.

Muhr, G. R.
1940   Available boron as affected by soil treatment. Soil Science Society of America Proceedings, 5:220–26.

Neely, James A.
1964   Unpublished field notes, drawings, maps and photographs from the Tehuacán Archaeological Reconnaissance and subsequent visits to the Tehuacán Valley and environs.
1966, 1970, 1971
       Unpublished field notes, drawings, maps, and photographs from the Hierve el Agua Project.
1967a Organización hidráulica y sistemas de irrigación prehistóricos en el Valle de Oaxaca. Instituto Nacional de Antropología e Historia, Boletín 27:15–17. México, D.F.
1967b Formative, Classic, and PostClassic Water Control and Irrigation Systems in the Valley of Oaxaca. Paper presented at the 32nd Annual Meeting of the Society for American Archaeology. Ann Arbor, Michigan.
1969   Correspondence addressed to William P. Hewitt. Dated June 11.
1970   Terrace and water control systems in the Valley of Oaxaca region: A preliminary report. In: Preliminary Archaeological Investigations in the Valley of Oaxaca, Mexico, 1966–1969, edited by Kent V. Flannery, pp. 83–87. A report to The National Science Foundation and the Instituto Nacional de Antropología e Historia de México. Museum of Anthropology, University of Michigan. Ann Arbor.
1972   Prehistoric Domestic Water Supplies and Irrigation Systems at Monte Albán, Oaxaca, Mexico. Paper presented at the 37th Annual Meeting of the Society for American Archaeology. Miami.
in press Paleoecología y Desarrollo Cultural de Hierve el Agua: Re-estudio de un sitio prehispánico en Oaxaca, Mexico. Boletín Semestral del Instituto Nacional de Antropología e Historia, No. 1. Mexico, D.F.
n.d.   Hierve el Agua: A Prehispanic Irrigation Agriculture Site in Oaxaca, Mexico. Manuscript.

Noguera, Eduardo
1975 Identificación de una saladera. Anales de Antropología, 12:117–51. México, D.F.: Universidad Nacional Autónoma de México.

O'Brien, M. J., R. D. Mason, D. E. Lewarch, and J. A. Neely
1982 A Late Formative Irrigation Settlement Below Monte Albán: Survey and Excavation on the Xoxocotlán Piedmont, Oaxaca, Mexico. Austin: Institute of Latin American Studies, University of Texas.

Orlandini, Richard J.
1967 A Formative Well from the Valley of Oaxaca. Paper presented at 32nd Annual Meeting of the Society for American Archaeology. Ann Arbor.

Parsons, Jeffrey R.
1971 Prehistoric Settlement Patterns in the Texcoco Region, Mexico. Memoirs, 3. Museum of Anthropology, University of Michigan. Ann Arbor.

Peterson, David A.
1976 Ancient Commerce. Ph.D dissertation. State University of New York, Binghamton.

Peterson, David A., Marcus C. Winter, and William P. Hewitt
1989 Reply to Doolittle. American Antiquity, 54(4):847–50.

Richards, L. A. (ed.)
1954 Diagnosis and Improvement of Saline and Alkali Soils. United States Department of Agriculture, Salinity Laboratory, Agricultural Handbook 60. Washington, D.C.

Scofield, C. S.
1936 The salinity of irrigation water. Smithsonian Institution Annual Report, 1935, pp. 275–87. Washington, D.C.

Sisson, Edward B.
1973 First Annual Report of the Coxcatlán Project. Robert S. Peabody Foundation for Archaeology. Andover, Massachusetts: Phillips Academy.

Stewart, G. R., and M. Donnelly
1943 Soil and water economy in the Pueblo South West. Scientific Monthly, 56:31–44, 134–44.

Vivo Escoto, J. A.
1964 Weather and climate of Mexico and Central America. In: Handbook of Middle American Indians, Vol. 1: Natural Environment and Early Cultures, edited by R. C. West, pp. 187–215. Austin: University of Texas Press.

Wentworth, C. K.
1922   A scale of grade and class terms for clastic sediments. Journal of Geology, 30:377–92.

White, D. E., J. D. Hem, and G. A. Waring
1963   Chemical composition of subsurface waters. In: Data of Geochemistry, 6th ed., edited by M. Fleischer, pp. F1-F67. United States Department of the Interior, Geological Survey Professional Paper 440-F. Washington, D.C.

Wilken, Gene C.
1969   Drained-field agriculture: An intensive farming system in Tlaxcala, Mexico. Geographical Review, 59:215–41.
1987   Good Farmers: Traditional Agricultural Resource Management in Mexico and Central America. Berkeley and Los Angeles: The University of California Press.

Winter, Marcus C.
1989   Oaxaca: The Archaeological Record. Editorial Trivia Mexicana, S.A. de C.V. Mexico, D.F.

Wood, W. W.
1985   Origin of caves and other solution openings in the unsaturated (vadose) zone of carbonate rocks—A model of CO_2 generation. Geology, 13 (11):822–24.

Woodbury, Richard B., and James A. Neely
1972   Water control systems of the Tehuacán Valley. In "Chronology and Irrigation" in The Prehistory of the Tehuacán Valley, vol. 4, edited by Richard S. MacNeish, pp. 81-153. Austin: The University of Texas Press for the R. S. Peabody Foundation.

Yermiyaho, U., R. Keren, and Y. Chen
1988   Boron sorption on composted organic matter. Soil Science Society of America Journal, 52.

Zárate, José C.
1917   Las Salinas de México y la Industria de la Sal Común. Anales del Instituto Geológico de México, vol. 1, no. 2. México, D.F.

5

SCIENCE AND SCIENCE FICTION IN POSTCLASSIC OAXACA
Or "Yes, Virginia, There is a Monte Albán IV"

Joyce Marcus and Kent V. Flannery,
University of Michigan

One of the most interesting episodes in Oaxaca prehistory is the one described in *The Cloud People* in the chapter entitled "The Changing Politics of A.D. 600–900" (Flannery and Marcus 1983). With the gradual decline of Monte Albán after A.D. 600, valley-floor centers like Zaachila, Cuilapan, Macuilxochitl, Lambityeco, Mitla, and Matatlán, as well as hilltop centers like Jalieza increased in importance. Stone monuments of a previously unknown type, called "genealogical registers" by Marcus (1983), indicate a concern with recording royal marriages and establishing the genealogical right to rule. Thus began a period of political balkanization during which the Zapotec were ruled not by one central capital, but by numerous competing centers (Marcus 1989:205–6).

Unfortunately, the outlines of this important period remain sketchy, for the simplest and most basic of reasons. The periods involved are Monte Albán IIIb (roughly A.D. 500–750) and Monte Albán IV (roughly A.D. 750–950); and unfortunately, the ceramics of Periods IIIb and IV are often difficult to distinguish. As we will see in the section below, the causes for this difficulty can be traced back to a decision made by Alfonso Caso in the early 1930s.

THE ORIGINS OF THE IIIB–IV CONFUSION

Alfonso Caso was the closest thing to a Renaissance man that Oaxaca has ever had. Given his monumental excavations at Monte Albán, his work at Monte Negro, his pioneering work on Zapotec hieroglyphs, and his analysis of the Mixtec codices, he may have been the most brilliant prehistorian ever to work in Oaxaca. One of his very few mistakes was his decision to try to make the break between Periods IIIb and IV correspond to an event, namely, the supposed "abandonment" of Monte Albán.

As nearly as we can tell from early articles and accounts, what happened was as follows. As Caso began to work his way through the architectural stratigraphy of the Main Plaza at Monte Albán, he found evidence for a succession of different pottery complexes. The earliest of these, found deep within the North Platform, he called Monte Albán I (Caso 1935: Fig. 50). So rich were these deposits that when Caso's student, Ignacio Bernal, decided to study them for his Master's thesis, he found enough stylistic change within the sequence to divide Period I into subphases Ia, Ib, and Ic (Bernal 1946). Monte Albán Ia ("Early I") and Ic ("Late I") have subsequently proven easy to identify, even on survey; Monte Albán Ib, which may simply represent the transition between the two, has not.

Stratigraphically above Period I remains in the Main Plaza came Monte Albán II, a ceramic complex notable for the presence of waxy red and waxy orange wares, whose cultural affiliations were clearly with Chiapas and the Maya area. Mammiform feet and rim flanges tied much of this pottery to the so-called "Q complex" or "Protoclassic" of southern Mexico, but there were also red wares and black wares with excised step-fret motifs; stuccoed vessels; and red *xicalcoliuhquis* painted on a cream background (Caso 1935: Fig. 52; Caso, Bernal, and Acosta 1967:61–77). This phase, in turn, was followed by the very distinctive grays and oranges of a ceramic complex contemporaneous with Teotihuacán, one Caso originally called Monte Albán III (Caso 1935: Figs. 53–54).

In the rubble above the abandoned structures of this Period III, Caso found a different complex of pottery, which he originally called Period IV (Caso 1935: Fig. 55). This was a much drabber ceramic assemblage, dominated by large crude bowls of the type we now know as G-35, but with a whole range of additional shapes like those shown in Figures 317 through 375 of Caso, Bernal, and Acosta (1967). Although there were effigy bat claw vessels, and incense burners or braziers studded with the kind of low spikes sometimes seen on dog collars, Period IV pottery was aesthetically unexciting compared to the more flamboyant ceramics of earlier periods. Because of the context in which he first found it, Caso assumed that Period IV pottery postdated the fall of Monte Albán.

Finally, near the surface and in occasional tombs, caches, and offerings, Caso found the obviously Postclassic complex he called Monte Albán V (Caso 1935: Fig. 56).

As Caso continued work at Monte Albán, however, he began to discover room repairs and new floors constructed during the period he had called "IV." Obviously, therefore, Monte Albán had not been "abandoned" as early as he had thought. In fact, today we know that although Monte Albán declined in size and importance, it was never fully abandoned. Even in the area of the Main Plaza, renovations and repairs continued for centuries; for example, the final construction of Building B on the North Platform dates to Monte Albán V (Bernal 1985:68).

At that moment, Caso could have made a decision that would have saved future generations of archaeologists a lot of grief. He could have said, "I now believe that I have a phase, called Monte Albán IV, which *brackets* the decline of Monte Albán. During the earlier part of the phase, major buildings were still being erected on the Main Plaza. Perhaps midway through the phase, major construction in the Main Plaza ended. During the latter part of the phase, offerings continued to be made in the rubble of the now largely abandoned buildings, some repairs were carried out, and a group of occupants evidently continued to live somewhere in the vicinity."

Instead, Caso made a different decision. He decided to rename his original Period III, calling it IIIa; and he decided to use the term IIIb for that part of the original "Period IV" sample which he felt predated the abandonment of the Main Plaza. Perhaps he felt that the shared use of the Roman numeral III would emphasize the notion that his new IIIa and IIIb both antedated the fall of Monte Albán, whereas his new Period IV postdated that fall. The problem was that, by so doing, he had made a phase division on the basis of an *event* (the supposed abandonment of Monte Albán), rather than on the basis of a striking change in the ceramic complex. This decision has led to confusion for decades.

The result of this division of one long ceramic phase into two different-sounding periods has been unfortunate. Caso's decision to create a "IIIb" out of what should simply have been the first half of Period IV has forced subsequent generations of Oaxaca archaeologists to search desperately for ways of telling IIIb and IV apart.

When the time came for Caso, Bernal, and Acosta (1967) to write the Monte Albán pottery volume, they found such a division so difficult that they simply gave up and assigned those chapters to "Monte Albán IIIb-IV". However, they also realized that one reason the separation was so difficult was that, while their collection of IIIb ceramics was large, their sample of IV was inadequate precisely because the Main Plaza was largely unoccupied at that time. They therefore suggested that the only way to define Monte Albán IV properly would be by future excavation at sites on the valley floor which had been occupied after the decline of Monte Albán. Toward this end, Bernal set out to excavate sites like San Luis Beltrán; later, John Paddock excavated an Early Period IV complex at Lambityeco (Paddock 1983). In the meantime, Jorge Acosta—who had continued to excavate at Monte Albán after Caso's work had ended—found a Period IV enclave on the north slope of that site (Acosta 1965).

This new work, although still far from widely published, made progress toward establishing better horizon markers for Monte Albán IV. First of all, the small enclave of Period IV occupation found by Acosta on the north slope of Monte Albán produced almost 40 tombs, many of whose vessels were of types not known from IIIb. For example, Acosta found specimens of Tohil Plumbate, a ware known to have been produced in Guatemala during the period A.D. 900-1200. He also found Y Fine Orange, a ware known to have been produced in Tabasco, which dates to A.D. 800-1000 at many Maya sites (among them Seibal, Chichén Itzá, and Altar de Sacrificios). Little by little, researchers also began to find local vessel types which could be assigned to Period IV, such as the bat claw vessel illustrated by Paddock (1966: Fig. 276) and some of the aforementioned spiked braziers.

Next, Paddock's work at Lambityeco in the 1960s suggested that certain vessels made in K11 and A7 wares were more common in Period IV than in IIIb. During Paddock's work at Lambityeco, he assigned Stephen Kowalewski, then a graduate student, the task of working on finer-grained ways of separating IIIb and IV. Kowalewski soon identified Puuc Slate (a northern Yucatec trade ware known to date from A.D. 800-1100) in the Early IV remains at Lambityeco. These early Period IV deposits also produced Balancán (or Z) Fine Orange, a Tabasco trade ware, known to date to A.D. 800-1000. Kowalewski subsequently went on to be one of the two or three people most confident about distinguishing between IIIb and IV ceramics. In addition, he has identified regional variation in IIIb and IV pottery, such as variants of G-35 bowls from the Central Valley of Oaxaca which are stylistically distinct from the G-35s at both Monte Albán and Lambityeco (Kowalewski 1983:190).

More recently, the settlement pattern surveys of the Valley of Oaxaca undertaken by Kowalewski, Feinman, Finsten, Blanton, and Nicholas during 1974-1980 have provided an opportunity to refine the diagnostics of Periods IIIb and IV still further. What the Settlement Pattern Project staff decided to do was to use (1) large sherd collections from Cerro de Atzompa (a pure IIIb subdivision of Monte Albán) as their type collection for IIIb, and (2) the large sherd collections from Lambityeco, a site already mentioned, as their type collection for Period IV.

Kowalewski et al. (1989:251) summarize the Atzompa IIIb collections as follows:

> Pastes are *gris-cremosa* and *gris*. . . . G-35 bowls, which make up the bulk of assemblages, are conical *cajetes* rather than the flaring-wall forms more typical of IIIA. "Reinforced" rims and "incipient annular bases" are common. Hollow and nubbin supports are sometimes present, as is the pattern burnished interior base. The next most common form is the conical necked *olla* equivalent to the G-35. Finer burnished bowls also occur, and they also have straight, outleaned walls. Other forms include G-35-like tall cylindrical vessels, *apaxtlis, molcajetes, gris-cremosa comales*, thin gray *ollas*, hollow-handle *sahumadores*, and mold-made, usually gray, figurines and urns.
>   Notably absent from the IIIB assemblages at Atzompa are . . . the polished black, Z Fine Orange, and Puuc Slate wares found at Lambityeco. Hemispherical bowls are uncommon . . .

These same authors go on to describe the Early Period IV assemblage from Lambityeco as follows (Kowalewski et al. 1989:251–52):

> Pastes are *gris*, with some *café* . . . G-35s still dominate assemblages. Reinforced rims and the *base incipiente* are less frequent. Hollow and nubbin supports, and stick-polished decoration are still used. Thick and thin gray *ollas* are common, as are hollow-handled *sahumadores*. Hemispherical bowls are more frequent than the thin, outleaned wall forms of Atzompa, barrel shapes are more frequent, and in general there is a greater variety of incurving, closed, and subspherical forms. G-3s tend to be more similar to the G-3Ms of Period V than in earlier periods. . . . Z Fine Orange, a distinctive polished black, and Puuc Slate occur in very small quantities. Figurines are small, flat-backed, mold-made, and tend to be orange rather than gray. There are many spiked braziers. An appliqué hill glyph or bifid tongue occurs more frequently in IV than in IIIB.

Thus, the differences between IIIb and IV are about what one would expect to find between the early and late subphases of one long phase. They do exist, but they are not as striking, let us say, as the differences between IIIa and IIIb, or between IV and V. In most cases, the differences between IIIb and IV involve *percentages* or *proportions* of one type to another, not simple presence or absence.

The Oaxaca Settlement Pattern Project found some 1073 sites of Monte Albán IIIb and IV; of these, 629 sites were assigned to IIIb, and 444 to IV. The distribution of these sites has sparked debate, however, since most localities assigned to IIIb occur in the Etla and Central valleys, while most localities assigned to IV occur in the Tlacolula and Zaachila-Zimatlán valleys. This suggests that there are *regional*, as well as *chronological*, differences involved; sites receiving their pottery from centers near the Atzompa-Cacaotepec clay sources may have had assemblages different from those at sites which received their ceramics from clay sources in the Tlacolula–San Marcos Tlapazola area, for example.

Kowalewski et al. (1989:252) suggest that readers who are made nervous by such regional differences can, if they choose, combine the Period IIIb sites (op. cit.: Map 6) and the Period IV sites (op. cit.: Map 7) into a single map, calling it "Monte Albán IIIb-IV." However, they warn that such a combination of sites would also mask some of the best chronological differences between IIIb and IV. For example, Z Fine Orange is absent at sites assigned to IIIb, even when they are large elite centers; it is present at sites assigned to IV, even in non-elite contexts.

Note also that the mere presence of Z Fine Orange at Monte Albán cannot be taken to mean that it was present in IIIb, since there were an estimated 4062 persons still living at Monte Albán in Period IV; these occupants were using a ceramic complex like that of Lambityeco (Kowalewski et al. 1989: Table 9.6). As we have indicated, the erroneous assumption that Monte Albán was "abandoned" at the end of IIIb has led to the needless rejection of perfectly good horizon markers for Period IV, slowing refinement of the sequence.

... AND MORE CONFUSION

Despite the gradual working out of the cultural sequence in the Valley of Oaxaca, described in the pages above, it is evident that some people remain very confused about the Classic-Postclassic transition. One of the most confused is Winter, who in a recent Dumbarton Oaks volume on the "Epiclassic" (Winter 1989) has set progress back several decades.

Not a little bewildered about the relationship between IIIb and IV, Winter proposes collapsing the two into a single, short phase, which he wants to end by A.D. 750. One source of his confusion seems to be the already-mentioned notion that Monte Albán was "abandoned" at the end of the Classic; he also seems to be puzzled as to why we don't have more radiocarbon dates for the period A.D. 750–1250.

To account for this shortage of dates, Winter further proposes that the entire Valley of Oaxaca was abandoned for 500 years between A.D. 750 and 1250. This would mean that an estimated 69,000 Zapotec Indians just got up and left. This was probably the largest mass exodus from a fertile farming area since Moses led the Hebrew people out of the Nile delta.

Perhaps the most astonishing part of Winter's paper, however, is his suggestion that although everyone left the Valley of Oaxaca, Zapotec culture somehow managed to persist in the area for 500 years after they were gone. Indeed, such is Winter's ambiguity that he alternates in his article between suggesting that the valley was abandoned, and arguing that the archaeological record shows strong continuity in architecture and artifacts from Monte Albán IIIb to V.

Gee! All through graduate school, our anthropology professors tried to convince us that culture could not exist apart from its human bearers. Now, in one bold stroke, Winter has suggested that Zapotec culture was so powerful that it could persist in a valley for half a millennium, receiving shipments of Tohil Plumbate, while all its bearers had left. And they say there aren't any new paradigms left!

As if Winter's own uncertainty weren't enough, his article has also confused William T. Sanders, who was asked to comment on the papers in the Dumbarton Oaks volume. "Monte Alban IIIa has always been difficult to separate from IIIb because Caso, Bernal, and Acosta's original definition was based upon grave lots and the presence of numerically rare Teotihuacan ceramic traits" Sanders asserts; "now it appears that IIIb cannot be distinguished from IV, and that we have a large chronological gap between IV and VI" (Sanders 1989:216).

We hesitate to blame Sanders too much for this statement, since we know that a lot of his disinformation is coming from Winter. We don't know where he got his ideas about Period IIIa, but they simply aren't true. Period IIIa is one of the most distinctive in the entire sequence; it has *never* been difficult to distinguish IIIa from IIIb, or from II, or from any other period. Nor is it known only from grave lots; Bernal wrote an entire doctoral dissertation on IIIa ceramics (Bernal 1949), and as if his study were not enough, there are tons of IIIa pottery available from other sites around the valley. One look at Figures 263 through 275 in Caso, Bernal, and Acosta (1967) or Figures 101 through 111 in Paddock (1966) should make it clear that, in addition to the cylindrical tripods and orange *floreros* which link IIIa to Teotihuacán, there are many other highly diagnostic IIIa types. For example, when walking over the surface of a site such as Santa Inés Yatzeche, one is almost overwhelmed by the G-23 gray bowls with "pseudo-glyphs" in cartouches (Fig. 5.1), not to mention the varieties of double bridgespout *ollas*.

Finally, we have to assume that Sanders was especially confused when he referred to "Monte Albán VI." If there were such a period, we suppose that it would start about A.D. 1530 and run to the time of Benito Juárez.

Figure 5.1. Example of a G-23 gray bowl with "pseudo-glyphs" in a cartouche, diagnostic of Monte Albán IIIa. (The two smaller vessels inside are attached to the floor of the bowl.)

We enjoy debating Sanders on a theoretical level, and although we know we will never wean him away from his environmental determinism, and he will never wean us away from our ethnohistorically based sociopolitical framework, we are willing to continue debating him until we all topple over. However, the debate will be fruitless unless we are all arguing about the same *facts*. We understand Sanders' temptation to follow the old Bedouin proverb, "The enemy of my enemy is my friend," but it makes for strange bedfellows. No one as smart as Sanders should ever be so eager for ammunition that he borrows wet gunpowder from a loose cannon.

Ironically, had Winter been less hasty in his criticism, Kowalewski might have been willing to teach him how to tell IIIb and IV apart for free; now, he'll probably have to pay. That shouldn't be too much of a burden, however, since we have recommended his Dumbarton Oaks paper for the 1989 Ray Bradbury Award for Science Fiction, and that carries a handsome stipend.

THE LATE PREHISTORIC SEQUENCE IN OAXACA: A SUMMARY

Let us end by summarizing the late prehistoric sequence in Oaxaca as we currently see it. We will begin with Monte Albán IIIa, a period whose clear diagnostics include vessels with crossties to Early Classic Teotihuacán. Surprising as it seems, we do not as yet have a single radiocarbon date for Monte Albán IIIa from the Valley of Oaxaca proper. (Does this mean that Winter will also propose that the Valley of Oaxaca was abandoned during IIIa? We hope not.) Fortunately, we have three dates from Hierve el Agua in the mountains east of Mitla, spanning the period from A.D. 350 to A.D. 500 (Neely, Caran, and Winsborough, Chapter 4).

The transition from IIIa to IIIb is thought to have occurred some time between A.D. 500 and 600, with Monte Albán IIIb running until 750 or even later. There are quite a few dates for the transition from IIIb to IV, and most are within one standard deviation of the expected date. Six dates from Mound 195 at Lambityeco, believed by Paddock to date "Early IV" material (material which, in fact, could be as early as Transition IIIb-IV), run from A.D. 640 to 755 (Drennan 1983). Adding one standard deviation would put these dates between A.D. 740 and 855, which brackets our expected date for the transition from IIIb to IV. Two dates from Early IV—or Transition IIIb-IV—from Guilá Naquitz Cave are A.D. 620 and 740. Adding one standard deviation would make these dates A.D. 750 and 780, once again near our expected transition. However, even an earlier transition would not bother us.

Now let us turn to Monte Albán IV, a period whose diagnostic traits include Z Fine Orange (A.D. 750–1000), Y Fine Orange (A.D. 800–1000), Puuc Slate (A.D. 800–1000), and Tohil Plumbate (A.D. 900–1200). Though Winter (1989) seems to believe that we have no C-14 assays to go along with these well-dated Maya trade wares, he either forgot, or doesn't know about the Monte Albán IV date of A.D. 940 ± 100 from Hierve el Agua (M-2105), and the date of A.D. 1055 ± 95 for Building 195-sub at Lambityeco (GX-1481). Of course, it would be nice if we had fifty dates for Monte Albán IV; perhaps some day we will.

Let us turn next to Monte Albán V. We strongly believe, on the basis of everything we have seen over the last fifteen years, that Monte Albán V begins much earlier than most people have thought. We also believe that, as it now stands, it is a period so long that it needs to be divided by future researchers.

Ignacio Bernal (personal communication) has for many years predicted that it will one day be possible to divide Monte Albán V into three phases, minimally defined as follows:

1. An Early V, growing out of Period IV, which contains the usual G3M gray ware, along with imported Yanhuitlán Red-on-cream from the Mixteca, but *lacks* polychrome.

2. A Middle V, in which polychromes of Mixteca-Puebla style (Fig. 5.2) join the already-present G3M and Yanhuitlán Red-on-cream, but which *lacks* metal.

Figure 5.2. Examples of tripod polychrome bowls, diagnostic of Monte Albán V.

3. A Late V, extending into the sixteenth century, which has all the elements of Middle V, plus metal (copper, silver, gold).

While such a division remains to be demonstrated, we tend to agree with Bernal. For one thing, our own excavations at San Sebastián Abasolo in the Tlacolula Valley in 1969 caught the transition from Monte Albán IV into something like Bernal's proposed "Early V." Our levels A5-A1 at Abasolo showed the G-35s of Period IV gradually giving way to G3Ms and occasional Yanhuitlán Red-on-cream, with polychrome appearing only later. (Needless to say, having observed this *in situ* evolution of V out of IV, we could hardly be expected to believe that the valley was abandoned during IV.)

Bernal himself found a similar transition at Cuilapan de Guerrero in the Zaachila Valley. In his excavations in the patio east of Mound II at Cuilapan, Bernal passed through two stucco floors whose pottery dated to the end of Monte Albán IV; as in the case of our work at Abasolo, this Late Period IV assemblage contained both the G-35 bowls typical of IIIb-IV, and some of the fine gray bowls and jars which were to become dominant in Monte Albán V (Bernal 1958). Since this material was sealed between floors (and since Monte Albán V was rare to absent in Bernal's excavations at Cuilapan), there was no threat of mixture there. Rather, we have a second case of Monte Albán V developing *in situ* out of IV.

A third place where the Monte Albán IV-V transition can be found is within Mound 5-W at Yagul, where it occurred above the level of Tomb 10 and below the level of Tombs 11 and 13 (see Drennan 1983:367).

Still a fourth transition could probably be found with a little patience at Mitla, where our 1967 riverbank excavations at Balah Bisyé, Balah Gui Wap, and Balah Gubesh (unfortunately still unpublished) produced remains of IIIb, IV, and V.

How early was the transition from Monte Albán IV to V? Drennan (1983:370), who put together the radiocarbon chart for *The Cloud People*, says: "The date A.D. 950 has been selected as the beginning date for Period V most compatible with the overall pattern of radiocarbon dates available at the moment, although 50, 100, or even more years later than this would do no great violence to the pattern." If Period V indeed began this early, it would make Monte Albán IV a relatively short phase, perhaps no more than 200 years long. This would not bother us (nor would we would mind seeing IV last until A.D. 1000 or 1050).

Such an early date for the beginning of Period V raises a very interesting possibility. Many Oaxaca specialists, including Caso, Bernal, Paddock, and Brockington, have long argued that many of the new elements appearing in the Valley of Oaxaca at the start of Period V have their origins in the Mixteca. One of the most expansionist rulers in the history of the Mixteca was 8 Deer "Tiger Claw" of Tututepec and Tilantongo, whose period of greatest conquest was A.D. 1043-1063 (Caso 1979). Of the 100 towns that he claims in the Codex Colombino to have conquered, some lie not very far from the Valley of Oaxaca. Could it be that the first arrival of Postclassic "Mixtec-influenced" elements in the Valley of Oaxaca coincided temporally with 8 Deer's military expansion? This is a possibility that should be investigated in the future.

If "Early Monte Albán V" dates to A.D. 950-1100 (or even 1000-1100), then "Middle Monte Albán V" should date to A.D. 1100-1300. Radiocarbon dates falling in this range include one from a fire basin in the Palace of the Six Patios at Yagul, A.D. 1200 ± 100 (M-1248) and another from a maguey roasting pit at Guilá Naquitz, A.D. 1270 ± 80 (SI-513). Radiocarbon dates for "Late Monte Albán V" are generally in the A.D. 1300-1500 range (Drennan 1983).

Looking at the data presented above, we see not the slightest evidence for a mass exodus of 69,000 Zapotecs in Early Postclassic Oaxaca. In fact, the striking cultural "continuity" to which Winter admits, over and over again, in his Dumbarton Oaks paper results from the fact that Oaxaca has one of the longest, most uninterrupted sequences of any valley in Mexico. Even if there were *no radiocarbon dates whatsoever* for the Valley of Oaxaca, we would still be able to date Period IIIa by its ties to Teotihuacán, Period IV by its trade wares from Tabasco, Yucatán, and Guatemala, and Period V by its Yanhuitlán Red-on-cream and Mixteca-Puebla polychromes. After all, that is how archaeologists dated things before radiocarbon chronology was invented.

Winter's catastrophic "mass abandonment" reminds us somewhat of the "giant lake" theory described in Chapter 2 of this volume. The reader will remember that as of January, 1966, we had not one single radiocarbon date from the Valley of Oaxaca which fell in the period 8000–500 B.C. This was supposedly explained by the presence of a giant lake which had prevented occupation of the valley before Monte Albán I.

Did this lack of radiocarbon dates mean that the Valley of Oaxaca was abandoned during the Archaic and Early Formative periods? Of course not. It simply meant that not enough work had been done on those periods. Does our relatively small set of radiocarbon dates for Monte Albán IV mean that the valley was abandoned for 500 years in the Early Postclassic? Of course not; it simply means that not enough work has been done on that period.

Consider this: roughly 90 percent of all Monte Albán IIIb and IV sites in the Central Valley of Oaxaca were "isolated residences, hamlets, or tiny villages with maximum populations of fewer than 290 people; 8% were somewhat larger villages (minimum 180–500, maximum 380–1000 people), and only 2% of the settlements were in the 1000–2500 range" (Kowalewski 1983:189). And how many of the isolated residences, hamlets, tiny villages, or somewhat larger villages of Monte Albán IV, which constitute 98% of the settlements, have ever been excavated? None. Thus we are talking about a phase with more than 400 sites and a set of clearly datable trade wares from other regions of Mesoamerica, none of whose major settlement types have ever been excavated. Small wonder we don't have enough dates.

If anyone wants to argue that Monte Albán IIIb and IV ceramics are tough to distinguish, that is fine with us. If anyone wants to argue that IIIb and IV are simply the early and late subphases of a single long ceramic phase, fine. If anyone further wants to argue that they will be convincingly separated in the future only by the analysis of more large excavated samples from good sealed contexts, this, too, is fine with us. Even Kowalewski, who has so far spent more time trying to separate the two complexes than any other archaeologist, would probably agree with those statements. But please, let's not throw up our hands and start proposing mass emigrations of thousands of Zapotecs. Our specimens of Tohil Plumbate, Puuc Slate, and Z and Y Fine Orange disprove such emigration, and so do the stratigraphic sequences at Abasolo, Cuilapan, Yagul, and Mitla. Let's just do more research.

During the twenty years between 1966 and 1986, intensive work on the Formative period in Oaxaca produced a sequence of five phases antedating Monte Albán I. A comparable twenty-year period of intensive work on the Postclassic—including the smaller sites which account for 98 percent of that period's settlements—could give us five redefined ceramic phases called Monte Albán IIIb, IV, Va, Vb, and Vc. Such phases should at least be recognizable in large excavated collections, where the percentages of one type to another could be calculated. Whether they would always be fully recognizable on survey is another story; small collections might still be difficult to tell apart, just as small San José and Guadalupe phase surface collections are.

We suggest that anyone interested in such a twenty-year project ask Kowalewski for a list of sites whose excavation might end the confusion. Doing it right will be a lot of work, but it will at least constitute science. The alternative, which we all know to be easier, is science fiction.

References Cited

Acosta, Jorge R.
1965   Preclassic and Classic architecture of Oaxaca. In: Handbook of Middle American Indians, vol. 3, part 2, edited by Robert Wauchope and Gordon R. Willey, pp. 814–36. Austin: University of Texas Press.

Bernal, Ignacio
1946   La Cerámica Preclásica de Monte Albán. Master's thesis. Escuela Nacional de Antropología e Historia, Mexico.
1949   La Cerámica de Monte Albán IIIa. Ph.D. dissertation. Universidad Nacional Autónoma de México, Mexico City.
1958   Exploraciones en Cuilapan de Guerrero, 1902–1954. Informes 7. Dirección de Monumentos Prehispánicos, Instituto Nacional de Antropología e Historia. México, D.F.
1985   Offical Guide: Oaxaca Valley. Mexico: Salvat Mexicana de Ediciones, S.A. de C.V.

Caso, Alfonso
1935   Las Exploraciones en Monte Albán, Temporada 1934–1935. Instituto Panameriano de Geografía e Historia, Pub. 18. Tacubaya, D.F., Mexico.

1979   Reyes y Reinos de la Mixteca. Mexico: Fondo de Cultura Económica.

Caso, Alfonso, Ignacio Bernal, and Jorge R. Acosta
1967   La Cerámica de Monte Albán. Memorias del Instituto Nacional de Antropología e Historia 13. Mexico.

Drennan, Robert D.
1983   Appendix. Radiocarbon dates from the Oaxaca region. In: The Cloud People: Divergent Evolution of the Zapotec and Mixtec Civilizations, edited by Kent V. Flannery and Joyce Marcus, pp. 363-70. New York: Academic Press.

Flannery, Kent V. and Joyce Marcus
1983   The changing politics of A.D. 600-900: Editors' introduction. In: The Cloud People: Divergent Evolution of the Zapotec and Mixtec Civilizations, edited by Kent V. Flannery and Joyce Marcus, pp. 183-85. New York: Academic Press.

Kowalewski, Stephen A.
1983   Monte Albán IIIb-IV settlement patterns in the Valley of Oaxaca. In: The Cloud People: Divergent Evolution of the Zapotec and Mixtec Civilizations, edited by Kent V. Flannery and Joyce Marcus, pp. 188-90. New York: Academic Press.

Kowalewski, Stephen A., Gary M. Feinman, Laura Finsten, Richard E. Blanton, and Linda M. Nicholas
1989   Monte Albán's Hinterland, Part II. Prehispanic Settlement Patterns in Tlacolula, Etla, and Ocotlán, the Valley of Oaxaca, Mexico. Memoirs, 23. Museum of Anthropology, University of Michigan. Ann Arbor.

Marcus, Joyce
1983   Changing patterns of stone monuments after the fall of Monte Albán, A.D. 600-900. In: The Cloud People: Divergent Evolution of the Zapotec and Mixtec Civilizations, edited by Kent V. Flannery and Joyce Marcus, pp. 191-97. New York: Academic Press.
1989   From centralized systems to city-states: Possible models for the Epiclassic. In: Mesoamerica After the Decline of Teotihuacan: A.D. 700-900, edited by Richard A. Diehl and Janet Catherine Berlo, pp. 201-8. Washington, D.C.: Dumbarton Oaks Research Library and Collection.

Paddock, John
1966   Ancient Oaxaca: Discoveries in Mexican Archaeology and History. Stanford: Stanford University Press.
1983   Lambityeco. In: The Cloud People: Divergent Evolution of the Zapotec and Mixtec Civilizations, edited by Kent V. Flannery and Joyce Marcus, pp. 197-204. New York: Academic Press.

Sanders, William T.
1989   The Epiclassic as a stage in Mesoamerican prehistory: An evaluation. In: Mesoamerica After the Decline of Teotihuacan: A.D. 700–900, edited by Richard A. Diehl and Janet Catherine Berlo, pp. 211–18. Washington, D.C.: Dumbarton Oaks Research Library and Collection.

Winter, Marcus C.
1989   From Classic to Post-Classic in Pre-Hispanic Oaxaca. In: Mesoamerica After the Decline of Teotihuacan: A.D. 700–900, edited by Richard A. Diehl and Janet Catherine Berlo, pp. 123–30. Washington, D.C.: Dumbarton Oaks Research Library and Collection.

6

SCALE AND COMPLEXITY
Issues in the Archaeology of the Valley of Oaxaca

Stephen A. Kowalewski,
University of Georgia

Now, almost two decades since the beginning of the regional survey of the Valley of Oaxaca, after several thousand pages of published reports, 2150 km^2 searched on foot, 2700 sites and 6153 components mapped and described, I would like to use this opportunity to discuss the archaeology of the Valley of Oaxaca in a different way. I want to emphasize how massive and how complex (in various senses of the term) the Mesoamerican archaeological record can be; what this says for useful theories about cultural evolution; and what it implies for archaeological methods.

The present paper leaves out the analytical procedures that helped us* reach our conclusions, and I try to avoid plowing the same ground that we have written about elsewhere. In this paper I rely more on illustration than on analysis and extended argumentation. The reader can find the details about the surface archaeology of the Valley of Oaxaca and various, alternative interpretations in our monograph (Kowalewski et al. 1989).

SCALE

The photographs and captions that form the body of this paper illustrate the spatial scales captured by a regional surface survey in Mesoamerica. My main methodological point in this regard is that archaeological methods have to be appropriate to the physical size of the objects being investigated. What I am speaking to, specifically, are

---
*Richard Blanton, Gary Feinman, Laura Finsten, Linda Nicholas, and Stephen Kowalewski.

studies that use methods appropriate for small objects, yet make claims about much larger objects. For example, small excavations in and of themselves say little about regional patterns. Conversely, regional surveys sometimes do not have the resolution, the fine-grain quality, to address in detail questions about intrasite variability. For example, regional survey is not appropriate for determining how many contemporary households there were at an alluvial, valley-floor site like Xoxocotlán (Fig. 6.14). We stretch our limits of resolution trying to determine the size of each component at the unusually complicated, multicomponent site of San José Mogote.

Hard fact does not reside only at one particular spatial scale; instead, real objects come in different sizes. One's methods and concepts have to be appropriate to the spatial scale of the objective phenomenon. In particular, archaeology could use more techniques that bridge the gap between the region and the excavation. The most productive insights seem to come when we can combine the results of investigations at various spatial scales, as the Oaxaca project has often shown.

It may be useful to review the sizes of the things that Mesoamerican (and other) archaeologists want to study. I begin at the micro and proceed to the macro. Assume that a fairly small thing that we want to see is a pattern of post holes forming the corner of a house. This corner might fit into a square meter or two, a test pit. A respectable-sized (not cheap!) excavation project might uncover a hundred square meters. Among our smallest sites in the Valley of Oaxaca are individual isolated residences, which cover roughly a tenth of a hectare. Digging all of a site like this would not be a small undertaking.

Now, a larger site in Mesoamerica—a San José Mogote, for instance—might have an area of a square kilometer. No archaeologist has ever excavated something as large as a square kilometer and lived to publish the results. Obviously we sample, as in fact Kent Flannery did at San José Mogote.

The largest Mesoamerican cities, however, are another order of magnitude larger. They may extend over 10 or 20 km^2. Other meaningful, patterned objects from the Valley of Oaxaca include the territories of the petty kingdoms from the Late Postclassic period. We could not see these until we plotted the site distributions on large-scale maps, and then they were obvious as concentrations of sites separated by nearly vacant stretches of land. These territories seen on the settlement pattern maps often coincide with the historically known polities of the sixteenth century. They measure roughly 100 km^2 in size. Highland valleys that formed more or less autonomous regions in Mesoamerica extend over several thousand square kilometers.

As Ignacio Bernal and John Paddock have written, in some sense Oaxaca is an archaeological region roughly coinciding with the boundaries of the modern state of Oaxaca. Conceivably, one might be able to plot artifact styles of various time periods in order to demonstrate this idea. The archaeological region of Oaxaca would cover about 100,000 km².

Finally, we should not neglect Mesoamerica, the culture area defined as a significant unit by Kirchhoff (1943) because it had a distinctive cluster of cultural traits. Mesoamerica measures somewhat over 1,000,000 km².

So archaeologists are concerned with things of significance that measure from less than a hectare to over a million square kilometers. It is difficult to comprehend this whole range of sizes without mentally condensing or shifting the scale of measurement. In the description just completed, I used the common terms of measurement: first I used square meters, then hectares when I described small sites, and then I shifted to square kilometers to deal with everything from the larger sites on up.

Changing the units of measurement makes it easier to talk about things, at the cost of obscuring the real relationships between sizes. Let us keep the same unit of measurement, square meters. The test pit is one square meter, the large site is one million, the petty kingdom is one hundred million, the Valley of Oaxaca survey area is two billion, and Mesoamerica is a trillion square meters. In terms of mental grasp, this may not be much better.

We can convert to a log scale. The large site is 1×10^6 square meters, the Valley of Oaxaca survey area is 2×10^9, and Mesoamerica is 1×10^{12} square meters. But again the compression into orders of magnitude makes the steps between sizes seem small and easy. If one tries to walk it or dig it, the distance between one order of magnitude and the next seems like more work than just adding another integer.

Perhaps we need a visual image, one that requires the reader's mind to do the work. The two printed pages open in front of you contain approximately five thousand characters. Suppose these five thousand characters represent the size of the Valley of Oaxaca survey area. Then each individual character would be about the size of a 40-hectare site (Tlaltinango or Tlalixtac, third-level centers of the Terminal Formative, or Cuilapan, a fourth-level center of the Classic period).

The analogy is still too cumbersome to handle something the size of a typical archaeological excavation. If one now expands or telescopes a single character (40 hectares) into the full two pages, then the 1/5000th represented by one character would be 80 square meters, about the size of an excavation. If one telescopes up the scale from our original visual image where the two pages equalled the Valley of Oaxaca, now letting the full two pages represent Mesoamerica, then the Valley of Oaxaca survey area would be about ten characters (we leave it to the reader to say which ten). Clearly, reading through this "Mesoamerica" would be easier than walking it, a conclusion that scholars have already reached without benefit of this reasoning.

Whatever visual, mental, or mathematical device one uses to comprehend the varying sizes of objects Mesoamerican archaeologists want to study, it seems clear that excavations and regional surveys, presently our most common methods, take in only limited, exclusive sectors of the total range of objects. In fact, when scaled in square meters, the abyss between the optimal sizes for excavations and surface surveys yawns over five or six orders of magnitude. Our field needs to develop better methods for seeing objects larger than the excavation. That such methods will sacrifice some detail or resolution, in comparison with excavation, should be obvious, but this fact should not stand in the way of their development and use.

A wonderful book called *Powers of Ten* (Morrison et al. 1982) stunningly illustrates how arrays of objects in the universe are randomly or structurally patterned, depending on the scale at which they are seen. For example, one can see the spiral-arm structure of a galaxy with telescopes that focus on things one hundred thousand light-years across. An instrument capable of discerning objects an order of magnitude smaller reveals more detail—but the spatial arrangement of these objects then loses its structure. *Powers of Ten* has many examples of phenomena that are patterned at one scale but apparently random at larger or smaller scales.

The common metaphor, of course, is not being able to see the forest for the trees. "Trees," the ever-smaller details, exist within "forests," or structures, at whatever scale. Stuctures have regular make-up and they are bounded—they are not random, arbitrary, or chaotic. This has methodological implications.

Mesoamerican archaeology has many kinds of different-sized, bounded objects with regular make-up: activity areas, cemeteries, field systems, neighborhoods, communities, sets of interacting communities, defensive systems, ceramic-style spheres, marketing spheres, political territories, and so forth. Several photographs in the body of this paper illustrate bounded spatial distributions and boundary phenomena.

Even the best program of excavations could be made more fine-grained, e.g. by a micro-stratigraphic, microscopic excavation of a single trash pit. A whole field season of surface collecting on part of a site will indeed produce more artifacts than a one-day inspection during a regional survey. If done correctly, the brief observation during the regional survey should, and usually does, produce the same broad pattern as the more intensive effort. That the smaller-scale, more intensive efforts will produce more information per unit area will surprise no one. But the practicing archaeologist might legitimately wonder what behaviorally significant structure or pattern the smaller-scale, intensive investigation will produce. To make a contribution to knowledge, scientific observations ought to find significant structure. Does the intensive survey of a single area at a site describe, for example, the range of wealth-statuses for the whole community or some integral segment of it? Does the finer-grain study identify bounded components of a larger structure, that is, constituents that are themselves structures? If not, the project makes little substantial contribution; it is a mechanical, methodological exercise; it is a waste of resources.

The objects of study have different sizes, they have specifiable and regular make-up, they have edges, and they have to be discovered empirically on the ground. If we imagine these objects as spatial distributions of items (they are more complicated, actually, because they are often co-occurrences or associations of features that we link together by inferences), we have to scale our recovery efforts to their size, plus a little more area to make sure we have correctly defined them. If we are to compare them, which we usually want to do, then we want to have several objects, not just one. For example, when we study a region or a site, we might delimit our site or region well, but for comparative, analytic purposes, we are actually limited to discussing not so much the object itself, but its constituent units, those on the next level of scale down. For the region, the "next levels down" mean the subregional, locality, and site constituents. For the site, the constituents or units of analysis may be sectors or household units.

When archaeologists sample a site they place sampling units across the whole site according to some informed design, in order to estimate parameters of the entirety. In sampling it is the whole, not the sampling units, that is of ultimate interest, so the well-collected sampling unit that is not logically tied to the whole is a shot that remains in darkness.

Archaeologists normally try to isolate objects, structures, or patterns that have a degree of unity or wholeness. To do so, they cover, at some degree of thoroughness, the whole thing, plus a little more. Excavating a trench through a house, without the rest of it, does not satisfy this criterion of a whole structure; nor would a survey, at whatever level of detail, whose boundaries were not designed to encompass or represent some significant object or structure.

We could plunk down a square kilometer grid of 100 ha at random anywhere within the Valley of Oaxaca and pick up every artifact within the grid. We doubt this would mean very much, because the items or patterns within the grid would not represent an anticipated or discovered whole. The grid unit could not be argued to represent the Valley of Oaxaca or even one of its subregions or localities. It might encompass, by chance, several small sites, thus comparing the collections between the sites might be of interest—but it might not; or the unit might catch a part of a large site, but we would not know what whole we were sampling. This is our argument against the mechanical use of "siteless" survey (Dunnell and Dancey 1983).

Some siteless surveys are designed to find the rare, isolated artifacts left from unintensive human activities. In these cases it may indeed be comforting to know that such artifacts are or are not where they are predicted to be, but it would be more informative to know something about the structure of their spatial distribution, including the spatial limits of the distribution. Spatial distributions of rare artifacts are structured, bounded objects of regular make-up too. Mere intensity of data recovery will not substitute for knowledge about the whole object.

Choosing the appropriate scale and resolution for making observations on bounded, structured distributions is a basic step in designing research. It is somewhat surprising to us that this major aspect of method has received as little attention as it has from the professional methodologists.

Another aspect of scale impinges on theories of cultural evolution. The fact is that many of the anthropological theories about cultural evolution fail to specify the spatial scale at which significant processes are supposed to take place. Recently the specification of scales has been receiving more attention. Having completed the regional survey and having been impressed by the mutual benefits of having both excavations and surveys in the Valley of Oaxaca, we think the time has come for more systematic treatment of the interactions of different processes involving different variables at different spatial scales. This topic is discussed by Blanton in this volume, and it also touches on the issue of complexity, which I address next.

COMPLEXITY

The photographs and captions in the body of this paper illustrate the complexities of surface archaeology in Mesoamerica. Complexity as a technical term means the number of functionally different parts in a system. But the word may also imply difficulty of understanding, due to a multiplicity of factors, parts, or required analytical steps. The illustrations allude to complexity in both senses. The archaeology is not easy to figure out, especially if we use a variety of different kinds of data and pay attention to the inherent variability in the data. The archaeology also implies real complexity in past social systems, complexity that is related to size but in different ways at different times, complexity that we think requires all the sophistication and nuance that social science theory can muster, and then some. At this point in the development of theory, understanding the evolution of urban systems in Mesoamerica requires more attention to variation, not less; more contrast, not more "blenderizing"; use of more variables, not fewer; and more use of appropriate raw data, rather than armchair discourse (such as this paper—I shall be brief, with pictures).

There is more to regional studies in archaeology than finding out where to dig or making models that predict site location. Exactly what else, of course, depends on one's theoretical approach. The Valley of Oaxaca settlement pattern project has emphasized the interplay of economic, political, and ecological factors. Evidence of past economic factors came from (among other things) obsidian, local chipped and ground stone, shell, pottery, and the distribution of settlements in relationship to the land and water resources necessary for farming. Evidence of political factors came from architecture—the spatial patterns, associations, and gross quantity of buildings and plazas, carved stone monuments, and patterns of specialized sites. Evidence of environmental/human interactions came from demographic estimates and the association of settlements with soils, water, vegetation, slope, and so on.

In analyzing these lines of evidence we paid a great deal of attention to patterns of spatio-temporal variability. One of several ways in which we exploited spatio-temporal variability was through the use of ideas borrowed from geography. Geographical models, modified by us to suit our needs, often proved fruitful. Some anthropologists have said such models cannot apply to Mesoamerica because they were designed for industrialized societies. In contrast, some geographers see such models as applicable only for preindustrial societies; we simply found them useful as tools to help us discover the nature of past regional systems.

It was geographically inspired analyses that let us describe the systems of central places as being linear and primate in the Formative, more integrated and less primate in the Early Classic, and less bounded, even more integrated, with a more complex lattice of central places in the Late Postclassic. Features of these three modes of the regional system are illustrated below.

How rich and robust are the survey data? Often with the survey data we would not know the meaning of, or trust the outcome of, a test or quantitative relationship measured at one time or place. But when the same relationship behaved in a regular, predictable way in different periods, in different parts of the region, under different environmental or survey conditions then we could be surer of the results.

For instance, in the field we noted obsidian fragments whenever we saw them. We did not systematically collect obsidian because we did not have time for special collections and because collecting would have adversely affected future studies. In spite of the lack of collecting, our observations are a good initial view of the relative abundance and spatial patterning of obsidian. When we say that a site had 17 pieces of obsidian in the Late Postclassic, it is obvious that further work would find more, but a site with 17 pieces is far more likely to have had more obsidian than a site on which we saw none, and this site should produce far less obsidian than a site on which we saw hundreds of pieces.

Our observations of obsidian and other items, including pottery, proved to be valuable data for reconstructing past economic, political, and ecological relationships. When coupled with the standard survey information such as site size and location, and the architectural data, the artifact patterns were useful beyond our initial expectations. Having these different kinds of data added complexity to the regional analysis (in the sense of difficulty of comprehension) and let us see a little better the real complexity of past social systems.

Any regional study combs with wider, coarser teeth than a local or site-specific study. Having had to walk over all the surface sites in the valley, we know better than most that finer-grain studies will produce more artifacts—and even greater complexity. But, to return to the question of how rich are the survey data, we conclude that the data are surprisingly rich, useful, and complex in the sense of being multifaceted and a bit difficult, as well as being enormously informative of the high degree of real complexity that characterized these past social systems. It seems to us that methods and theories in archaeology should respect and anticipate the real complexity of Mesoamerican societies.

SCALE AND COMPLEXITY 215

The following photographic tour of the Valley of Oaxaca is by no means complete, but it will illustrate our points about scale and complexity and appropriate theory and method. Along the way I add details, so that the reader might pick up a feeling for the nature of the surface archaeology and our interpretations of it.

We begin, as the project did, with Monte Albán and the surrounding Central area, which has become rapidly urbanized since the 1970s. Settlement in the Central and Etla areas illustrates the pulses of demographic growth in the Late Formative, Late Classic, and Late Postclassic. Several photographs also show boundary phenomena, both regional and local.

Beginning with Figure 6.10 we move to Tlacolula, the eastern arm of the valley, showing more boundary phenomena, architecture, and the size and changing composition of central places. The Early Classic regional system had a high degree of functional differentiation and integration. Figures 6.14 through 6.17 provide examples of functionally different Early Classic sites in the Valle Grande, the southwestern part of the valley. Figure 6.18 illustrates the pattern of settlement over a fairly broad area in the southeastern Ocotlán district.

In this paper we tied together the scale and complexity of the archaeological record with the idea that archaeological theory and method should be capable of handling the various scales of objects that constituted these complex societies. I use Figures 6.19 through 6.24 – all photographs of Jalieza, one of Mesoamerica's largest sites – to describe regional complexity and appropriate method. Shortcomings of the regional survey, along with benefits, are shown in the original field map in Figure 6.25. The final figure depicts one of the hazards in our line of work.

A Photo Tour of the Valley of Oaxaca

Figure 6.1 [*below*]. Aerial view of the Cerro de Atzompa. The Cerro de Atzompa is the northernmost barrio (site subdivision 11) of Monte Albán, built and occupied mainly during the Monte Albán IIIb phase (Late Classic). A crew of five mapped, collected, and described 467 residential terraces here over a season of two months. The trail ascending the northeast ridge follows a major ancient road. Note the large artificial terraces on the north ridge.

Atzompa and most of the other site subdivisions at Monte Albán are about the same scale – in numbers of inhabitants and mound construction – as the secondary and tertiary centers out in the valley. Atzompa, physically the closest site subdivision to the Etla arm of the valley, has artifact assemblages similar to those of Etla; likewise, the southern and eastern subdivisions as Monte Albán had their closest ties to the southern and eastern arms of the valley.

North is at the top. The photograph measures about 3.6 km east-west. [Valley of Oaxaca Settlement Pattern Project (VOSPP) grid square N13E6. Compañía Mexicana Aerofoto.]

SCALE AND COMPLEXITY 217

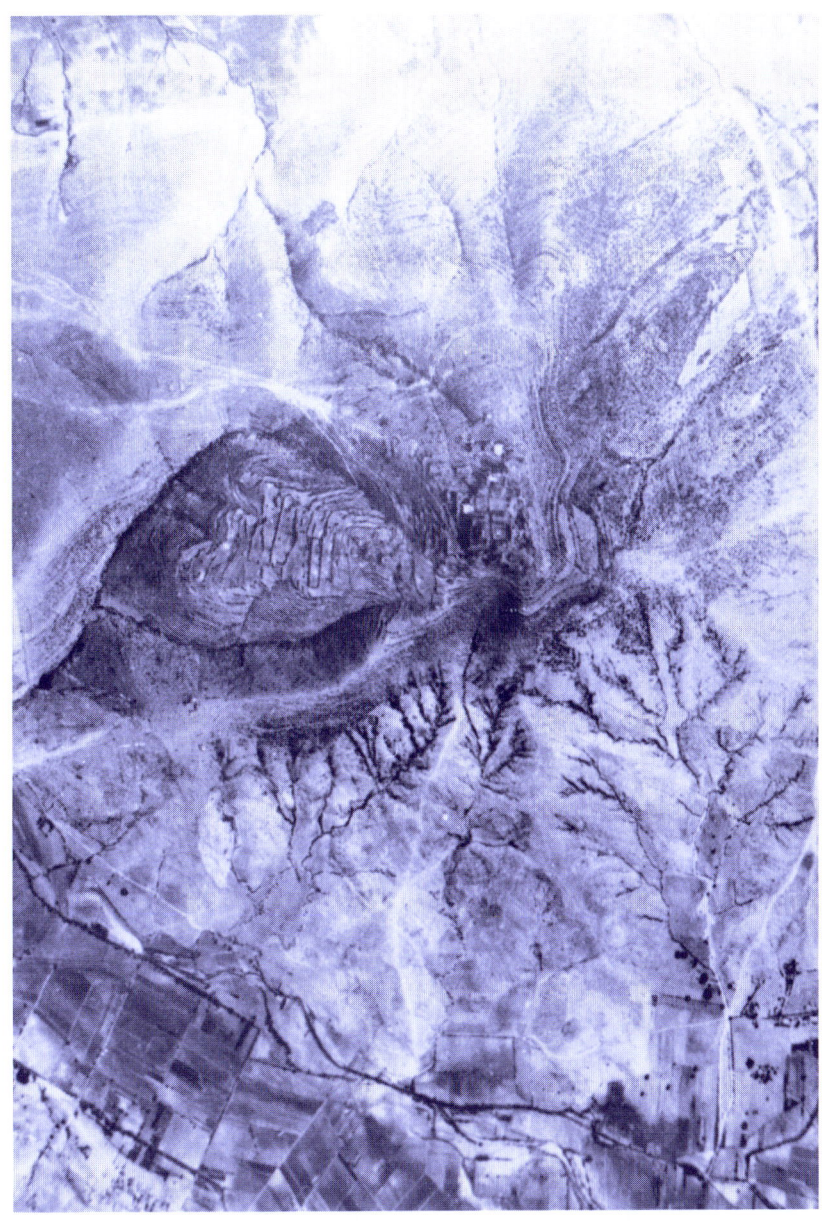

Figure 6.2 [*below*] Monte Albán from the east, in 1974. Site subdivision 12 is on the closest ridge in the center of the photograph; site subdivision 5 is higher and just to its right. Site subdivision 10 is the lower ridge on the right side of the photograph, where Richard Blanton found a small amount of Aztec III pottery.

The 200–700-meter-wide strip of alluvium, between the Atoyac River and the mountain, and some of the lower slopes are now completely urbanized and inaccessible to survey. We found Monte Albán Ia (Middle Formative) settlements about every 2 km along the edge of the piedmont from here into the Etla Valley and in the opposite direction into the Valle Grande. This pattern is not different from the Central area around Monte Albán, in spite of the presence of the city—a fact that supports the interpretation that Monte Albán's role was special, and not that of a typical farming town.

[North is to the right. The scene takes in approximately 2.5 km. [VOSPP grid N12E6. Photo by S. Kowalewski.]

SCALE AND COMPLEXITY 219

Figure 6.3 [*below*] Aerial view of the middle and high piedmont north of Oaxaca City. The city is in the lower left corner. The towns across the high piedmont are, from west to east, San Felipe del Agua, Donají, San Luis Beltrán, and San Andrés Huayapan.

Virtually the entire area of this photograph, taken in the mid-1960s, is now urbanized and inaccessible to archaeological survey. The area's heaviest occupations were in Monte Albán V (Late Postclassic), when there were over 80 sites, and in Monte Albán Ic (Late Formative). Periods Ic and V are two of the phases of demographic expansion in the piedmont of the Central area and Etla. Mounds at the San Luis Beltrán site excavated by Ignacio Bernal show up as two dark rectangles in the center of the photograph.

North is at top. The distance from the top to the bottom of the photograph is about 6 km. [VOSPP grids N13E7-9, N14E7-9. Compañía Mexicana Aerofoto.]

SCALE AND COMPLEXITY 221

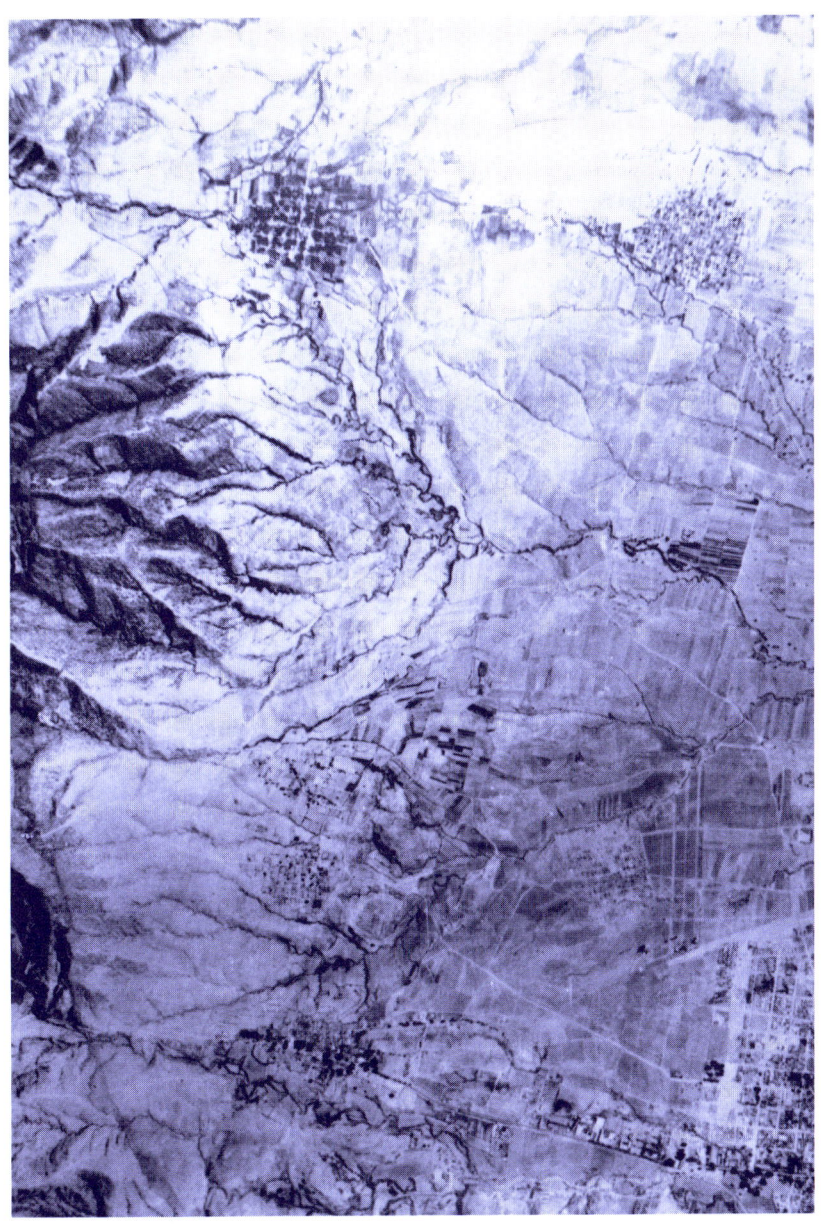

Figure 6.4 [*below*] The middle piedmont north of Oaxaca City, from the west. This photograph was taken in 1974, from the heights on the far west [left] side of Figure 6.3. The village of Dolores is in the center, with San Agustín Yatareni and Tlalixtac de Cabrera beyond it, and Santa María del Tule on the valley floor in the far distance. The north edge of Oaxaca City in 1974 was on the right, but today this whole landscape is urbanized. In 1974 we mapped many Monte Albán Ic (Late Formative), IIIb-IV (Late Classic–Early Postclassic), and V (Late Postclassic) sites here, including localities 2-6-76, 2-9-157, and 2-11-194, located in the flat field with the solitary house on the left of the photograph.

North is on the left. The most distant visible point on the valley floor is about 11 km away. [VOSPP grids N13E7-9. Photo by S. Kowalewski.]

SCALE AND COMPLEXITY 223

Figure 6.5 [*below*] Northwest from Monte Albán. Monte Albán's terraces below the North Platform are visible in the foreground, El Gallo (Monte Albán site subdivision 15) is in the center, and the Cerro de Atzompa (Fig. 6.1) is to the right. On the highest knobs of the whitish hills in the distance, we mapped sites with small, squarish mounds (e.g. 2-9-24, 2-9-114) that may have marked a boundary between communities in the Atzompa drainage on this side of the hills and the Cacaotepec-Tejalapan drainage on the far side of the hills. Strings of single-mound sites, possibly marking territorial boundaries of communities, are a common pattern in some phases, including Etla and the Central area in Monte Albán IIIb-IV (probably IIIb, Late Classic), but not at other times (e.g., Monte Albán V, the Late Postclassic).

North is in the direction of the Cerro de Atzompa on the right edge of the photograph. From the point where the picture was taken to the top of the white hills is about 9 km. [VOSPP grids N12E5-6, N13E4-5. Photo by S. Kowalewski.]

Figure 6.6 [*right*]. Aerial view of the hills west of San Andrés Ixtlahuaca. These hills are 10 km west of Monte Albán. The western edge of the survey area is the Jalapillas stream, at left. Elevations range from 1700 m in the Jalapillas valley to 1850 m on the highest ridges. The white hills appear in the northern third of the photograph.

The hill crests in this scene have a few small habitation sites dating to as early as Monte Albán Ic (Late Formative), but there was substantial settlement—amounting to several thousand people—in Monte Albán IIIb-IV (Late Classic, Early Postclassic) and V (Late Postclassic). In the Central and Etla areas there was heavy use of the piedmont during these three time periods, but in the intervening phases (Monte Albán II, IIIa) the same piedmont areas were abandoned.

The El Mirador site (Fig. 6.7) sprawls over the high ridges in the center of the photograph. El Mirador must have served as a local center for the several thousand people living in these hills in Monte Albán IIIb.

North is at the top. From the top to the bottom of the photograph the distance is about 6 km. [VOSPP grids N13E3, N12E3. Compañía Mexicana Aerofoto.]

Figure 6.7 [*below*]. The El Mirador site, looking north. This is a view of the mounds that can be seen on the ridge crest near the center of Figure 6.6 at El Mirador (2–6–1, 2–9–1 etc., 2–11–9 etc.). Structure 7, closest to the camera, is about 4 m high and Structure 6, beyond it, is 1 m high. Between the two mounds is a 24 x 21 m plaza. El Mirador's architecture also includes four other mounds, several plazas, a ballcourt, and over 30 residential terraces. Another hilltop site, shown in Figure 6.8, is in the far distance to the left of the mound. El Mirador and the site in Figure 6.8, in addition to serving local needs, probably had functions related to their positions on the regional system's boundary.

The camera looks north at the mounds. [VOSPP grid N13E3. Photo by S. Kowalewski.]

SCALE AND COMPLEXITY 229

Figure 6.8 [*right*]. ET-SFT-SFT-48, a terraced site above San Felipe Tejalapan. The site is strategically located on a major route between the Mixteca Alta and the Etla and Monte Albán areas. Quartz-working took place on several terraces; Terrace 4 had evidence of magnetite-working; and Terraces 4, 55, and 78 had sherd discs, possibly spindle whorls for spinning. The site has a bit of Monte Albán Ic (Late Formative), a substantial amount of Monte Albán II (Terminal Formative), a tiny amount of Monte Albán IIIa (Early Classic), and a heavy IIIb-IV (probably IIIb, Late Classic) occupation. In the Terminal Formative this was a second-or third-ranking center in the region's hierarchy; it was a third-or fourth-ranking center in the Late Classic. This photo shows the 1:5000 amplification we used in the field, with the original pencil retraced in ink, following our standard practice.

North is toward the top of the photograph. The scene covers about 1300 m from north to south. [VOSPP grid N14E3. Compañía Mexicana Aerofoto.]

Figure 6.9 [*below*]. Plaza 1 at ET-SFT-SFT-48. This is the large plaza visible in Figure 6.8. In this photo, taken from the north, the plaza is the light-colored, open area in mid-ground. The ballcourt is in the trees at the end of the plaza closest to the camera. Unlike the two other plazas, which are small and secluded, Plaza 1 is large (over 8000 m^2) and accessible. At other sites we have interpreted the large, accessible plazas as possibly having market functions. If this plaza served as a market (an idea that remains to be tested), one might consider exchange with peripheral villages outside the valley as a significant function of these boundary towns.

North is toward the camera, south is at the top of the photograph. The plaza is 153 m north-south. [VOSPP grid N14E3. Photo by L. Nicholas.]

SCALE AND COMPLEXITY 233

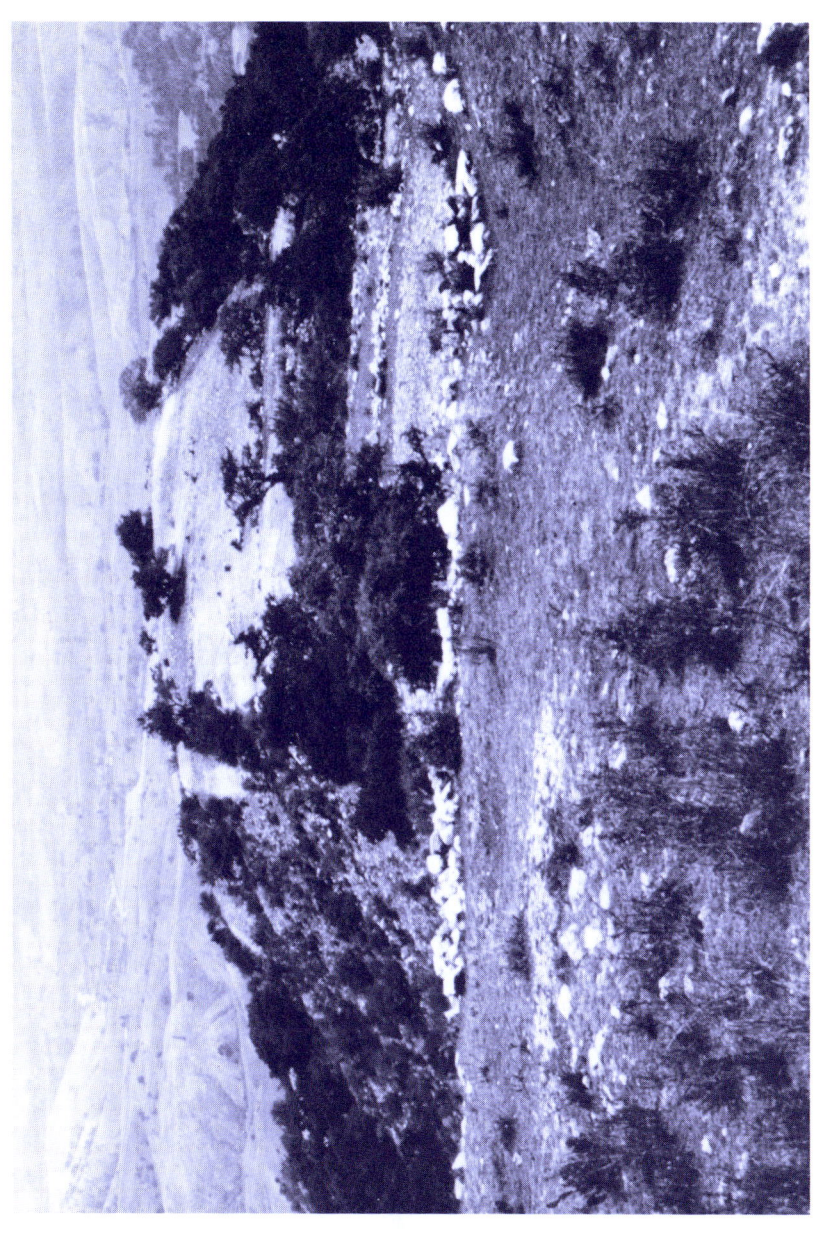

Figure 6.10 [*below*]. The hill above San Mateo Macuilxochitl. The modern town with its church is at the base of the hill. The Dainzú archaeological zone is 1 km to the south (off the left edge of the photograph). Ancient terraces, now under cultivation and heavily eroded, are clearly visible.

The Macuilxochitl, Tlacochahuaya, and Dainzú area had a first- or second-ranking center in the region's hierarchy in every phase from Monte Albán II (Terminal Formative) through Monte Albán V (Late Postclassic) – although the nature of the Formative, Classic, and Postclassic centers was quite different. Only later in the Colonial period did the area begin to lose regional importance. The top of this hill had a very secluded mound group since Monte Albán IIIa; it has a prominent symbolic place on the map of Macuilxochitl accompanying the 1580 *Relación geográfica* (Asensio 1580); and today it features a substantial Catholic shrine.

North is to the right of the photograph. The hill measures about 900 m long (north-south) and rises 200 m above the valley floor. [VOSPP grid N11E12. Photo by L. Nicholas.]

Figure 6.11 [*below*]. Teotitlán del Valle. The survey found few archaeological remains in the dry fields in the foreground. But all through the town (in the center of the photograph) we found evidence of Monte Albán IIIa (Early Classic) and Monte Albán V (Late Postclassic) occupation, as well as remains of settlement dating to earlier periods. The Late Postclassic settlement continues at about the same elevation as the modern town around the base of the hill to the left. In prehispanic times, floodwater farming (Kirkby 1973) and small-scale irrigation were probably practiced here. This area is part of the Monte Albán V community that sprawled from Santiago Ixtaltepec 4 km to the west, to Santa Ana del Valle 6 km to the east, and to Guadalupe 7 km to the southwest.

The survey recorded (but did not collect) obsidian. Interestingly, the five or six largest Monte Albán V cities, including the Macuilxochitl-Teotitlán sprawl, have much more obsidian per hectare than the smaller centers. Obsidian and other evidence of crafts tend to be dispersed in Late Postclassic sites, but concentrated near site centers in Classic period sites.

One does not map towns that go on for 10 km on hands and knees, picking up every artifact. Nor (as an initial strategy) would a small, probabilistic surface sample or a series of test pits be productive. The Macuilxochitl-Teotitlán complex is a good example of how a regional survey approach is necessary for defining the outlines and basic composition of settlements and the general characteristics of craft specialization.

The pinnacle on the left has residential terraces from Monte Albán IIIa and Monte Albán V, and it was a famous sacred landmark of the town of Teotitlán in the sixteenth century. Teotitlán is situated in a strategic position on a route into the Sierra. Teotitlán and other Late Postclassic commercial centers, such as Mitla, had important shrines that attracted pilgrims. The pinnacle here, as well as the Macuixochitl hill in Figure 6.10, are reminders that prehispanic people partitioned and marked the landscape in ways that we could not discover by studying population and land use alone.

The photograph was taken toward the north. At the elevation of the town the scene takes in about 2.5 km. [VOSPP grids N11E12, N12E12. Photo by S. Kowalewski.]

SCALE AND COMPLEXITY   237

Figure 6.12 [*below*]. Everardo "Lalo" Olivera inspects the four-mound group at Cerro Guirún (TL-SLA-SLA-2). This site extends along the dividing ridge between San Lorenzo Albarradas and Xaagá, on the eastern edge of the survey area (about 66 km from the western edge of the survey area in Fig. 6.6). The site has Monte Albán IIIa, IIIb, IV, and V (Early Classic through Late Postclassic) occupation. The architecture in the photograph has been partially reconstructed by the landowner, who planted corn and keeps the bees. The original construction dates to Monte Albán IIIb-IV (probably IV, Early Postclassic). The open, cruciform tomb of Cerro Guirún is 150 m upslope. Our collection from the construction around the tomb had 47 sherds from Monte Albán IIIb-IV and 3 from Monte Albán V.

The photograph was taken looking south. The interior courtyard measures 23 m in length. [VOSPP grid N8E18. Photo by S. Kowalewski.]

SCALE AND COMPLEXITY 239

Figure 6.13 [*below*]. The ballcourt at Cerro Guirún. The ballcourt is adjacent to the south end of the four-mound group in Figure 6.12. It also has been partly reconstructed by the landowner, who was presumably responsible for the medial wall just to Everardo Olivera's right. The Cerro Guirún site fits the Valley of Oaxaca pattern of ballcourts located on the frontiers of the region (see Figs. 6.6–6.8, 6.17). All the sherds from this structure indicate a Monte Albán IIIb-IV date (probably Early Postclassic). In the distance is the *raya* marking the present San Lorenzo Albarradas-Xaagá boundary.

Looking south. The length of the ballcourt on the interior is 21 m. [VOSPP grid N8E18. Photo by S. Kowalewski.]

SCALE AND COMPLEXITY 241

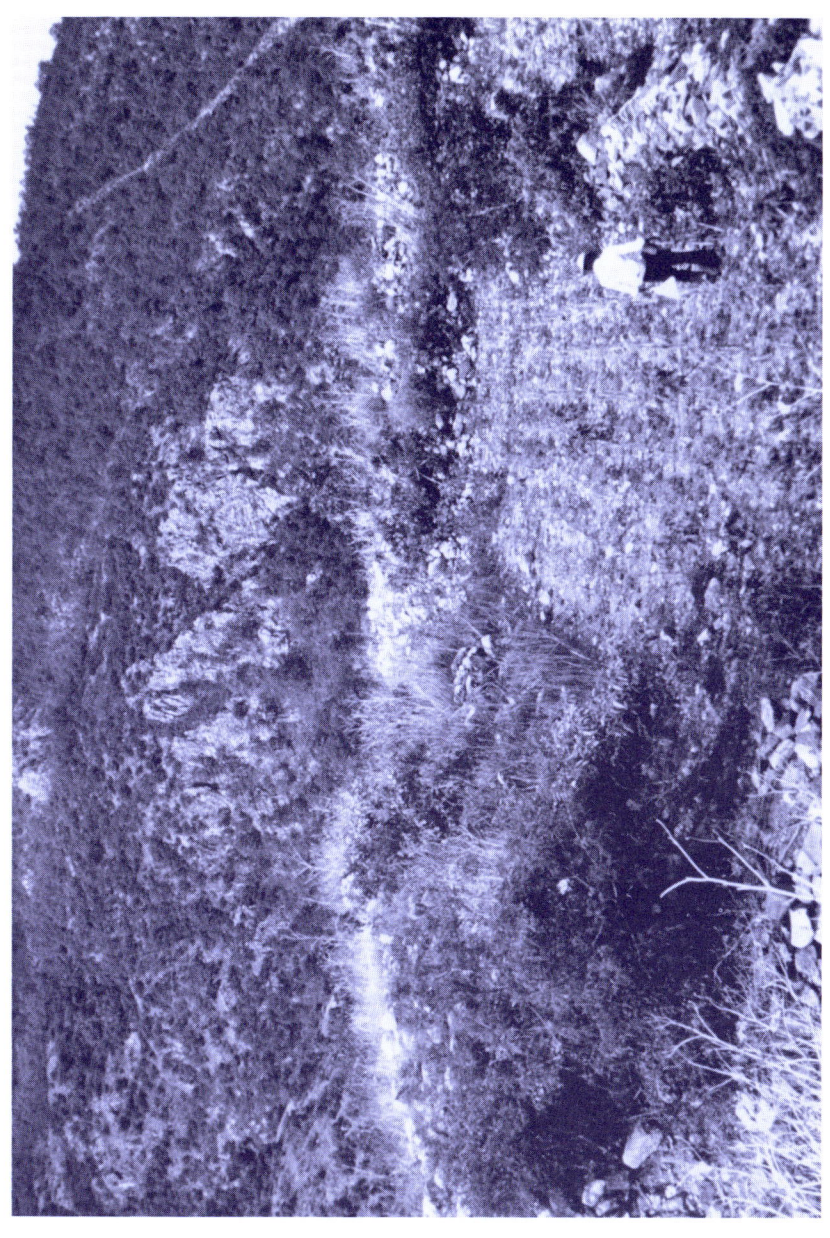

Figure 6.14 [*right*]. Xoxocotlán. Santa Cruz Xoxocotlán is at the top of the photograph. A tall, conical mound and a lower, broad mound at a small center (2-8-16) are visible in the bright area at the southwestern corner of the town. Running along the east (right) edge of the town and slanting across the length of the photograph is the railroad. About in the center of the picture, just to the east (right) of the railroad, is the four-mound group and the large southern mound of the major Monte Albán IIIa town of Xoxocotlán (2-8-17). The rest of the site, including five more large mounds, occupies the light-colored, somewhat sandy alluvium between the mound group and the eastern edge of the photograph. The site has a total area of 115 ha.

Impressive as Xoxocotlán is, especially with its monumental construction and rich artifacts (Saville 1899; Marcus 1983), in Monte Albán IIIa nine other places in the Valley of Oaxaca had larger populations, and fifteen other places had more mounds. Xoxocotlán is one of about twenty Early Classic towns in the alluvium on the west side of the Atoyac river that had unusually large pyramid mounds. Our analysis suggested that such towns had quite different functions in the regional system than the contemporary upland and hilltop settlements.

North is at the top of the photograph. The distance between the north and south edges of the photograph is 3 km. [VOSPP grid N11E7. Compañía Mexicana Aerofoto.]

SCALE AND COMPLEXITY 243

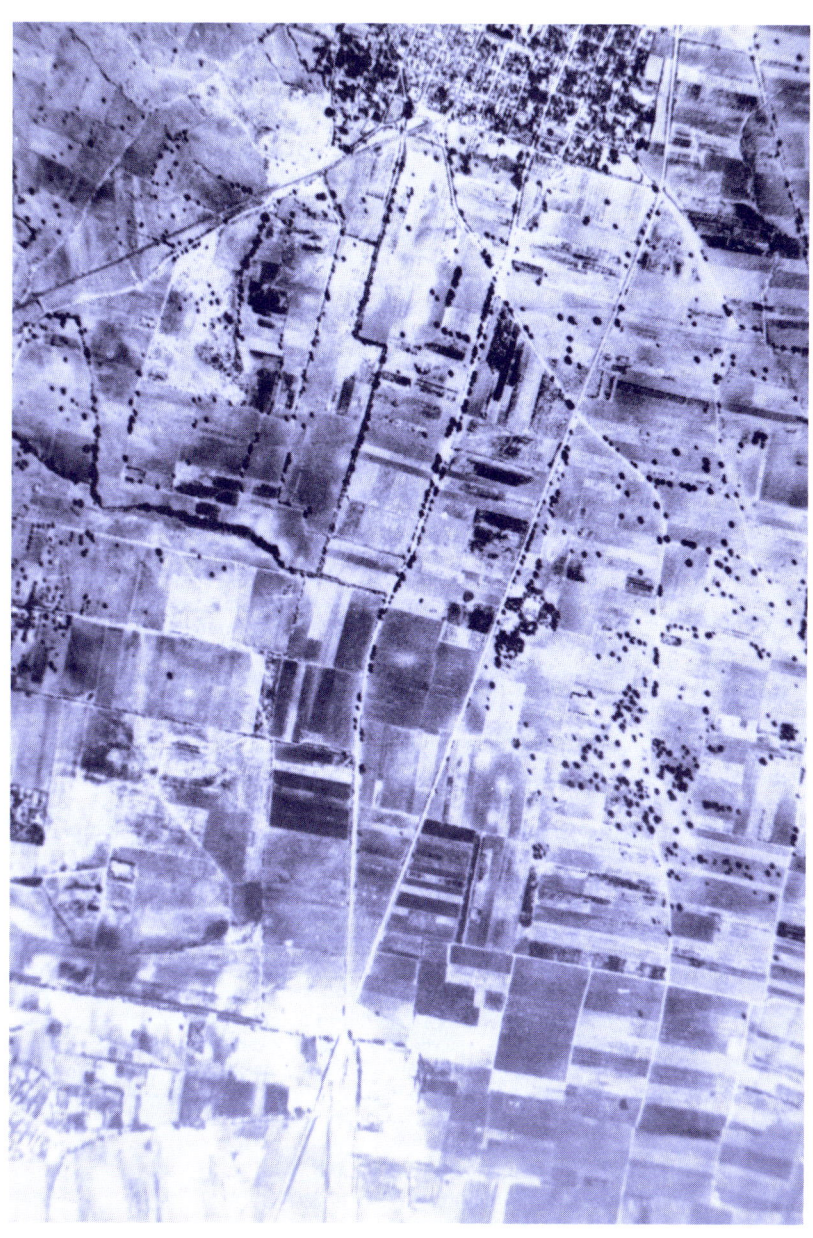

Figure 6.15 [*right*]. Hilltop and valley floor sites at Santa Ana Tlapacoyan (ZI-SAT-SAT-2). Tlapacoyan is in the southwestern part of the survey area, about 34 km south of Monte Albán. The fields south of town show signs of continuous occupation from the Tierras Largas phase (Early Formative) to Monte Albán V (Late Postclassic). The most extensive settlement is in Monte Albán IIIa (Early Classic), when the entire southern half of the Valley of Oaxaca was most heavily settled. Across the Atoyac River from the main site is a low hill ringed by 92 residential terraces dating to Monte Albán IIIa (3-8-250) (see Fig. 6.16 for two more contemporary terraced sites nearby). In Monte Albán V, dispersed settlement covered many of the fields north of the modern town.

The Tlapacoyan vicinity is a microcosm illustrating some of the main changes in the Valley of Oaxaca regional system. It has an Early Formative hamlet probably like those excavated at Tierras Largas, Fábrica San José, and Tomaltepec. The area experienced fairly rapid growth when it was a frontier or periphery of the Monte Albán state in the Late Formative. The Terminal Formative saw a decline and nucleation of population. In the Early Classic there were more people than at any time during the prehispanic sequence. At that time the area was closely drawn into the total regional system, which indeed had a decidedly southern valley orientation. The towns of the Tlapacoyan vicinity, like those elsewhere in the Early Classic (e.g. Figs. 6.14, 6.16-6.25), clearly had a variety of functional roles to play in the regional system of centers. Late Classic and Early Postclassic remains are present but hardly prominent. Finally, Tlapacoyan had the typical Late Postclassic pattern of a high population living in dispersed settlements, although the area seems to have functioned somewhat separately from the rest of the Valley of Oaxaca.

North is at top. The distance covered from north to south is about 2.6 km. [VOSPP grids N3E4, N4E4. Compañía Mexicana Aerofoto.]

SCALE AND COMPLEXITY 245

Figure 6.16 [*right*]. Two terraced sites on the Río Mixtepec. Full regional coverage reveals broad spatial patterns, such as the occurrence of ballcourts on frontiers (e.g., Fig. 6.13), and the ring of terraced sites on the southern and eastern frontier of the valley in the Early Classic. These two examples, on the conical hills just north and south of the stream, are 4 km northwest of the terraced site at Tlapacoyan in Figure 6.15. The northern one has 141 terraces, and the southern site has 13 terraces. Some of the terraces supported more than one house. Small Monte Albán IIIa sites are located on elevated ground up and down the stream. Monte Albán V sites, however, tend to be farther downstream, both on the heights and on the valley floor.

The modern irrigation system of the Río Mixtepec was one of the localities studied by Susan Lees (1973). The modern town to the east (right) is El Trapiche de Santa Cruz, which in the 1980s organized a cooperative *ejido*; the other village, upstream to the west, is Rincón de Tlapacoyan.

North is at top. From north to south the distance is about 3 km. [VOSPP grid N4E3. Compañía Mexicana Aerofoto.]

SCALE AND COMPLEXITY 247

Figure 6.17 [below]. El Choco. This is the hilltop terraced site west of Santa María Ayoquezco de Aldama, dating mainly from Monte Albán IIIa (Early Classic) and Monte Albán IIIb-IV (probably Early Postclassic). The local name refers to a historical battle that took place on this mountain. One of the platform mounds is clearly visible on top of the knoll at the pine tree and others are discernible to the right of the tree. The upper slopes are covered with ancient residential terraces (we mapped 524). This telephoto lens shot makes the site appear deceptively accessible, but in fact it is a fifty-minute fast walk between the center of the site and the valley floor. In the Early Classic there were eight terraced sites in a span of 18 km in this southwestern part of the valley, including those in Figures 6.15 and 6.16.

The view is toward the southwest. The distance along the top of the ridgelines from the pine tree to the right-hand edge of the photograph is about 500 m. [VOSPP grid N2E3. Photo by L. Nicholas.]

SCALE AND COMPLEXITY 249

Figure 6.18 [*below*]. Aerial view of southern Ocotlán. This photograph illustrates patterning over a somewhat broader area than that of the Tlapacoyan vicinity (Fig. 6.15). A crew of four could cover this 79 km² area in about a month.

The earliest occupation here was in the Rosario phase (Middle Formative). We found two small Rosario phase sites in the piedmont on the lower edge of the photograph. For the succeeding Monte Albán Ia phase there are six sites, located both on middle piedmont hilltops and in the low piedmont near streams. The hilltop locations, especially given the fact that so few people lived in the agriculturally more productive low piedmont, show that local ecological relationships are only one factor in regional settlement patterns. We suspect that Ocotlán's relationship to the rest of the regional system, and perhaps raiding or warfare, had a role in determining site locations.

By Monte Albán Ic (Late Formative) the number of sites in the area covered by the photograph had quadrupled, keeping pace with the general growth of the valley's population during Monte Albán I. There was a well-established community on a terraced site on a middle piedmont hilltop about a kilometer north of the town (Praxedis G. Guerrero) near the right edge of the photograph. Examples of contemporary valley-floor sites are several small ones on the edge of the town on the north side of the arroyo in the center of the photograph.

Southern Ocotlán settlement declined slightly and nucleated in Monte Albán II (Terminal Formative), as it did generally in the Valley of Oaxaca. We doubt that this could be predicted from the local environment and demographics alone.

As everywhere else in the southern and eastern Valley of Oaxaca (but not in the north, i.e. Etla and the Central area), populations expanded here in Monte Albán IIIa (Early Classic), to about 5000 people at the height of the expansion. A major settlement lies between Santa Lucía Ocotlán (the town in the center of the photograph) and San Pedro Reforma (downstream from Santa Lucía). Small settlements are scattered elsewhere on the low piedmont. The area has six terraced sites, located on hilltops in the southwestern corner, the northwest edge, and along the eastern edge of the photograph.

Monte Albán IIIb-IV (Late Classic and Early Postclassic) sites are scarce in this area. The largest was a town at San Pedro Reforma, with an estimated population of about 1800 people.

Southern Ocotlán again had a major demographic boom in Monte Albán V (Late Postclassic). The area may have had 8000 people living in a hundred sites. In contrast to the middle phases of the sequence, most people and most sites were in the low piedmont. From San Pedro Reforma and Magdalena Ocotlán (the town in the southwestern corner) across to Praxedis G. Guerrero at the right edge of the picture, the entire area is covered by dispersed settlement. Floodwater farming and small-scale irrigation must have been important.

The land in this photograph was one of the more developed areas in the Central Valleys of Oaxaca during Monte Albán V; but it may have collapsed before the sixteenth century, since we can find few early colonial documents referring to the area. Colonial and nineteenth-century mining and massive grazing in the mountains just to the east caused large-scale erosion (as seen in the eastern third of the photograph), and perhaps contributed to catastrophic flooding on the plain to the west.

North is at top. The photograph measures 10.4 by 7.6 km. [VOSPP grids N4E7-10, N3E7-10. Compañía Mexicana Aerofoto.]

Figure 6.19 [*below*]. Aerial view of Jalieza. The prehispanic site occupies the rectangular area from the knoll at top left, south to Santo Tomás Jalieza at center left, then due east to the right edge of the photograph, plus another half-kilometer beyond the right and top edges – roughly 10 km^2. In sheer area, Jalieza is the largest site in the Valley of Oaxaca.

The whole 10 km^2 area was never occupied all at once. The western half dates to Monte Albán IIIa (Early Classic), the eastern half to Monte Albán IIIb-IV (probably Early Postclassic), and the top of the north ridge to Monte Albán V (Late Postclassic). The site has only minor occupations prior to the Early Classic.

In 1977 we mapped Jalieza in the same way we did other terraced and non-terraced sites. It took several crews six weeks, but our survey left many questions unanswered. Finsten returned to carry out controlled surface collections on carefully selected, representative groups of terraces in 1988 and is currently analyzing the results. We think this multistage strategy is better than "siteless" (or "mindless") surface pickups because the regional survey provides better context, broad delineation of entities, and the necessary, prior information about representativeness.

North is at top. The scene measures 4.8 by 3.4 km. [VOSPP grids N7E8,9; N6E8,9. Compañía Mexicana Aerofoto.]

SCALE AND COMPLEXITY 253

Figure 6.20 [below]. The view from atop the eastern ridge at Jalieza. The leading town of the southern Valley of Oaxaca changed location in every phase since the Middle Formative. Every one of these southern valley "district capitals" is visible in this photograph.

The Rosario phase and Monte Albán I center was at the base of the hill immediately behind the dark ridge in middle ground (about 6 km away). In Monte Albán II (Terminal Formative) this site was abandoned, and power shifted to the top of the same hill. In Monte Albán IIIa (Early Classic) the southern valley's most important city was clearly Jalieza, whose center was the hill in the cloud shadow in the lower left. Monte Albán IIIb (Late Classic) is not well represented at Jalieza (Finsten has found some at the IIIa civic-ceremonial center). The photographer stands on the Monte Albán IV (probably Early Postclassic) part of Jalieza. At the time of occupation it was the most populous place in the whole valley. Finally, the ridge in mid-ground, on the right side of the photograph, is the center of Monte Albán V (Late Postclassic) Jalieza, for a time the most important city in the southern valley.

The movement of the southern valley's leading center from place to place is related to the configuration of the larger regional system. When the region had its greatest development in the north, the leading center was located on the pass from Ocotlán into the northern Valle Grande, in the direction of Monte Albán. Jalieza in Monte Albán IIIa was situated to control movement from the southern valley to western Tlacolula. The move to the eastern ridge in Monte Albán IV reflects the region's greatest development in Tlacolula in the Postclassic. This is an example of how the location of cities in networks of central places depends more on the configuration of the whole network than on purely local conditions.

The photograph looks west. The distance from the camera to the Cerro "Teta de María Sánchez," the prominent hill left of center, is 9.5 km. [VOSPP grids N7E7-9. Photo by S. Kowalewski.]

Figure 6.21 [*below*]. The center of Early Classic Jalieza. On top of the hill is the civic-ceremonial center. This is the same hill that is at the top left of Figure 6.19 and the lower left of Figure 6.20. Surface visibility is good – excised bowls, plain pottery, obsidian, white chert, figurines, bone, grinding stones, building stone, etc., litter the ground. All the slopes seen here were terraced, and occupational remains are also found on the flat ground. A possible mano workshop is located on the western slope of the hill, to the left. At the base of the hill are several low mounds that we interpreted as high-status residences. Isolated on top of the hill are two mounds with a plaza in between.

Looking northwest. The hill rises 200 m above this point, and is 800 m away. [VOSPP grid N7E8. Photo by S. Kowalewski.]

Figure 6.22 [*below*]. Monte Albán IV Jalieza. Jalieza was the largest city in the valley at about A.D. 700, with over 16,000 people. The photograph was taken from the north (Monte Albán V) ridge. Jalieza offers a pass to the Tlacolula (eastern) arm of the valley, seen here opening to the left. Tlacolula was the most developed part of the valley at this time. The trail visible in Figure 6.19 was an ancient road crossing the pass and running through the center of the site. Many of the fields follow old terrace retaining walls. Note the mounds on the ridge line. Jalieza has 37 mounds, second to Macuilxochitl's 67 at the time.

Looking southeast. The mounds are about a kilometer away. [VOSPP grids N6E9, N7E9. Photo by S. Kowalewski.]

SCALE AND COMPLEXITY 259

Figure 6.23 [*below*]. Terrace retaining wall at Jalieza. The photographer stands on one terrace and looks past the intervening outcrop to the next terrace. Often, residential terraces seem to have been constructed or modified in small groups, rather than one at a time, and connecting ramps suggest a supra-terrace organization of households. Finsten's sampling strategy for her 1988 Jalieza project was designed to investigate the possibility of such social units. This photograph was taken on the north side of the main IIIa hill in the dry season of 1977. [VOSPP grid N7E8. Photo by E. Kowalewski.]

SCALE AND COMPLEXITY 261

Figure 6.24 [*below*]. Inspecting artifacts on a terrace at Jalieza. The eastern, Monte Albán IV part of Jalieza lies in the distance. Beginning with the Monte Albán project and continuing with the valley surveys, we have used the terrace as the basic unit of mapping and analysis on this type of site. The terrace was the artificially created activity area for one or more domestic units. Terraces were built by cutting into the slope (right) and building up behind a retaining wall (left). These retaining walls may be several meters high.

Survey crews take into account several post-depositional factors in mapping and collecting terraces. Erosion and plowing sometimes obliterate features. Artifacts sometimes have washed in from the terrace above.

In this vicinity the 1977 survey found many excised bowls (type G-23) of a greenish color identical to that of a distinctive local rock. G-23s are specific to Monte Albán IIIa and occur in the Jalieza area in high frequencies. Interestingly, they are also found in high frequencies at Monte Albán, in that city's southern barrios—those nearest Jalieza.

The camera looks southeast. The terrace measures about 6 m in width. [VOSPP grid N7E8. Photo by E. Kowalewski.]

SCALE AND COMPLEXITY 263

Figure 6.25 [*right*]. A chert tool and debitage scatter near San Marcos Tlapazola, southern Tlacolula. This portion of our 1:5000 air photo used in the field illustrates strengths and weaknesses of the regional survey method. The crew mapped the outlines of the artifact scatters for each of the ceramic phases present, Monte Albán IIIa and V. The IIIa component (solid line) measures 14 ha. For the "field number" TL-TL-SMT-1 the phase-specific "site numbers" are 4-8-225 (IIIa) and 4-11-353, 354 (V). The crew mapped the mounds, took two collections of pottery on this part of the site (which later confirmed the field assessment, adding more detail), and mapped the general distribution of chert. The crew took note of the unusually large amount of chert of various colors and qualities, and remarked that this appeared to be an area where large nodules and cores were reduced to smaller cores and flakes. The isolated residence labeled TL-TL-SMT-4 may have had smaller flakes, representing a later reduction stage compared to the large decortication flakes seen on the rest of the site. Later in the lab we noticed the general association between prehispanic chert working areas in Tlacolula and present-day maguey growing, and wondered if the two had been associated in the past.

These are interesting observations, but we carried out no collecting strategy for chipped stone and we have little firm evidence of what was going on here, or when. Obtaining a description of chert working on the regional scale will require more systematic, specialized observations at an intelligently selected sample of the chert-bearing sites we found on the regional survey.

North is at the top of the photograph. The distance between the north and south edges is 1 km. [VOSPP grid N8E12. Compañía Mexicana Aerofoto.]

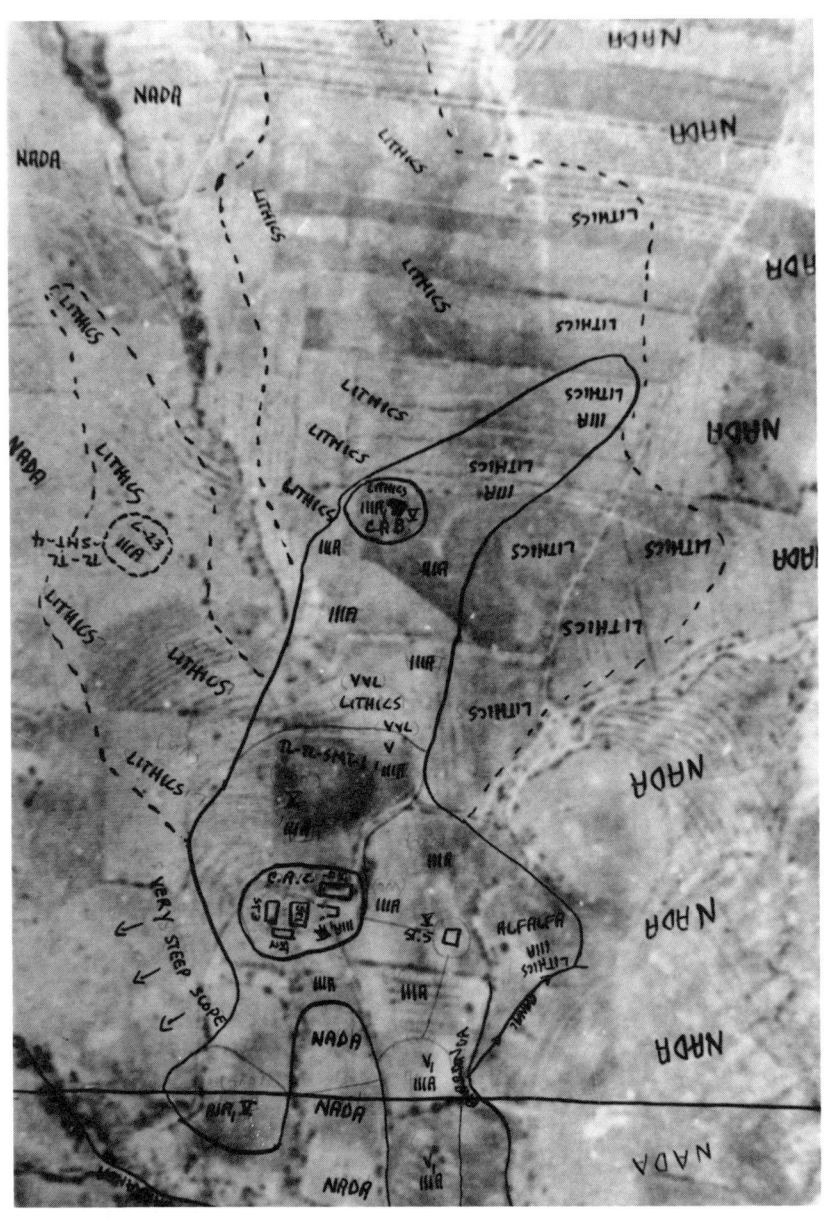

Figure 6.26 [below]. Structure 3 at Unión Zapata (Loma Larga). Not only were prehispanic Mesoamerican societies large in scale and complex in make-up and variation, but at times the evidence lies deeply buried due to Domesticated Bovine Transforms (DBTs). The bovine pictured is a simple input/output device that contributes along various links of its behavioral chain (or tether) to the formation processes of the archaeological record. Of concern here is the output function. According to some (but not us), processes such as these constitute six-sevenths of Archaeological Theory.

Looking west. The mound is 2.5 m high and measures 26 by 13 m at the base and 11 by 5 m at the top. It dates to Monte Albán Ia, Ic, and II. [VOSPP grid N9E15. Photo by S. Kowalewski.]

Acknowledgments

I am grateful for the support given to the Valley of Oaxaca Settlement Pattern Project by the National Science Foundation, the Social Science Research Council, the Canadian Social Science and Humanities Research Council, the City University of New York, Purdue University, the University of Arizona, the University of Georgia, Arizona State University, the University of Wisconsin, and McMaster University. Authority to carry out fieldwork, and valuable assistance, was granted by the Instituto Nacional de Antropología e Historia and the Centro Regional de Oaxaca, directed by Manuel Esparza, Rogelio González, and Ma. de la Luz Topete. I thank the many members of our field and lab crews, and the Oaxacans whose land we walked over. I thank my colleagues Richard Blanton, Gary Feinman, Laura Finsten, Kent Flannery, Joyce Marcus, and Linda Nicholas for discussing these issues with me. I thank Robert Sharer and Elin Danien for the opportunity to present our work to the Fifth Annual Northeast Mesoamerica Conference in Philadelphia in 1987.

References Cited

Asensio, Gaspar de
1580   Relación de Macuilsúchil u su partido. In: Papeles de Nueva España: segunda serie, Geografía y Estadística, vol. 4, edited by Francisco del Paso y Troncoso, pp. 100–104. Madrid (1905).

Dunnell, Robert C. and William S. Dancey
1983   The siteless survey: A regional scale data collection strategy. In: Advances in Archaeological Method and Theory, vol. 6, edited by Michael B. Schiffer, pp. 267–87. New York: Academic Press.

Kirchhoff, Paul
1943   Mesoamérica: Sus límites geográficas, composición étnica y carácteres culturales. Acta Americana, 1:92–107.

Kirkby, Anne V.T.
1973   The Use of Land and Water Resources in the Past and Present Valley of Oaxaca, Mexico. Memoirs, 5. The Museum of Anthropology, University of Michigan. Ann Arbor.

Kowalewski, Stephen A., Gary M. Feinman, Laura Finsten, Richard E. Blanton, and Linda M. Nicholas
1989   Monte Albán's Hinterland, Part II. Prehispanic Settlement Patterns in Tlacolula, Etla, and Ocotlán, the Valley of Oaxaca, Mexico. Memoirs, 23. Museum of Anthropology, University of Michigan. Ann Arbor.

Lees, Susan
1973   Socio-Political Aspects of Canal Irrigation in the Valley of Oaxaca, Mexico. Memoirs, 6. Museum of Anthropology, University of Michigan. Ann Arbor.

Marcus, Joyce
1983   Lintel 2 at Xoxocotlán. In: The Cloud People: Divergent Evolution of the Zapotec and Mixtec Civilizations, edited by Kent V. Flannery and Joyce Marcus, pp. 150–52. New York: Academic Press.

Morrison, Philip, Phyllis Morrison, and the Office of Charles and Ray Eames
1982   Powers of Ten: A Book about the Relative Sizes of Things in the Universe and the Effect of Adding another Zero. New York: W. H. Freeman.

Saville, Marshall H.
1899   Exploration of Zapotecan tombs in southern Mexico. American Anthropologist, (n.s.)1:350–62.

UMMA Backlist

Four series of publications are available from the Publications Office of the University of Michigan Museum of Anthropology. The Occasional Contributions, published from 1932 through 1956, and the Anthropological Papers, begun in 1949, are two series of short monographs, while the Memoirs, first published in 1970, are longer, more detailed studies. The fourth series, Technical Reports, begun in 1971, are brief, highly technical discussions of recent advances in several areas of anthropological study. New subseries will be added to the Technical Reports from time to time. Contributions to all of the series are prepared by staff members, associates, and friends of the Museum and include descriptions of museum collections and field work, results of research in various anthropological fields, and discussions of field and museum techniques.

Henry T. Wright, Director
Museum of Anthropology

The books below may be ordered from the Museum of Anthropology, 4009 Museums, University of Michigan, Ann Arbor, MI 48109. Libraries and members of the Michigan Archaeological Society receive a 20% discount. Checks must be in U.S. funds drawn on a U.S. bank. Please include $2 postage for all orders less than $10, $4 postage for orders over $10.. Prepayment is required.

Occasional Contributions

6. The Younge Site: An Archaeological Record from Michigan, by Emerson F. Greenman. 1937. Reprinted 1967. Pages 172, 33 plates, 9 figures, 10 maps. Price $3.00.
15. Araucanian Culture in Transition, by Mischa Titiev. 1951. Pages 164, 17 plates, 9 figures, 2 maps. Price $2.50.

Anthropological Papers

13. The Puerto Rican Population: A Study of Human Biology, by Frederick P. Thieme. 1959. Pages 156, 4 figures, 2 maps. Price $2.50.
14. Tell Toqaan: A Syrian Village, by Louise E. Sweet. 1960. Pages 280, 54 figures. Price $2.50.
34. The Prehistory of the Burnt Bluff Area, edited by James E. Fitting. 1968. Pages 140, 47 figures. Price $3.00.
39. Rules of Descent: Studies in the Sociology of Parentage, by Guy E. Swanson. 1969. Pages 108. 4 figures, 7 tables. Price $2.00.
41. The Archaeology of Summer Island: Changing Settlement Systems in Northern Lake Michigan, by David S. Brose. 1970. Pages 236, 31 tables, 17 figures, 35 plates. Price $3.00.
42. The Occupations of Migrants in Ghana, by Polly Hill. 1970. Pages 84, 11 tables. Price $2.00.
43. Prehistoric Biological Relationships in the Great Lakes Region, by Richard Guy Wilkinson. 1971. Pages 168, 40 tables, 33 figures, 2 plates. Price $3.50.
44. Property Control and Social Strategies: Settlers on a Middle Eastern Plain, by Barbara C. Aswad. 1971. Pages 180, 16 tables, 33 figures, 2 plates. Price $3.50.
48. The Wardell Buffalo Trap 48 SU 301: Communal Procurement in the Upper Green River Basin, Wyoming, by George C. Frison. 1973. Pages 111, 29 figures, 6 tables, 14 plates. Price $3.00.

50. Faction and Conversion in a Plural Society: Religious Alignments in the Hindu Kush, by Robert Leroy Canfield. 1973. Pages 142, 11 figures, 4 tables, 1 appendix. Pricce $3.00.
55. The Ait Ndhir of Morocco: A Study of the Social Transformation of a Berber Tribe, by Amal Rassam Vinogradov. 1974. Pages 128, 11 figures, 13 plates. Price $4.00.
59. An Analysis of Effigy Mound Complexes in Wisconsin, by William M. Hurley. 1975. Pages 466, 63 figures, 48 tables, 45 plates. Price $8.00.
60. Yerbas de la gente: A Study of Hispano-American Medicinal Plants, by Karen Cowan Ford. 1975. Pages 438, 1 figures. Price $5.00.
62. The Demography of the Semai Senoi, by Alan G. Fix. 1977. Pages 123, 17 figures, 38 tables. Price $5.00.
63. Economic and Social Organization of a Complex Chiefdom: The Halelea District, Kauai, Hawaii, by Timothy Earle. 1978. Pages 205, 27 figure, 7 tables, 6 plates. Price $6.00.
64. Wāsita in a Lebanese Context: Social Exchange Among Villagers and Outsiders, by Frederick Charles Huxley. 1978. Pages 174, 6 figures, 47 tables, 5 plates. Price $6.00.
65. Meadowood Phase Settlement Patterns in the Niagara Frontier Region of Western New York State, by Joseph E. Granger, Jr. 1978. Pages 403, 73 figures, 113 tables, 35 plates. Price $8.00.
66. The Snodgrass Site of the Powers Phase of Southeast Missouri, by James E. Price and James B. Griffin. 1979. Pages 189, 80 figures, 2 tables, 17 plates. Price $6.00.
67. The Nature and Status of Ethnobotany, edited by Richard I. Ford. 1978. Pages 428, 33 figures, 28 tables, 24 plates. Price $10.00.
68. The Biological and Social Analyses of a Mississippian Cemetery from Southeast Missouri: The Turner Site, 23BU21A, by Thomas K. Black III. 1979. Pages 170, 7 figures, 69 tables, 10 plates. Price $6.00.
69. The Ait Ayash of the High Molouuya Plain: Rural Social Organization in Moroco, by John Chiapuris. 1980. Pages 186, 15 figures 9 maps, 12 plates. Price $6.00.
70. An Early Woodland Community at the Schultz Site 20SA2 in the Saginaw Valley and the Nature of Early Woodland Adaptation in the Great Lakes Region, by Doreen Ozker. 1982. Pages 273, 27 tables, 33 figures, 15 plates. Price $10.00.
71. Persian Diary, 1939–1941, by Walter N. Koelz. 1983. Pages 227, 2 maps, 68 photos. Price $10.00.
72. Lulu Linear Punctated: Essays in Honor of George Irving Quimby, edited by Robert C. Dunnell and Donald K. Grayson. 1983. Pages 354, 39 figures, 19 plates, 20 tables. Price $12.00.
73. Paleoethnobotany of the Kameda Peninsula Jomon, by Gary W. Crawford. 1983. Pages 200, 27 figures, 12 tables, 23 plates. Price 48.00.
74. The Archaeology of the Sierra Blanca Region of Southeastern New Mexico, by Jane Holden Kelley. 1983. Pages 527, 85 figures, 10 maps, 41 tables, 87 plates. Price $15.00.
75. Prehistoric Food Production in North America, edited by Richard I. Ford. 1985. Pages 411, 39 figures, 22 tables. Price $15.00.
76. Primitive Polluters: Semang Impact on the Malaysian Tropical Rain Forest Ecosystem, by A. Terry Rambo. 1985. Pages 104, 5 figures, 5 tables, 16 plates. Price $8.00.
77. Jumano and Patarabueye: Relations at La Junta de los Rios, by J. Charles Kelley. 1986. Pages 180, 14 figures, 9 plates. Price $10.00.
78. Protohistoric Yamato: Archaeology of the First Japanese State, by Gina L. Barnes. 1988. Pages 473, 94 figures, 17 tables. Price $15.00.
79. The Foxie Otter Site: A Multicomponent Occupation North of Lake Huron, by Christopher C. Hanks. 1988. Pages 203, 21 figures, 14 tables. Price $12.00.
80. Living in a Lean-to: Philippine Negrito Foragers in Transition, by Navin K. Rai. 1990. Pages 184, 4 figures, 10 plates, 12 appendices. Price $12.00.
81. The Bridgeport Township Site: Archaeological Investigation at 20SA620, Saginaw County, Michigan, edited by John O'Shea and Michael Shott. 1990. Pages 326, 50 figures, 68 tables, 1 appendix. Price $15.00

Memoirs

2. The Burial Complexes of the Knight and Norton Mounds in Illinois and Michigan, by James B. Griffin, Richard E. Flanders and Paul F. Titterington. 1970. Pages 216, 177 plates. Price $7.00.
3. Prehistoric Settlement Patterns in the Texcoco Region, Mexico, by Jeffrey R. Parsons. 1971. Pages 447, 8 tables, 14 maps, 88 figures, 57 plates. Price $8.00.
4. The Schultz Site at Green Point: A Stratified Occupation Area in the Saginaw Valley of Michigan, edited by James E. Fitting. 1972. Pages 317, 84 figures, 70 tables, 2 appendixes. Price $8.00.
7. Formative Mesoamerican Exchange Networks with Special Reference to the Valley of Oaxaca, by Jane W. Pires-Ferreira. Prehistory and Human Ecology of the Valley of Oaxaca, Vol. 3. Pages 111, 44 figures, 27 tables, 4 plates. Price $6.00.
8. Fábrica San José and Middle Formative Society in the Valley of Oaxaca, by Robert D. Drennan. Prehistory and Human Ecology of the Valley of Oaxaca, Vol. 4. 1975. Pages 300, 10 tables, 2 maps, 75 figures, 29 plates. Price $8.00.
9. Studies in the Archaeological History of the Deh Luran Plain, by Frank Hole. 1977. Pages 369, 94 tables, 119 illustrations, 55 plates. $10.00.
10. Part 1. The Vegetational History of the Oaxaca Valley, by C. Earle Smith, Jr. Pages 39, 1 table, 2 maps, 10 plates. Part 2. Zapotec Plant Knowledge: Classification, Uses, and Communication About Plants in Mitla, Oaxaca, Mexico, by Ellen Messer. Pages 149, 29 figures, 1 map, 10 plates. Prehistory and Human Ecology of the Valley of Oaxaca, Vol. 5. 1978. Price $8.00.
11. An Archaeological Survey of the Keban Reservoir Area of East-Central Turkey, by Robert E. Whallon. 1979. Pages 309, 211 figures, 20 tables, 2 plates. Price $10.00.
12. Excavations at Santo Domingo Tomaltepec: Evolution of a Formative Community in the Valley of Oaxaca, Mexico, by Michael E. Whalen. Prehistory and Human Ecology of the Valley of Oaxaca, Vol. 6. 1981. Pages 225, 38 tables, 58 figures, 73 plates. Price $13.00.
13. An Early Town on the Deh Luran Plain: Excavations at Tepe Farukhabad, edited by Henry T. Wright. 1981. Pages 462, 99 figures, 96 tables, 21 plates. Price $15.00.
14. Prehispanic Settlement Patterns in the Southern Valley of Mexico: The Chalco-Xochimilco Region, by Jeffrey R. Parsons, Elizabeth Brumfiel, Mary H. Parsons, and David J. Wilson. 1982. Pages 504, 128 figures, 115 tables, 40 maps, 31 plates. Price $16.00.
15. Monte Albán's Hinterland, Part 1: The Prehispanic Settlement Patterns of the Central and Southern Parts of the Valley of Oaxaca, Mexico, by Richard E. Blanton, Stephen Kowalewski, Gary Feinman, and Jill Appel. Prehistory and Human Ecology of the Valley of Oaxaca, Vol. 7. 1982. Pages 506, 43 tables, 139 figures. Price $20.00.
16. A Fuego y Sangre: Early Zapotec Imperialism in the Cuicatlán Cañada, Oaxaca, by Elsa M. Redmond. Studies in Latin American Ethnohistory and Archaeology, Vol 1. 1983. Pages 216, 75 figures, 46 tables, 42 plates. Price $15.00.
17. Irrigation and the Cuicatec Ecosystem: A Study of Agriculture and Civilization in North Central Oaxaca, by Joseph W. Hopkins, III. Studies in Latin American Ethnohistory and Archaeology, Vol. 2. 1984. Pages 148, 13 figures, 3 tables, 16 plates. Price $15.00.
18. Aztec City-States, by Mary G. Hodge. Studies in Latin American Ethnohistory and Archaeology, Vol. 3. 1984. Pages 166, 64 figures, 30 tables. Price $15.00.
19. Early Neolithic Settlement and Society at Olszanica, by Sarunas Milisauskas. 1986. Pages 319, 160 figures, 153 tables, 51 plates. Price $20.00.
20. Chipped Stone Tools in Formative Oaxaca, Mexico: Their Procurement, Production and Use, by William J. Parry. Prehistory and Human Ecology of the Valley of Oaxaca, Vol. 8. 1987. Pages 178, 42 tables, 52 figures, 20 plates. Price $18.00.
21. Conflicts Over Coca Fields in XVIth-Century Perú, by María Rostworowski de Diez Canseco. Studies in Latin American Ethnohistory and Archaeology, Vol. 4. 1988. Pages 314, 21 figures, 2 tables. Price $19.50.

22. Agricultural Intensification and Prehistoric Health in the Valley of Oaxaca, Mexico, by Denise C. Hodges. Prehistory and Human Ecology of the Valley of Oaxaca, Vol. 9. 1989. Pages 146, 6 figures, 42 tables, 4 appendices. Price $16.00.
23. Monte Albán's Hinterland, Part II: Prehispanic Settlement Patterns in Tlacolula, Etla and Ocotlán, the Valley of Oaxaca, Mexico, by Stephen Kowalewski, Gary Feinman, Laura Finsten, Richard Blanton and Linda Nicholas. 1989. Pages 1146 (in 2 vols.), 141 figures, 116 tables, 8 plates, 9 appendices. Price $40.00.

Technical Reports

2. LONGTERM and PEAKSCAN: Neutron Activation Analysis Computer Programs, by Thomas Meyers and Mark Denies. Contributions in Computer Applications to Archaeology, No. 2. 1972. Pages 76, 43 pages computer output, 2 figures. Price $1.00.
3. Data on the Abnormal Hemoglobins and Glucose-6-Phosphate Dehydrogenase Deficiency in Human Populations, by Frank B. Livingstone. Contributions in Human Biology, No. 1. 1973. Pages 289. Price $2.50.
4. An Arachaeological Investigation on the Loboi Plain, Baringo District, Kenya, by William R. Farrand, Richard W. Redding, Milford H. Wolpolff, and Henry T. Wright. Research Reports in Arcaeology, No. 1. 1976. Pages 59, 10 figures. Price $3.50.
5. Digging for Gold: Papers on Archaeology for Profit, edited by William K. Macdonald. Research Reports in Archaeology, No. 2. 1976. Pages 86. Price $3.50.
6. An Investigation of Ethnographic and Archaeological Specimens of Mescalbeans (*Sophora seconiflora*) in American Museums, by William L. Merrill. Research Reports in Ethnobotany, No. 1. 1977. Pages 167, 3 figures, 3 tables, 25 plates. Price $5.00.
7. Excavations at Quachilco: A Report on the 1977 Season of the Palo Blanco Project, by Robert D. Drennan. Research Reports in Archaeology, No. 3. Pages 81, 18 figures. Price $4.00.
10. Archaeological Investigations in Northeastern Xuzestan, 1976, edited by Henry T. Wright. Research Reports in Archaeology, No. 5. 1979. Pages 140, 52 figures, 20 tables. Price $6.00.
11. Prehistoric Social, Political, and Economic Development in the Area of the Tehuacan Valley: Some Results of the Palo Blanco Project, edited by Robert D. Drennan. Research Reports in Archaeology, No. 6. 1979. Pages 260, 46 figures, 26 tables. Price $6.50.
12. Late Prehistoric Bison Procurement in Southeastern New Mexico: The 1978 Season at the Garnsey Site, by John D. Speth and William J. Parry. Research Reports in Archaeology, No. 7. 1980. Pages 384, 39 figures, 32 tables, 34 plates. Price $9.00.
14. Archaeological Settlement Pattern Data from the Chalco, Xochimilco, Ixtapalapa, Texcoco and Zumpango Regions, Mexico, by Jeffrey R. Parson, Keith W. Kintigh, and Susan Gregg. Research Reports in Archaeology, No. 9. Pages 222. Price $8.00.
15. The Garnsey Spring Campsite: Late Prehistoric Occupation in Southeastern New MExico, by William J. Parry and John D. Speth. Research Reports in Archaeology, No. 10. Pages 228, 24 figures, 27 tables, 24 photos. Price $8.00.
16. Regional Archaeology in the Valle de la Plata, Colombia: A Preliminary Report on the 1984 Season of the Proyecto Arqueológico Valle de la Plata, edited by Robert D. Drennan. Research Reports in Archaeology, No. 11. 1985. Pages 195 (including complete Spanish translation), 43 figures, 16 tables. Price $8.00.
17. Zooarchaeology of Six Prehistoric Sites in the Sierra Blanca Region, New Mexico, by Jonathan C. Driver. Research Reports in Archaeology, No. 12. 1985. Pages 103, 29 tables, 8 figures, 1 appendix. Price $5.00.
18. The Henderson Site Burials: Glimpses of a Late Prehistoric Population in the Pecos Valley, by Thomas R. Rocek and John D. Speth. Research Reports in Archaeology, No. 13. 1986. Pages 348, 118 figures, 63 tables. Price $13.00.

19. Medicinal Plants of Native America, by Daniel E. Moerman. 1987. Pages 912 (in 2 vols.). Price $30.00.
20. Late Intermediate Occupation at Cerro Azul, Peru, by Joyce Marcus. 1987. Pages 112, 70 figures. Price $8.00.
21. The Inscriptions of Calakmul: Royal Marriage at a Maya City in Campeche, Mexico, by Joyce Marcus. 1987. Pages 205, 65 figures, 7 tables. Price $8.00.

Special Publications

The Williams Collection of Far Eastern Ceramics, Chinese, Siamese, and Annamese Ceramic Wares Selected from the Collection of Justice and Mrs. G. Mennen Williams in the University of Michigan Museum of Anthropology, by Kamer Aga-Oglu. 1972. Pages 73, 85 black and white photographs. Price $4.00.

The Williams Collection of Far Eastern Ceramics—Tonnancour Section, by Kamer Aga-Oglu. 1975. Pages 185, 183 black and white photographs, 18 color photographs. Price $8.00.